Schooling, society and inclusive education

an Afrocentric perspective

Chinedu Okeke • Micheal van Wyk • Nareadi Phasha

OXFORD

UNIVERSITY PRESS

SOUTHERN AFRICA

OXFORD
UNIVERSITY PRESS
SOUTHERN AFRICA

Oxford University Press is a department of the University of Oxford.
It furthers the University's objective of excellence in research, scholarship,
and education by publishing worldwide. Oxford is a registered trade mark of
Oxford University Press in the UK and in certain other countries
Published in South Africa by
Oxford University Press Southern Africa (Pty) Limited

Vasco Boulevard, Goodwood, N1 City, P O Box 12119, Cape Town,
South Africa
© Oxford University Press Southern Africa (Pty) Ltd 2014

The moral rights of the author have been asserted

First published 2014

Schooling, society and inclusive education

ISBN 978 0 19 907780 9

Typeset in Palatino LT Std 10pt on 12pt
Printed on 70gsm Woodfree

Acknowledgements
Publishing manager: Alida Terblanche
Publisher: Marisa Montemarano
Project manager: Kelly Williams
Editor: Catherine Damerell
Designer: Shaun Andrews
Illustrators: Matthew Ackerman and André Plant
Indexer: Adrienne Pretorius
Typesetter: Marco Casati
Cover Image: Gallo Images 175398627
Printed and bound by: Creda

Contents

Foreword

This much needed teacher education textbook introduces students at undergraduate and postgraduate levels to the realities and complexities associated with education in South Africa, and on the wider African continent. It confronts the interrelatedness between schooling, society and inclusive education, articulating the knowledge and skill repertoires needed for prospective teachers to make sense of an increasingly challenging professional and socio-economic environment. The text, through its coherent organisation, links between chapters, thorough and grounded research, and scientifically discussed issues, makes this entire volume an invaluable resource to have. The contributions made by various authors are focused on equipping future teachers to respond to, facilitate, and manage educational issues and schooling demands, in a practical, yet contextualised manner.

Some of the other important features of this book include the following:
- It shows the connection between education theory and its relevance to the teaching profession.
- It supports the notion of inclusivity by exploring indigenous knowledge and an African theory of knowledge in understanding diverse educational challenges.
- It provides prospective teachers with guidelines on how to respond to and manage various forms of learner behaviour and related socio-economic conditions.
- It presents ideas on how to support learners with barriers to learning and development, in an inclusive education system.
- It is written in line with SAQA requirements, follows an interactive approach, and provides clear learning outcomes, many case scenarios, stop and reflect activities, projects, summaries of discussions, and suggestions for further reading and research.
- It stimulates interest and serves as a knowledge base for prospective teachers to think critically about their roles and future personal growth, as well as their professional development trajectories, within a challenging yet vital profession.

This volume is certain to support the prospective teacher in getting an insight to contemporary educational issues and how contentious societal challenges should be viewed and addressed. It serves as an essential vehicle for building professional teacher competence, while acknowledging the demands of the mainstream world context.

Gregg Alexander, Central University of Technology

Preface

As teacher educators with specialities in the dynamics of schooling, society, inclusive education, and curriculum studies, the authors and editors of this volume address the dearth of primary resources that clearly and comprehensively addresses the subject of this book – inclusive education from an African perspective. While it may be convenient for academics and other education professionals who are working in the field of education and society, to handle the numerous existing texts that have compartmentalised topics into various textbooks, experience shows us that many students grapple with doing the same. Given the economic circumstances in which most students undertake their academic programmes, we believe that the availability of a primary text of this kind will come as relief to most students.

Therefore, *Schooling, society and inclusive education: An African perspective* is designed to cater for the needs of all students who are engaged in teacher education, with the intention of becoming professional teachers. For this reason, the issues covered in this book have been carefully thought out so that students, and other readers, will be well-grounded in the dynamics of schooling, society, and inclusive education. Such knowledge is necessary if they are to be effective and successful in their everyday activities as practising teachers. We hope that the three parts of this textbook will particularly provide students with a long sought resource enabling them to succeed in their training endeavour.

Part 1: Alternative ways of knowing, which covers the first four chapters of the book, looks at various theories in education, as well as their applications to teaching and learning. The unique importance of this part is that it represents a new approach to the theoretical understanding of education. With this book we believe we are providing for the first time an examination of education theories with an indigenous African approach within the context of schooling, society and inclusive education. Accordingly, Chapter 1 looks at the origin, meanings and uses of theories in education. Experience over the years has shown that students as well as professionals appear to struggle with the application of theory both in their research and in classroom teaching. So this chapter has been designed to ground students' understanding of theory, and to show them how to apply theories to their everyday classroom experiences and research. The remaining chapters of this part (Chapters 2, 3 and 4) are at the heart of this book from the perspective of Afrocentric pedagogy.

Part 2: The child and dynamics of the environment comprises six carefully selected chapters that relate directly to children, their development, and their environmental dynamics (Chapters 5, 6, 7, 8, 9 and 10). At the end of this part, students should be able to discuss the theory on which the ecology of the child is based; explain the various layers of the theory; explain the interconnectedness of the home, school and society in the overall environment of the child; apply the experiences gained from this section to their everyday dealings in their classrooms; and understand the implications of this theory to the overall development and wellbeing of the child.

At the end of Chapter 5, students should be able to understand the central concepts of Bronfenbrenner's ecological model in an African perspective, as well as discuss the ecological model in its application to individual, family, classroom, school, and community settings. Most importantly, this chapter is aimed at equipping readers with the essential skills that will enable them to explain and apply an ecological model of child development from an African perspective. Chapter 6 draws the readers' attention to the relatively silent consequences of cyber bullying. The chapter describes the differences between traditional bullying and cyber bullying by identifying the various types, situations and consequences of cyber bullying. The educational–psychological impacts of cyber bullying are also highlighted in this chapter. Chapter 7 attempts to deepen our understanding of sexual violence by highlighting the usually neglected existence of the problem amongst learners with intellectual disabilities.

In Chapter 8 the management of violence at school is discussed and strategies to deal with it are proposed. At the end of Chapters 6, 7 and 8, students should be able to identify and explain various forms of violence within our schools; discuss the impact of school violence; examine school violence prevention and management models; and understand how to manage violence and potentially violent situations through teaching and learning in their classrooms and school environment. The last two chapters in Part 2, Chapters 9 and 10, deal with the crisis of poverty in sub-Saharan Africa. They are included to enable students to understand the meaning of poverty in their classrooms, schools, communities, and country. They should be able to discuss how poverty can be contextualised, examine various ways in which poverty is measured, identify the deep impact of poverty on the South African child, family and society, including the educational impacts of poverty, discuss various strategies in which education can serve as tool for tackling poverty; and particularly apply the knowledge gained from this discussion in dealing with learners' experiences with poverty.

The final section, *Part 3: Understanding inclusive education*, consists of four closely-linked chapters. This part is carefully structured within the context of 'Education for All'. Chapter 11 presents a brief historical overview of inclusive education in South Africa and summarises the main education policies and developments that have shaped inclusive education in South Africa. In addition, the chapter outlines key barriers to the realisation of inclusive education in South Africa, and critically discusses how these can be overcome in the future to realise true transformation in South Africa. Chapter 12 takes a more practical approach by looking at the application of teaching and learning approaches to achieve inclusive education in South African classrooms. Finally, in Chapters 13 and 14, the issues that surround barriers to learning are discussed. While Chapter 13 takes a general approach to barriers to formal learning, Chapter 14 looks specifically at the crucial issue of language as a barrier to learning in classrooms in South Africa.

As noted earlier, the unique nature of this book is such that it represents the first attempt to offer a primary reader to assist university students come to terms with the realities of everyday schooling in contemporary South Africa and other African societies. Throughout the text a reader-friendly interactive approach has been used, providing many opportunities for active engagement with the material, and the application of its ideas, so that this book achieves the aim for which it is designed. We hope you find this book a companion during your journey as a student teacher.

The authors

Contributors

Chinedu I. O. Okeke is Senior Lecturer and Leader: Early Childhood Development Research, Faculty of Education, University of Fort Hare, South Africa. He has taught at universities in Swaziland and Nigeria. His interest in qualitative research culminated in a Vice-Chancellor's Prize-winning doctoral thesis at the University of Nigeria, Nsukka in 2003. He also holds a Master's degree in Educational Studies and Bachelor of Arts in Educational Foundations and History. He has published numerous local and international papers, books and book chapters, and has spoken at various national and international conferences on issues relating to higher education, curriculum, research methods, research supervision, and sociology of education generally. His main research areas include gender and education, gender-based violence, and early childhood development (ECD). He is also the lead editor of another OUP-commissioned book project entitled: *Research methods: An African approach.*

Micheal van Wyk is a Professor in the Department of Curriculum and Instruction Studies in the School of Teacher Education at the College of Education, University of South Africa. He has more than 28 years of teaching experience at primary, secondary, and higher education levels. He is a National Research Foundation (NRF)-rated researcher in Economics education. He has published more than 40 research articles in accredited journals in the last five years, reading 47 papers at educational conferences; he has written three academic books, and contributed four chapters in research publications. He has delivered several keynote addresses at various teacher education conferences. He also received an award for Outstanding Education Research Paper at an international conference in Dublin, Ireland in 2010. In 2011 he received an award for the Best Researcher in Education category, in the Faculty of Education at the University of the Free State. Professor van Wyk is an international reviewer for several international journals, as well as for South African journals. He serves on a number of academic boards. In 2012 he published the article: *(Re)claiming the Riel as Khoisan Indigenous Cultural Knowledge.* He serves on various committees in the College of Education, Unisa. Professor van Wyk's research interests are technology-integrated teaching and learning strategies, indigenous knowledge systems (IKS), social entrepreneurship, and Economics education.

Nareadi T. Phasha holds the degrees, BEd; BEd Hons (UNIN, Turfloop); MEd Special Education (Virginia State University, US); and PhD (University of Cambridge, UK). She is Professor in the College of Education, University of South Africa. Her research interests include: inclusivity in education, sexuality and disability issues, maltreatment, abuse, and violence against school learners.

Charles Chikunda is currently a stakeholder facilitator and professional development trainer: natural resources management, and basin resilience planner, at Award, an NGO based in Limpopo. His work entails project design, research design and stakeholder facilitation, professional support, skills development, and professional training in water and biodiversity management. At the time of writing he was Manager of the Professional Development Centre in the Faculty of Education at Rhodes University, Grahamstown. Dr Chikunda recently completed his PhD. He is a science teacher by profession and has been in teacher education since 1997, working in Zimbabwe and South Africa. At Rhodes University he was involved in coordinating the in-service teacher development programme, as well as lecturing in Science Education and Environmental Education. His research interests include sustainability and professional teacher development, gender, and science education.

Thembinkosi Mfundo Dlamini is a Governance Manager with Oxfam GB, based in Johannesburg. He obtained his LLM at the University of Sydney, Australia, which focused on international taxation. A former Swaziland Ministry of Finance official, he completed his junior degree in agricultural economics at the University of Swaziland. His keen interest in economic governance issues led him to pursue a career in research, advocacy and capacity development, focusing on fiscal transparency, accountability and participation. His energies are channelled towards campaigning for pro-poor tax policies to address the injustice of poverty and inequality. He was previously a senior researcher at Idasa, leading the design and implementation of the Right to Know, Right to Education project in six African countries. It focused on empowering poor rural communities with skills to govern local schools in order to achieve better education outcomes and reduce poverty.

Melanie Drake has taught at both private and public primary schools in South Africa, while her doctoral research explored education in rural and township communities of South Africa. She has recently moved back to South Africa after a five-year period abroad in New Zealand, where she lectured and completed her PhD at the University of Auckland, New Zealand, as an International Commonwealth Scholar. She now lectures at the University of Fort Hare in East London, and still keeps in touch with schools by conducting schools-based research. Her areas of interest include: values education; school practice; school leadership; teacher motivation; organisational development; and qualitative research methods.

Ntombozuko Stunky Duku is Associate Professor in the School for General and Continuing Education (SGCE), Faculty of Education, University of Fort Hare. She teaches pre-service, in-service and postgraduate programmes. She is also responsible for coordinating faculty postgraduate studies (Masters and PhD). She was involved in a number of research and capacity-building projects, including the Imbewu Project in which she was responsible for training SGBs and principals, commissioned by CEPD (Centre for Education Policy Development, Evaluation and Management), on engaging communities in educational development through CLINGs (Community Literacy and Numeracy Groups). She participated in a comparative analysis of educational inclusion and exclusion in India and South Africa. Most recently, she was a member of a national research team that carried out a feasibility and impact study of the Advanced Certificate in Education (ACE) for school principals in South Africa. Her areas of research and publication include: policy planning, development, monitoring and evaluation, school governance, multicultural education, African indigenous theories in education, and issues of access and success in education.

Ellen Lombard is a Senior Lecturer in the Department of Afrikaans and Theory of Literature at the University of South Africa, where she teaches Afrikaans linguistics. Her research interests include language pragmatics, forensic linguistics and open distance learning.

Moshweu Simon Mampe is a Lecturer in the School of Teacher Education and Training, Faculty of Education, North West University. His qualifications include an MEd in Special Education. Mr Mampe lectures the following modules: English methodologies for second-, third-, fourth-year students, and PGCE students. He also lectures Educational Psychology for second-year students and Inclusive Education for third-year students. He engages in other school-related activities like quality assurance and research activities.

Boitumelo Moreeng is a Lecturer in the Faculty of Education, University of the Free State. He has a PhD in Curriculum Studies from the University of the Free State. His research interests are in History education and teacher training.

Muzwa Mukwambo is a Science and Mathematics Education Lecturer in the Faculty of Education, University of Namibia (Katima Mulilo Campus), Namibia. He is a Physics and Mathematics teacher by profession. In the Education Department, he is involved with mathematics and science teacher education. He is the author of *Understanding trainee teachers' engagement with prior everyday knowledge and experiences in teaching physical science concepts: case study; Trainee teachers' perceptions on engagement with Indigenous Knowledge, and explanations of natural phenomena when teaching physical science concepts;* and Understanding the challenges and how trainee teachers source distilled water for practical work in science in under-resourced schools.

Kenneth Mlungisi Ngcoza is a Senior Lecturer in Science Education in the Faculty of Education, Rhodes University, Grahamstown. He is a mathematics and science teacher by profession. In the Education Department, he is involved with science teacher education (both pre- and in-service) and is the coordinator of school experience for PGCE students. He is the chairperson of the SAARMSTE Eastern Cape Chapter, and his research interests include professional development, science curriculum, cultural contexts, and indigenous knowledge. He peer reviewed the book, *The Professional Knowledge Base of Science Teaching,* edited by Deborah Corrigan, Justin Dillon and Richard Gunstone (2011).

Vussy Alby Nkonyane is a Senior Lecturer in the Department of Curriculum and Instructional Studies of the College of Education at the University of South Africa (UNISA). In his current position he forms part of a team of scholars whose focus is on the academic productivity of the College of Education, in publishing articles in accredited journals. He has presented and published papers both nationally and internationally and contributed book chapters. Dr Nkonyane has 21 years of teaching experience in primary and high schools, and seven years of tertiary education experience as a lecturer. He serves on various committees (Research; Community engagement; and Archiving African Indigenous Knowledge Systems). He is most passionate about poverty, socio-economic class and race issues and how these manifest themselves in education (academic performance). His research is informed by Afrocentricity, education for social justice, and critical race theory. His research niche is decolonisation pedagogy: how to change dysfunctional schools with poor backgrounds into functional and productive centres of excellence through cultural identity formulation.

Doris Nyokangi holds a PhD in Inclusive Education from the University of South Africa. Dr Nyokangi completed her MEd degree in Gender and International Studies at the Institute of Education in London. She is a researcher and works at UNISA on a contract basis. Her research focus is on violence in schools for learners with disabilities.

Juliet Ramohai is a Lecturer in the School of Education Studies at the University of the Free State. She is currently responsible for courses in undergraduate, postgraduate, and teacher education offered within the discipline of Inclusive Education. She received her MEd in Psychology of Education from the University of the Free State in 2008. Currently, she is pursuing a PhD in Higher Education Studies, focusing on the broader field of transformation in South African higher education.

Namhla Sotuku holds a PhD in Education Management and Policy Formulation. She is a Senior Lecturer in the School for General and Continuing Education (SGCE), Faculty of Education, University of Fort Hare. Dr Sotuku has wide experience as a teacher educator and draws from a varied background as a Foundation Phase teacher, language lecturer at a teachers college, a researcher, curriculum trainer, author of Foundation Phase Language school textbooks, university lecturer, materials developer for teacher development programmes, and a school support officer. Most recently, she was a member of a team that designed and developed the innovative UFH Distance Education Course, and also produced polysemic materials that have attracted international interest and have won awards locally. The materials are being uploaded as open educational resources.

Walter Sukati is Associate Professor and Director of the Institute of Distance Education at the University of Swaziland. He holds two bachelor's degrees, two master's degrees and two doctoral degrees. One of the doctoral degrees was earned from the University of South Africa in Comparative Education and the other was earned from Harvard University in Administration, Planning and Social Policy. Professor Sukati has occupied several positions within the Swaziland Ministry of Education and the University of Swaziland. His research interests and areas he has lectured and published in, include educational policy and planning, comparative education, open and distance education, and economics and politics of education. Among his publications are a co-published book, chapters in books, and many articles in refereed journals.

Ramodungoane Tabane is a registered Educational Psychologist and a Senior Lecturer in the Department of Psychology of Education at the University of South Africa, where he is involved in the teaching of undergraduates, and the training and supervision of Masters and PhD students. His research interests lie in innovative qualitative research methodologies; educational psychology; guidance and counselling; and cross-cultural psychology in the fields of child development, assessment, learning, psychological and emotional adjustment.

Matshidiso Joyce Taole holds a PhD degree in Curriculum Development from the University of North West (Mafikeng campus). She is an Associate Professor at the University of South Africa, College of Education, in the Department of Curriculum and Instructional Studies. She has presented papers at local and international conferences in the field of curriculum development and implementation, and is a member of various academic associations. She is the Associate Editor for the *African Journal of Pedagogy and Curriculum* (AJPC). She is presently involved in teaching practice supervision, and undergraduate and postgraduate teaching and research supervision in the field of Curriculum Studies. She has published with local and international journals.

Joseph Tchatchoueng is currently a Master's research student. He holds a BA in Philosophy (cum laude). He also obtained a PGCE at the University of KwaZulu-Natal in 2011, and an Honours degree (summa cum laude) in Educational Psychology at UKZN in 2012. Mr Tchatchoueng is now doing a Master's degree by research in Educational Psychology at UKZN under the supervision of Professor Kamwendo and Dr Ntombela. The main focus of his research project is on English as barrier to learning and development among black South African students, and inclusive education vis-à-vis the languages of minority groups.

Acknowledgements

The authors would like to use this opportunity to express their gratitude to the reviewers of the earlier draft for the time they spent reading various chapters of this book. Particularly, the authors want to acknowledge the high level of professional acumen they shared with them in their searching reviews of the manuscript. They also take this opportunity to recognise their colleagues at Oxford University Press, Cape Town, for their professional roles in making this book a reality.

The authors and publisher gratefully acknowledge permission to reproduce copyright material in this book:

Chapter 2
James A. Banks's guidelines 'Dimensions of Multicultural Education': Reprinted with permission of James A. Banks from James A. Banks, CULTURAL DIVERSITY AND EDUCATION: FOUNDATIONS, CURRICULUM AND TEACHING (6th Edition). Boston: Pearson, 2015, page 5.

Chapter 3
p. 39 picture credit: Gallo Images/Getty Images/Simon Hayter
p. 40 picture credit: Photo of Professor Joe L. Kincheloe reprinted by permission of Professor Shirley R. Steinberg
p. 50 McLaren, P & Giroux, H. A. 1990. Critical pedagogy and rural education: A challenge from Poland. *Peabody Journal of Education*. 67(4):154–165. Published by Taylor & Francis. Copyright © 1990 Routledge. http://www.informaworld.com.
pp. 51–3 Shockley, K.G. 2011. Reaching African American students: Profile of an Afrocentric teacher. Journal of Black Studies. 42(7):1027–1046. Copyright © 2011 by SAGE Publications. Reprinted by permission of SAGE Publications.

Chapter 6
p. 104 O' Moore, M. & Kirkham, C. 2001. Self-esteem and its relationship to bullying behaviour. *Aggressive Behaviour*. 27(4):271. Copyright © 2001 Wiley-Liss, Inc. Reprinted by permission of John Wiley and Sons.

Chapter 8
p. 130 Prinsloo, L.J. 2005. How safe are South African schools? *South African Journal of Education*. 25(1):5–10. Reprinted by permission of the Executive Editor: *South African Journal of Education*
p. 139 picture credit: Sibongile Mashaba/Sowetan 2013

Chapter 9
p. 167 Reprinted from International Journal of Educational Development Vol. 31 No. 3. Ginsburg, C., Richter, L.M., Fleisch, B. & Norris, S.A. 2011. An Analysis of Association between Residential and School Mobility and Educational Outcomes in South African Urban Children: The birth to twenty cohort. *pp.213–222*. Copyright © 2011 Elsevier, with permission from Elsevier.

Chapter 11

p. 204 Lomofsky, L. & Lazarus, S. 2001. South Africa: First steps in the development of an inclusive education system. *Cambridge Journal of Education*. 31(3): 311–312. University of Cambridge, Faculty of Education, reprinted by permission of Taylor & Francis Ltd, www.tandfonline.com on behalf of University of Cambridge, Faculty of Education.

Chapter 14

p. 275 poster reprinted with permission of Inclusive Education Western Cape. © Inclusive Education Western Cape, www.included.org.za

1

The meaning and practice of educational theory

Chinedu Okeke

Chapter overview

This chapter looks at one of the **epistemological** choices you will be required to make when you embark on your learning endeavour that involves research, reading, and writing. Over the years, our experience as teachers shows that students often fail to make a connection between theory and its relevance to their studies. We have also learned from our dealings with students that most of them struggle to locate the theory or theories relevant to their field of specialisation. These students are, consequently, not able to demonstrate knowledge of the application of theory to their studies. By reading this chapter we hope you will understand, from now on, that theories are essential learning and research tools, without which the outcome of your learning and research may be of little or no value to you and others. To develop this chapter, we will:

- look briefly at the meaning of educational theory
- outline the functions of educational theory
- explain the different categories and kinds of educational theories
- examine the concept of conceptual framework
- discuss what theoretical framework and perspective represent
- look at two concepts of theoretical or literature reviews
- look briefly at the implications of our discussion for educational practice
- summarise our discussion
- present some activities, and
- explore a list of further readings.

epistemology
(noun): simply means the theory of knowledge. It deals with what we mean by knowledge itself and what is it to know something. So an epistemological *(adjective)* choice is one that requires 'knowing what it is to know'.

Learning outcomes

By the end of this chapter you should be able to:

- Explain the meaning and functions of educational theories
- Name the different categories of theories
- Outline the different kinds of educational theories
- Differentiate between conceptual framework, theoretical framework or perspective, theoretical or literature reviews
- Discuss the implications of educational theories for educational practice
- Try out some reflective activities.

What does educational theory mean?

What you are about to read represents our attempt to help you understand the meaning of educational theory. This section is important because our experience as teachers working with students over the years has shown that most of you often find it difficult to understand what we mean when we talk of 'theory'. By reading this section, you will become familiar with the terms *theory*, and *educational theory* in particular. So, put simply, an educational theory is a systematic discussion of related educational concepts. Theories represent a particular kind of explanation. Klette (2012) defines theory as an organised body of concepts and principles intended to explain a particular **phenomenon**. Theories provide the analytical concepts and the language to use when doing research (or investigating something), as well as when you are writing the reports of such an investigation.

> A **phenomenon**, in the context of education, represents something – concepts, events or facts – which you are interested in understanding, e.g. poverty, violence, academic achievement or failure, etc.

Theories provide us with the concepts we can use to identify, as well as understand issues, processes, and social developments. The range of chapters in this book have been carefully put together to enable you to understand some of these issue, and to apply various theories, presented in Part 1 of this book, in explaining these issues. Theories attach meaning to concepts that ordinarily may mean nothing to you. According to Henning (2004:14), "theories are human constructions: they are derived from information that people collect by seeing, hearing, touching, sensing and feeling". This information is put together through the process of theorising. When you engage in a process of theorising, you are simply arranging your collection of ideas in a systematic manner in order for you to understand the particular phenomenon you may be studying or observing.

You should note the importance of the word 'systematic', which we use throughout our discussion here. To be systematic in this context is to be properly and consciously organised in your attempts at formulating a theory. Without being systematic, it will be difficult for you to arrive at any theory. More so, it will be equally difficult for you to understand any existing theory if you fail to be systematic in your reasoning. A theory, then, is a systematic way of looking at, as well as understanding, events within a given situation. Therefore, one rule that you have to observe when you engage in the process of theorising, is to be systematic in your own way of thinking. Theories may also be viewed as verifiable facts which create awareness of a particular kind, linking the identifiable effects to the causes, with the aim of providing solutions toward understanding particular educational problems (Creswell, 2003). Thus, a theory explains how and why a particular thing, issue, or social development functions or occurs as it does. Furthermore, a theory is an organising tool that tries to explain why society, or an aspect of society, functions in a particular way.

From our discussions so far, you should find that you are developing a clear idea of what theory means. People do not always understand the difference between a theory and a hypothesis, and perhaps you are wondering about this too. So let us use the rest of this section to try to understand the difference between theory and hypothesis. A hypothesis is a tentative 'guess', a working assumption, which a researcher formulates to guide the processes of an educational investigation or research endeavour. It is a statement that tries to predict what the investigator or researcher thinks will be the outcome of the investigation. Unlike a theory, a hypothesis states the relationship between two or more variables or phenomena under investigation. Usually, a hypothesis will try to suggest some form of answer or solution to problems. This is not what a theory does; instead, theory offers evidence-based explanations about the nature of a particular educational problem. Hypothesis is aimed at defining the direction of an investigation. It will also assist you by sharpening your focus on a problem, as well as providing the direction in which the solution to the problem might be found. Theory is simply a tool of analysis. It is a lens that enables you to direct your thinking on a particular course when you are engaged in the examination of educational issues.

 Stop and reflect

We hope you are finding this discussion useful. What have you learned so far from the discussion? Can you define a theory? Are you clear about what theory means? Are you able to differentiate between a theory and a hypothesis? Take a few minutes to write down your responses to these questions. The act of writing will organise and clarify your thoughts and ideas.

Explanation of concepts linked to theory

In your readings about educational theory, you will encounter certain concepts that are related to (and are often confused with) theory. This section of the chapter is just as important because students often appear to confuse these concepts or rather, use some of them interchangeably. By reading this section, you will begin to appreciate the differences between these concepts while equally appreciating their functions. These concepts include the following: *theoretical or literature review, conceptual framework, theoretical framework,* and *theoretical perspective.*

The following diagram describes the relationships that exist between these concepts.

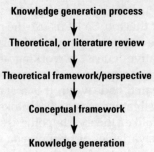

Figure 1.1   Process relationship between concepts in theory-driven research

Now, while your attention is still on Figure 1.1, let us begin to explain the concepts in greater detail to enable you to understand their various functions, and relationship with one another.

Theoretical, or literature review

When you want to study or research a particular phenomenon (note that we have already explained what a phenomenon means), you engage yourself in an activity known as a theoretical or literature review. Theoretical or literature reviews represent a comprehensive study of related literature or materials of interest on a particular issue or issues you may be investigating. These materials may include papers, articles, published books, documents, brochures, technical reports, personal communication, video recordings, television broadcasts, electronic books and internet resources (websites and web pages). It is also an exercise you embark on because you want to show what has been covered by previous investigators or researchers in the area you want to investigate. In addition, a theoretical review may also be an activity you undertake in order to explore existing theories within a particular field of learning. However, merely showing the existence of such theories is not enough. You will be on the right track when you take the additional step of demonstrating how a particular theory will influence your thinking and investigations, from this review process through until you have finalised your research report. This practice will enable you to construct and bring into focus the theoretical framework of your study. So what does theoretical framework mean?

Theoretical framework

A theoretical framework is driven by your **theoretical orientation**, an analytical engine which propels your thinking. This is something like the wheels of your study when you are engaged in an investigation. Note that your role in this investigative journey will be to drive the research vehicle around. However, the satisfaction you will get from riding this research vehicle depends on the explanatory power which

theoretical orientation: in this context, means the direction or angle from which you want to project your study; and you want others to view your study

characterises the activity. A theoretical framework therefore is the explanatory mechanism that enables you to understand as well as to explain the verbal and non-verbal interactional **dynamics** amongst the participants in a particular study. It is meant to guide the research process by determining what things you must measure, as well as what statistical relationships you must seek to establish. A theoretical framework enables you to put together your conceptual framework (to be discussed shortly) in a particular manner. Henning (2004:25) notes that a theoretical framework helps you to make **explicit** the "assumptions about the interconnectedness of the way things are related in words. A theoretical framework is like the lenses through which you view the world." A well-established theoretical framework functions to direct your conceptual framework in a way that makes your investigation clear, as well as its purpose; and equally, makes a good link with the literature review, already discussed earlier. Henning (2004) also notes the complementary role of a good theoretical framework to the review of literature or theoretical review when she states that it facilitates dialogue between both your literature and your investigation: they are able to 'talk' to each other.

A concept that is related to theoretical framework is *perspective*. Sometimes these terms are used interchangeably to mean the same thing; sometimes they are used to denote different things. To be clear, it is worth looking at the concept of perspective. The word 'perspective' refers to a **worldview**, a school of thought, an established opinion, a theory that tries to give a picture of something, an event, or society at large. So it is important to note that theoretical perspective often means the same as theoretical framework.

Conceptual framework

The difference between theoretical and conceptual frameworks can be confusing. You should be able to see by now that both terms perform slightly different, but related functions in the process of knowledge generation. Since we have already covered the meaning of theoretical framework, let us turn to understanding the meaning of conceptual framework.

Unlike a theoretical framework, which serves as the lens through which to conduct your research (your second eye), a conceptual framework provides the structure that your research will take on. A conceptual framework is a schematic diagram, which tries to explain the entire process of the inquiry or research. According to Jabareen (2009:51), a conceptual framework is "a network of interlinked concepts that together provide a comprehensive understanding of a phenomenon" or set of variables. Let us use an example to demonstrate this explanation. Suppose you want to study inclusive education in the classroom (see Part 3, Chapter 12), your conceptual framework would concentrate on explaining certain key concepts that may include:
- features of the inclusive education classroom
- the way inclusive education is practised in the classroom

dynamics: the influences or forces that make something shift or change
explicit: made clear and precise

worldview: a representation of one's own way of seeing and reasoning about something, and about life generally. A person's worldview is also influenced by his or her beliefs and thoughts.

- strategies that are used by teachers
- available support systems – the family and community support for the teacher, school-based and district support, etc.

In providing your conceptual framework, your role is to present in a very simple, articulate, and comprehensive manner a full description of how the listed phenomena or variables relate to one another in making sense of inclusive education in a particular classroom situation. You would have realised at this point that there is a strong relationship between developing a conceptual framework and literature review. Your conceptual framework is usually and necessarily informed by the quality of your literature review. The quality of your conceptual framework is hugely dependent on the strength of your literature review; it allows you to know what has already been covered by other investigators in the same field on the specific phenomenon you are studying. Henning (2004) notes that one major function of conceptual framework would be to position you as the researcher within the context of your study. A well-written conceptual framework allows you to establish clearly your own interest in the study.

The following table presents a summary of the differences and relationship between theoretical and conceptual frameworks.

Table 1.1 The relationship between concepts: Theoretical framework and conceptual framework

	Theoretical framework	**Conceptual framework**
Meaning	Theoretical orientation, worldview, perspective, analytical engine, research lens, explanatory mechanism, etc.	A schematic diagram, a descriptive presentation of a network of concepts, a structure or direction that tries to describe which way you may be leading on a particular phenomenon, etc.
Purpose	To provide your study with a particular identity. Also, to position your discussion within a particular theoretical discipline.	To enable you to put some sequence or order in your style of presentation. This will help to prevent unnecessary overlapping or repetition of ideas.
Function	Directs your conceptual framework in a manner to make the purpose of your investigation clear. It also enables you to put aside your personal assumptions while working from a particular theoretical orientation.	Makes for well-planned, organised, and clear presentation of connected and interlinked ideas and concepts that explain the phenomenon or variable.

By now you have learned from the discussion that both theoretical and conceptual frameworks perform different but related functions during the course of knowledge production. To make sure you are clear in your reading of this chapter, you need to see theoretical frameworks in terms of that which gives you the language to conduct your inquiry. In contrast, a conceptual framework functions to put some structure or order in the approach you use to argue, arrange, and present the analysis of your literature search. Before we discuss the various functions of an educational theory, take some time and reflect on what we have discussed so far.

Stop and reflect

Reflect on the following questions: Do you have a particular personal theory? Or have you ever thought that you could have a personal theory? Take a few minutes to write down your personal theory on a piece of paper. Now think about how your personal theory may be different from some of the educational theories you have come across before. How might your personal theory be different from the theories you will study in later chapters of this book? And how has your personal theory influenced your approach to life generally? Write down as much as you like in response to these questions. (Remember to keep in mind what you now understand by the concept, theory.)

Functions of educational theory

So far, we have explored what theory means. You have also been exposed to various concepts that are linked with that of theory. Theories perform many **functions**. In this section, you will learn some of the very useful functions of any educational theory. Henning (2004), Jabareen (2009), Kawulich (2009), and Klette (2012) discuss some of the important roles of educational theories, which include the following:

First, educational theories provide us with **empirically** backed justifications to make predictions about a particular event, phenomenon, variable, or society at large. You may remember that theories are themselves products of time spent on a well thought-out process of investigation (sometimes lasting for many years). All human inventions are based on some form of theory that resulted from a long period of empirical investigation. Such theories are usually adopted as given, relative to the explanations that would necessarily inform guidelines for actions and behaviour. From a simple micro-classroom investigation to a large-scale government-financed investigation, classroom adjustments as well as big governmental policy formulations are all supposedly informed by some form of theoretical explanation. Theories therefore provide us with the justification for forecasting into the future, while explaining the rationale for doing so, based on what we know from the data informing the theory.

Second, we have already noted that theories are like lenses that enable us to direct our thoughts in a particular direction when we engage in the examination of educational issues. Remember that theories do not present a uniform lens to every educational theorist. Instead, educational theories offer different lenses to different people, depending on what they want to observe, study, and analyse. For instance, when studying poverty (which you will encounter in Part 2), or school violence (in Parts 2 and 3), an educational psychologist, sociologist, or philosopher would not necessarily approach the issue from theoretical lenses that are in agreement with one another's theoretical standpoint or orientation. This diversity is possible because educational theories do not operate from one particular direction;

function: in this context, means notions such as role, contribution, or importance of educational theory to the generation of knowledge
empirically: describes an approach to research that is based on what can be verified by observation or experience, rather than only theory or deduction

instead, the individual is usually offered a multi-dimensional approach at the level of explanation (Okeke, 2009).

Third, because all human inventions are based on theory, often resulting from a long period of empirical investigation, it would it is unlikely that opinions or speculations would lead to any theory. All educational theories are based on empirical data that serve to provide a safeguard against unreasoned approaches to solving educational problems. So instead of some form of abstract generalisation, theories that are soundly informed by empirical data and evidence help to guard against speculative assumptions since all conclusions would be drawn from data – and verified by data.

Fourth, one very important area in which educational theory is useful toward knowledge generation is in making possible widespread comparative analysis. Klette (2012) notes that theory functions as a means of building analogies and universal generalisations, especially about the natural sciences. Researchers with this orientation share the idea that the central aim of knowledge generation is to discover universal laws in the positive data of experience, pure logic, and pure mathematics (Wagner & Okeke, 2009). Such researchers regard the products of such process as true, given, and universal.

Fifth, another benefit of educational theory is to allow the investigator to go beneath the surface to show the inherent meaning of something. As an interpretive tool, theory enables us to ask hard questions and to go extra lengths to really understand the phenomenon under study. Klette (2012) notes that it is a merit of theory to push for deeper understanding and not to relax before we have a complete analysis of, for example, teenage pregnancy; persistent lateness for school; incidence of truancy, amongst a particular set of learners, etc.

Finally, educational theories enable us to guard against what Klette (2012) refers to as the 'triviality of empiricism'. Empiricism here refers to simple recording of individual facts with no method of analysis, generalisation, or theoretical framework. Note that while recording facts may constitute data, only by applying the explanatory tool of theory can the researcher extract the meaning that is buried in the data. So theory in this case functions to enable you to guard against assuming that the way your collected data may explain things.

At this stage we are making progress in terms of our discussion and understanding of the meaning and relevance of educational theory to knowledge generation. Remember, however, that no textbook will supply you with all the information you need about a particular issue you want to understand. You need to read more about the development of theory on your own. You will discover that each chapter of this book includes some readings to guide you through a more comprehensive exploration of issues about the meaning and practice of educational theory. For now, let us look at the many kinds of educational theories.

Stop and reflect

Earlier, you were asked to take a few minutes to write down your personal theory. Refer to it now. Are you happy with what you have written? Can you write down four reasons why your personal theory is important to you? Please go back again and read the functions of educational theory in the last section. Do you find any similarity between these, and the significance of your personal theory? Continue to read until you find some similarities.

Categories and kinds of educational theories

You are already aware that this particular book takes the position of an *African perspective* to issues around schooling, society and inclusive education. For this reason, we will divide our discussion on the kinds of educational theory into two, namely: *Eurocentric* theories, and *Afrocentric* or *indigenous* theories. We will look at each of these more closely. But before we go on with our discussion, be aware that Chapters 2, 3, 4 and 5 have detailed contributions on some aspect of our discussion in this section. So our focus here is mainly to foreground the detailed groupings you will encounter in forthcoming chapters.

Eurocentric theories

The first category of theories is the Eurocentric category. By Eurocentric, we mean all Western (educational) theories that have been adopted both theoretically and practically within the African knowledge industry. Theories that fall within this category can be sub-divided into two kinds, namely: micro-level and macro-level theories.

Micro-level theories are concerned with the nature of everyday human social interactions on a very small scale. Typically, this is the study of small groups within a social setting. Researchers working from the perspective of micro-level theories are interested in understanding how people make sense of their everyday interactions in small units. Within such small units as the school, the micro-sociologist or education researcher would be concerned with the understanding of such interactional dynamics involving learner–learner, teacher–teacher, and teacher–learner relationships. Micro-level theories tend to focus attention on the actions of individuals in groups, and how the groups affect, and are affected by, our values, beliefs, and behaviours. Some examples of micro-level theories include:

• Symbolic interaction
• Labelling theory
• Rational choice theory
• Ecological development of the child.

Macro-level theories are concerned with the understanding of people in a broad way. They are mainly about human societies. It is this type of theoretical approach that led to a sociological approach that analyses societies, social systems, or populations on a large scale. Macro-level theories in education focus on the dynamics of systems and structures. A major difference between the micro- and macro-level theories in education is that micro-level theories focus directly on the interactions within and among individuals in classrooms. In contrast, the macro-level takes in other human interactions from the broader society. Some examples of macro-level theories include:

* Functional theory
* Conflict theories
* Reproduction and resistance theories.

You will find more detail about these theories in Chapter 5 (on the ecological development of the child). Next, we will look at the Afrocentric category of theories.

Afrocentric or indigenous African theories

The second category of theories is classified as Afrocentric theories. Afrocentric theories refer to all theories that have originated from within the African continent rather than being 'imported' from elsewhere, as with Eurocentric theories. Theories within this category would include:

* Africanisation
* Ubuntu
* African indigenous knowledge.

The concept of *Africanisation* directs our attention to the need for educational theories that will relevantly reflect African educational, economic, political, and social lives. Africanisation demands a re-telling of the African experience and history that would necessarily de-emphasise over-reliance on Eurocentric theoretical interpretations of Africa and its development. Moreover, Africanisation reflects a call to all people who call themselves Africans, but also to all institutions responsible for the training of the mind, to the need for the African intellectuals to begin theoretically changing our world through a reflection of ourselves. Naude & Naude (2005) refer to the concept of Africanisation as an ideology, highlighting the need for an education programme that must be inherently inclusive. This is highly pertinent because any attempt towards the rethinking of Africa's higher education must confront the issue of policy diversity within Africa's institutions of higher learning, since this appears to be at the heart of Africanisation. This seems to be what Naude and Naude (2005) mean when they say that cultural justice is indeed a crucial dimension of the Africanisation of higher education. Again, the concept of Africanisation reminds Africans that something is missing. Thus an African perspective to this transformation is believed to be a step in the right direction. In Chapters 2, 3 and 4 you will learn about this concept in detail.

A second kind of Afrocentric or indigenous theory refers to *Ubuntu*. This is a theoretical ideology that resonates with the humanistic spirit that intends to clearly define the ethos of the African peoples. Ubuntu (in South Africa, an Nguni word; an eastern Nigerian synonym for *igwebuike*, an Igbo word) implies humanity, unity, and togetherness of Africa's peoples. You may notice that the word 'Ubuntu' emerged out of the political tumult prior to the 1990s when peacemakers wanted to ensure that in the process of creating a new framework, they formulated a sentiment that would become part of the defining vision of democracy (Msila, 2008). Thus the Ubuntu philosophy is a worldview which was popularised under the democratic dispensation in South Africa because it contains some basic values of humanity and compassion. Moreover, because the Ubuntu philosophy is informed by aspects of village and kin relations in many contexts within contemporary African societies, it serves equally as a social survival strategy that developed from the adverse social and geographical circumstances in which people had to cooperate to survive (Msila, 2008). It is believed by many African intellectuals that these sentiments are not usually accounted for by most existing Eurocentric theories, hence the push for Afrocentric approaches in theorising about African affairs: educational, political, economic, and social. In Chapters 2, 3 and 4 you will learn in greater detail how the Ubuntu ideology impacts the act of knowing and the generation of knowledge.

The third and final kind of theory listed in this subsection, is *African indigenous knowledge*. This indigenous theoretical orientation refers to the totality of the knowledge and skills that are possessed by a particular group of people, which enables them to get on with their lives within a particular geographic community. Micheal van Wyk (in Chapter 3) defines indigenous knowledge as a lived world, a form of reasoning that informs and sustains people who make their homes in a local area. From their perspective, indigenous knowledge is a bridge between human beings (communities of practice) and their environments (nature). Please refer to Chapter 3 (and also Chapters 2 and 4) to read more about *African indigenous knowledge systems*. Before proceeding to the final section of this chapter, which looks at the implications of our discussion so far on theories for educational practice, let us stop once more and think about what we have learned.

 Stop and reflect

Reflect on what we have discussed so far in this subsection. Do you understand the categorisation of theories in terms of Eurocentric and Afrocentric? Does this section perhaps interest and appeal to you more than others? Why do you think this is so? What, in your opinion, are the differences between these two categories of theories? Go back and read the section again if you are unsure.

Implications of theories for educational practice

Educational theories have implications for how we generate knowledge through research, and how education policies are formulated. Note therefore that the lack of a clear-cut theoretical base during the process of the generation of knowledge or research would certainly result in you making wrong or very weak conclusions about a particular study. Research problems represent the constructs of your mind which you intend to unpack through an empirical or fieldwork process. Be aware that during the conduct of such fieldwork, the problems will be brought into concrete existence through the conceptual frames which you formulate. This exercise can only proceed through a particular approach which resonates with your language structure. Remember, it is this language structure that we earlier referred to as your theoretical framework. You also need to remember that you can only select from a whole body of existing language that which best represents your conceptual, as well as contextual, thinking in relation to the problem(s) you want to study. Any study or research endeavour that fails to follow this basic requirement would most certainly result in a very weak outcome.

The centrality of theories for the explanation of the human dynamics has long been established by many researchers (some examples include Creswell, 2003; Henning, 2004; Maxwell, 2009). Theories are orienting strategies that inform you how to conduct your studies especially when human beings are involved. When theories are applied appropriately they will help you know the kind of questions to ask, and the kind of information to seek in your study. This practice is what will help you accomplish the objectives you set out to achieve through a particular study. That is why theories represent a comprehensive way of explaining human personal, social, and behavioural dynamics. A good study or research report is able to demonstrate how a particular theory or theories have influenced the entire process of knowledge generation from the literature review until the process is completed.

From the perspective of the sociology of education (sometimes referred to as 'school and society'), note that sociological theories have been influencing the conduct of research in universities for centuries. These influences have a history dating back to the eighteenth and nineteenth centuries. For instance, when sociology was first introduced as a resource for researching the human world, its main approach was through the science of **positivism**, in which researchers looked for scientific laws. This led researchers to the idea that social phenomena can only be explained through the collection and quantification of data (Okeke, 2009; Wagner & Okeke, 2009). More recently, in the 1950s, the development of **humanist** approaches challenged positivist ideas (Glesne & Peshkin, 1992). A major effect of this development was the emergence of various competing theoretical perspectives which we earlier grouped as micro- and macro-theories, with each establishing a unique way of viewing the

positivism: a philosophy which emphasises things that can be seen and observed rather than those based on abstract reasoning or speculation
humanism: a concept in social psychology which relates to an approach that studies the whole person, and the uniqueness of each individual. Humanist psychologists look at human behaviour not only through the lens of the researcher, but through that of the person doing the behaving.

social world. Let us now consider a few examples of the different theoretical approaches to knowing and knowledge generation.

Functionalist views of education assume a dimension in which education is perceived as performing certain basic functions including the transmission of culture; promotion of social and political integration; social control; and change. Note that the views of conflict theorists are different from those of the functionalists. Conflict theorists view education in relation to the dynamics of capitalism and are more interested in understanding how schools respond to the demands of the workplace and economy. Similarly, a theory-guided study of the role of education in society would establish the links between power, ideology, education, and the relations of production within capitalist society. This is the type of theoretical orientation that has dominated research on schooling processes since the 1950s. On a different note, feminist-conflict theoretical views on the educational processes centre on the issues of gender and subjugation. These views are also committed to a type of research aimed at equity and emancipation in a world that creates, maintains, and reproduces unequal power relations within society (Henning, 2004).

> **functionalism:** an approach in social psychology that interprets phenomena in terms of the functions they perform within a whole system

A symbolic interactionist approach to a theory-guided study would seek an understanding of the meanings embedded in individuals' actions and interactions within a social setting such as the school. Thus a symbolic interactionist's study starts with an attempt to uncover the meanings in the language and actions of the individuals within the social setting. In this manner, symbolic interactionist researchers have questioned the justifications of such school practices as typifying, labelling, and streaming. They have also questioned the issue of stereotyping in schools. The interactionist view is that the way individuals and teachers (in particular) perceive human actions and human beings would certainly influence the outcome of such perceptions. In this way, interactionists warn of the dangers that are inherent in the way teachers in particular perceive and assess their learners.

Researchers within the domain of sociology of education and education in general have been applying various theories in researching such issues as the relationship between education and society, schooling and inequality, culture, gender, school violence, school discipline, school dropouts, poverty, multiculturalism, **cultural hegemony** in schools, school performance, the family, the relationship between the school and the state, and so on. Such research endeavours have led to various theories and models which offer the foundations for educational policy-making, educational planning and management, and the evaluation of education systems in general. Next, in Chapter 2 you will be exposed to aspects of theory development and professional practice in much greater detail. Always keep in mind the Afrocentric importance and focus of this book. Further chapters, namely Chapters 3, 4, and 5, have all been carefully designed to introduce you to many aspects of the African epistemological ways of knowing. Enjoy learning about who you are.

> **cultural hegemony:** describes a social situation where one group's identity, values and views dominate over all other groups'

Summary of discussion

In this chapter we have discussed the meaning and practice of educational theories. You are now well grounded in the meaning of educational theories and various concepts that are linked with the use of theory. Always keep in mind the various functions that theories perform in the field of education. Remember, too, the two major categories of theories that we have discussed in this chapter – the Eurocentric and the Afrocentric. We also noted various theories associated with each of these categories. You should now be able to contrast and explain the differences between these two categories of theories. Further, we outlined the many functions that theories perform as we embark on the task of knowledge generation, which we refer to as research. You will recall that we discussed the differences between conceptual framework, theoretical framework or perspective, and theoretical or literature review. Many activities and reflections have been carefully designed in this chapter, and throughout this book, to help you understand and engage with the ideas it contains. The next chapter takes you into theory in practice in multicultural classrooms, and the implications for professional practice.

Closing activities

Self-reflection
Think back on our discussions in this chapter:
• What are your personal theories?
• What you have learnt from this chapter?
• Can you now define a theory?
• Are you able to differentiate between various theoretical concepts?
• Are the functions that theories perform clear to you?
• Do you perhaps need to read the chapter again?

Questions to answer in writing
• List and discuss five functions of educational theories.
• Discuss the major differences between the two categories of theories.
• What differences are there between a conceptual framework and a theoretical framework of a study?
• Discuss some of the implications of educational theories for educational practice.

Micro-classroom-based research
• As an intending professional teacher, provide a conceptual model of a particular classroom problem within a given classroom or school setting.
• In not more than 14 words, provide a title for what you have conceptualised.
• Write two purposes for your chosen title.
• In your own words, mention and briefly discuss one micro-level theory relevant to your topic.
• Finally, give two reasons why you have chosen this theory.

References and further reading

Arum, R., Beattie, I.R. & Ford, K. (Eds). 2011. *The structure of schooling: Readings in the sociology of education.* London: Sage.

Ballantine, J.H. & Spade, J.Z. (Eds). 2012. *Schools and society: A sociological approach to education.* London: Sage.

Creswell, J.W. 2003. *Research design: Qualitative, quantitative, and mixed methods approaches.* London: Sage Publications.

Glesne, C. & Peshkin, A. 1992. *Becoming qualitative researchers: An introduction.* London: Longman.

Henning, E. 2004. *Finding your way in qualitative research.* Pretoria: Van Schaik Publishers.

Jabareen, Y. 2009. Building a conceptual framework: Philosophy, definitions and procedure. *International Journal of Qualitative Methods.* 8(4):49–58.

Kawulich, B. 2009. The role of theory in research. In M. Gardner, C. Wagner, & B. Kawulich (Eds). *Teaching research methods in the social sciences.* (37–47). London: Ashgate.

Klette, K. 2012. *The role of theory in educational research.* Norway: The Research Council of Norway.

Maxwell, J.A. 2009. Review of theory and educational research by Jean Anyon. *Education Review.* 13:1–9.

Msila, V. 2008. Ubuntu and school leadership. *Journal of Education,* 44:67–84.

Naude, P. & Naude, E. 2005. "We must recover our own selves ..." Cultural justice as ethical issues in higher education. *Journal of Education.* 37:59–77.

Nwana, O.C. 1981. *Introduction to educational research.* Ibadan, Nigeria: Heinemann Educational Books Limited.

Ofo, J.E. 1994. *Research methods and statistics in education and social sciences.* Lagos, Nigeria: Joja Educational Research and Publishers Ltd.

Okeke, C.I.O. 2010. School and Society: A-300 level course material. Kwaluseni, Swaziland: Institute of Distance Education Print Shop.

Okeke, C.I.O. 2009. Issues pertaining to the theoretical framework of a study: Reflections from some universities in three African countries. *The Nigerian Journal of Guidance and Counselling.* 14(1):58–70.

Okeke, C.I.O. 2010d. *Gender and schooling: A qualitative study of teens' perceptions of schooling in a Nigerian suburb.* Germany: VDM Verlag Dr. Muller.

Parelius, A.N. & Parelius, R.J. 1978. *The sociology of education*. New Jersey: Prentice-Hall.

Rimer, B.K. & Glanz, K. 2005. *Theory at a glance: A guide for health promotion practice*. Washington, DC: US Department of Health and Human Services.

Suppes, P. 1974. The place of theory in educational research. *Educational Researcher*. 3:3–10.

Wagner, C. & Okeke, C.I.O. 2009. Quantitative or qualitative: Ontological and epistemological choices in research methods curricula. In M. Gardner, C. Wagner & B. Kawulich (Eds). *Teaching research methods in the social sciences*. (61–69). London: Ashgate.

2

Indigenous African theories in multicultural education

Namhla Sotuku and Ntombozuko S Duku

Chapter overview

This chapter introduces an Afrocentric philosophy which argues against views and approaches that often perceive indigenous knowledge (IK) as the historical and outdated practices of African people. We argue instead that indigenous knowledge is a process of learning and sharing social life, histories, identities, economic and political practices, unique to each cultural group in the context of inclusive education. This chapter also supports the notion of inclusivity by presenting an African theory of knowledge, and argues for its place in multicultural classroom contexts. In this chapter therefore, we examine multiculturalism, its possibilities and challenges; and then we build an argument for how Ubuntu, an African philosophy and value, could be infused into school curricula to meet the challenges of multiculturalism.

Learning outcomes

By the end of this chapter you should be able to:
- Identify the core elements of multicultural education
- Examine teachers' practices and experiences in multicultural classrooms
- Critically analyse the criticisms of multicultural education
- Identify core elements of Ubuntu
- Demonstrate an understanding of how Ubuntu could be used as a strategy to manage some of the challenges that multiculturalism poses in South African schools.

CASE STUDY 1

Pam has just graduated from an English-medium multiracial teachers' college. However, when she was at college she almost never mixed with students from other language backgrounds. She tended to interact with only English-speaking students. During lectures, when the students in Pam's class were asked to work in groups, they would often group themselves by race and home language.

Today is Pam's first day of teaching at Pama Primary School. On entering her classroom her heart beats faster. She is greeted by a class of 45 eager Grade 3 learners.

Before long she remembers that at college they were taught to do a profile of their learners. She quickly decides to give her new learners the task of writing on the topic 'Who am I'?

Later on, this is the mind map she drew after reading through her learners' narratives:

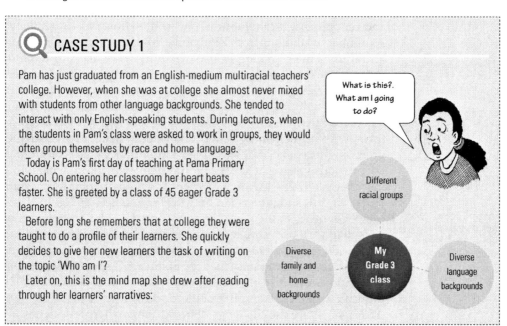

What is this?. What am I going to do?

Different racial groups

My Grade 3 class

Diverse family and home backgrounds

Diverse language backgrounds

Stop and reflect

1   What is your understanding of the concepts 'diverse language backgrounds', 'diverse home backgrounds', and 'diverse racial backgrounds'?
2   How will having learners with 'diverse language backgrounds', 'diverse home backgrounds', and 'diverse racial backgrounds' influence teaching and learning in Pam's class? Discuss both the strengths and challenges inherent in such a diverse classroom.
3   What did Pam miss out on at college that would have prepared her for this diverse classroom that she now faces?
4   If this was your class, how would you feel, and why?

Introducing the challenges of multiculturalism

South Africa exhibits social diversity in the starkest possible forms. It is the home of a breathtaking range of different languages, religions, ethnic groups, and cultural traditions and practices. The term 'rainbow nation' has been used to highlight and exemplify this rich diversity. The diversity is not only visible in our wider society but also in spaces – physical and psychological – closer to our future generations, like schools and classrooms (Brown & Shumba, 2011).

When the South African Schools Act (Act No. 84 of 1996) was published, it formalised the process of desegregation of schools in South Africa. It created the opportunity for learners from diverse cultural backgrounds to attend public schools of their choice. African students flocked to historically white and Indian schools in search of quality education. Besides this, the desegregation of schools in South Africa also introduced the phenomenon of intra-black dynamics and xenophobia, as the emphasis now shifted from race to 'ethnicity'. A number of students from Zimbabwe, Malawi, Nigeria and Kenya also entered the schooling system of South Africa. Teaching has thus become a multicultural encounter of many dimensions. Daily, teachers are faced with the challenge of teaching and managing learners of unfamiliar cultures, social class, languages, and backgrounds. This has placed tremendous pressure on teachers and has impacted on their own sense of identity, beliefs, and value systems. Many currently practising teachers completed their initial training as educators in the previously segregated education system, with the understanding that they would be teaching learners from a particular race group. However, this situation is not only synonymous with South Africa. Many countries in the world have become more **heterogeneous** as a result of various social, economic and political developments, and increased global mobility. Public spaces such as schools have become cultural crossroads because they are points where people of different orientations, or with different sub-cultures, converge (Morrow, 1998). Education policymakers all over the world, but particularly in South Africa, now face the challenge of how to serve diverse societies.

heterogeneous: not of the same kind; different in nature and type

In this chapter, we seek to examine multiculturalism, its possibilities and challenges, and then to build an argument for how Ubuntu, an African theory and value could be infused into school curricula to enrich multicultural school contexts, and help to overcome the challenges of multiculturalism.

The origins of multicultural education (ME)

Multicultural education is a philosophical concept built on the ideals of freedom, justice, equity, and human dignity (Nussbaum, 2003). James Banks, a pioneer in the field, traces the beginnings of multicultural education to have emerged during the civil rights movement of the 1960s and 1970s, in the United States. It grew out of the demands of minority ethnic groups for recognition and inclusion in the curricula of schools, colleges, and universities. Although multicultural education is an outgrowth of the ethnic studies movement of the 1960s, it has deep historical roots in the African-American ethnic studies movement that emerged in the late nineteenth and early twentieth centuries.

Initiated by scholars such as George Washington Williams, Carter G. Woodson, W.E.B. DuBois, and Charles H. Wesley, the primary goal of the early ethnic studies movement was to challenge the negative images and stereotypes of African-Americans prevalent in mainstream scholarship, by creating accurate descriptions of the life, history, and contribution of African-Americans. These scholars had a personal, professional, and enduring commitment to the upliftment of African-Americans. They believed that creating positive self-images of African-Americans was essential to their collective sense of identity and liberation. They also believed that stereotypes and negative beliefs about African-Americans could be effectively challenged by objective historical research that was also capable of transforming mainstream academic knowledge.

assimilation: the process of absorbing and integrating people, ideas or culture

 What are the perceived features and goals of multiculturalism?

Proponents of multiculturalism believe that multiculturalism emerged in reaction to the ideology of **assimilation**. Assimilation is an approach which places emphasis on minimising cultural differences, and encouraging social conformity and continuity. Multicultural education, on the other hand, is based on an acknowledgement that all cultures are equally valid and should be respected, in the school context. Lemmer, Meier and Van Wyk (2012:14) referring to Banks et al. (Banks, 2006; Banks, 2009; Baruth & Manning, 2000), identify the following features and goals of multicultural education:

* *Multicultural education encourages acculturation and cultural preservation.* This kind of education aims to provide learners with educational experiences that will enable them to maintain a commitment to their community of origin.
* *Multicultural education recognises and accepts the rightful existence of different cultural groups.* A major goal of multicultural education is therefore to reform schools, colleges and universities so that students from diverse groups will have equal opportunities to learn.
* *Multicultural education views cultural diversity as an asset rather than a handicap.* Multicultural education therefore attempts to accustom each ethnic and cultural group to the unique nature and value of other groups.

- *Multicultural education acknowledges the equal rights of all cultural groups in a society.* Learners should therefore be taught to recognise, acknowledge, and fight for the rights of all other groups.
- *Multicultural education advocates equal educational opportunities.* One of the major objectives of multicultural education is to ensure the success of all learners.
- *Multicultural education requires the reform of the total school environment.* Multicultural education is not achieved by simply, for example, changing the curriculum. The school as a whole needs to be restructured so that all learners will acquire the knowledge, attitudes and skills needed to function in ethnically and racially diverse communities and nations.

Given that these are the expected outcomes in contexts where multicultural education is implemented, what should inform teacher practice when implementing multicultural education? This chapter is dedicated to exploring the answer to this question.

The dimensions of multicultural education

James A. Banks's guidelines, called Dimensions of Multicultural Education (Banks, 2006), are used widely by school districts to conceptualise and develop courses, programmes, and projects in multicultural education. The five dimensions are: 1) content integration; 2) the knowledge construction process; 3) prejudice reduction; 4) an equity pedagogy; and 5) an empowering school culture and social structure. Although each dimension is conceptually distinct, in practice they overlap and are interrelated.

- **Content integration:** Content integration deals with the extent to which teachers use examples and content from a variety of cultures and groups to illustrate key concepts, principles, generalisations, and theories, in their subject area or discipline. The infusion of ethnic and cultural content into a subject area is logical and not contrived when this dimension is implemented properly. According to Grant and Sleeter, this means that content in subject areas or disciplines needs to be reworked so that it represents diverse perspectives, experiences, and contributions, particularly those that tend to be omitted or misrepresented when schools conduct 'business as usual':

> More opportunities exist for the integration of ethnic and cultural content in some subject areas than in others. There are frequent and ample opportunities for teachers to use ethnic and cultural content to illustrate concepts, themes, and principles in the social studies, the language arts, and in music. Opportunities also exist to integrate multicultural content into math and science. However, they are less ample than they are in social studies and the language arts. Content integration is frequently mistaken by school practitioners as comprising the whole of multicultural education, and is thus viewed as irrelevant to instruction in disciplines such as math and science.
> (Grant & Sleeter, 2007:162)

- **The knowledge construction process:** The knowledge construction process describes teaching activities that help students to understand, investigate, and determine how the implicit cultural assumptions, frames of references, perspectives, and biases of researchers and textbook writers influence the ways in which knowledge is constructed. Multicultural teaching involves not only infusing ethnic content into the school curriculum, but changing the structure and organisation of school knowledge. It also includes changing the ways in which teachers and learners view and interact with knowledge, helping them to become knowledge producers, not merely the consumers of knowledge produced by others.

  The knowledge construction process helps teachers and learners to understand why the existing cultural identities and social positions of researchers need to be taken into account when assessing the validity of knowledge claims. Multicultural theorists assert that the values, personal histories, attitudes, and beliefs of researchers cannot be separated from the knowledge they create. They consequently reject the positivist claims of **disinterested** and distanced knowledge production. They also reject the possibility of creating knowledge that is not influenced in some way by the cultural assumptions and social position of the knowledge producer. In multicultural teaching and learning, paradigms, themes, and concepts that exclude or distort the life experiences, histories, and contributions of **marginalised** groups are challenged. Multicultural pedagogy does not so much seek to challenge the prevailing Western outlook but to reconceptualise and expand it, to make it more representative and inclusive of a country's diversity, and to reshape the frames of references, perspectives, and concepts that make up school knowledge.

- **Prejudice reduction:** The prejudice reduction dimension of multicultural education seeks to help learners develop positive and democratic attitudes. Research shows that children often come to school with many negative attitudes and misconceptions about different racial, religious, and ethnic groups. On this issue, Aboud (2009) suggests that interventions to modify children's attitudes should therefore have a dual objective: to overcome the children's currently held bias; and to add more positive attitudes about different racial or cultural groups. The prejudice reduction dimension also helps learners to understand how ethnic identity is influenced by the context of schooling, and the attitudes and beliefs of dominant social groups. Prejudice can be reduced by interracial and intercultural contact if the contact situations have these characteristics: 1) they are cooperative rather than competitive; 2) the individuals experience equal status; and 3) the contact is **sanctioned** by authorities such as parents, principals, and teachers. By reducing prejudices, teachers help learners develop positive attitudes towards racial, ethnic, and cultural groups.

disinterested: impartial, not taking sides, or influenced in a particular direction

marginalisation: a condition of being always on the outside, or left out of the mainstream of social, cultural and economic life

sanctioned: allowed, approved or supported

- **Equity pedagogy:** Equity pedagogy exists when teachers modify their teaching in ways that will facilitate the academic achievement of learners from diverse racial, cultural, socio-economic, and language groups (Banks, 2006). This includes using a variety of teaching styles and approaches that are consistent with the range of learning styles within various cultural and ethnic groups. Teachers should adapt their instructional processes in the classroom so that they support high expectations, build on the strengths that diverse learners bring to the classroom, and actively engage learners in working with and producing knowledge (Grant & Sleeter, 2007). Multicultural theorists describe how cultural identity, communicative styles, and the social expectations of learners from marginalised ethnic and racial groups often conflict with the values, beliefs, and cultural assumptions of teachers. For example, the middle-class mainstream culture of schools tends to create a cultural **dissonance** and disconnects those privileged students who have internalised the school's cultural codes and communication styles, from those who have not. Teachers' practice becomes culturally responsive teaching when equity pedagogy is implemented. These teachers use instructional materials and practices that incorporate important aspects of the family and community culture of their learners. Culturally responsive teachers also use the cultural knowledge, prior experience, frames of reference, and performance styles of ethnically diverse learners to make learning encounters more relevant to, and effective for, them (Banks, 2006).

dissonance: not being in harmony with something, clashing, not fitting in

Reviewing what we know

From this discussion of multicultural education, the following conclusions can be drawn.

Baruth and Manning (2000) sum up by asserting that the current goal of multicultural education is to foster cultural pluralism within a culturally diverse, globally connected, and interdependent society, through teaching that is based on democratic values and beliefs.

The pathway towards this goal incorporates three strands of transformation:

1. *Transformation of self.* Teachers have a dual responsibility: on one hand, they have to engage in a critical and continuous process to examine how their prejudices, biases and assumptions inform their teaching, and thus affect the educational experience of learners. On the other hand, teachers have to engage learners in order to examine their own prejudices, and how these could affect the teaching and learning environment. To be an effective multicultural teacher two principles should guide one's teaching agenda: self-examination and transformation.
2. *Transformation of schools and schooling.* ME calls for a critical examination of all aspects of schooling. These include: teaching methodologies; curriculum; learning and teaching support materials (LTSM); school and classroom climate; school governance and rules.
3. *Transformation of society.* The ultimate goal of ME is to contribute progressively to the transformation of society, and to the application and maintenance of social justice and equity.

Multicultural education at play in South Africa's classrooms: Teachers' practice

South Africa can be regarded as still being in its infancy stages of multicultural schools and education (Cox, 2002). At the centre of multiculturalism are schools which have become the sites of cultural convergence – where previously diverse and divided cultures meet for the first time on supposedly 'equal ground' (Mpisi, 2010). Many black parents are sending their children to former white schools, which are perceived as better, more stable and supportive (Arendse, 2012). Teachers in such schools now teach and manage learners with cultures, languages and backgrounds that may be unknown to them (Meier & Hartell, 2009). Consequently, teachers and learners do not always cope effectively with the changes brought about by the introduction of multicultural education (Cox, 2010).

The following are some practices and experiences from multicultural classrooms. These include assimilationist approaches, hidden curriculum, and pluralistic co-existence.

Assimilationist approaches

Vandeyar (2010), Jansen (2004), and Mpisi (2010) reveal that teachers often apply an assimilationist approach when dealing with multiculturalism in the classroom. According to Banks (2006), assimilation occurs when one ethnic or cultural group acquires the behaviour, values and perspectives, ethos, and characteristics of the previously dominant group. This may be an unintentional strategy to deny differences between people, rather than an authentic multicultural approach. Under such circumstances, the members of the less powerful culture are accepted only if they give up their original identity, values, behavioural styles, language, and non-verbal communication styles. In South Africa, many schools work from the premise of assimilation; only the learner composition has changed. In most cases, the staff and school governing body (SGB) profiles remain unchanged.

Allied to the perspective of assimilation is the 'colour blindness' approach (Vandeyar, 2010). Colour blindness occurs when teachers suppress any negative images they hold of learners of other races. The 'colour blind' approach, especially towards the curriculum, is one way in which schools continue to maintain the *status quo* (in other words, the former segregation bias). Educators claim to 'see children and not colour' and studiously ignore race or colour in their dealings with learner diversity. Cox (2002:52–53) notes that teachers use expressions such as 'children are children' as a blanket statement to protect them from having to re-think and re-plan their approach to teaching. This is not only directed at issues of cultural and racial diversity, but also at diverse learner abilities and learning styles. By denying these differences, teachers expect learners to adjust to the system, and not the other way round.

CASE STUDY 2

Ms Kay teaches Grade 3 learners. Her class consists of diverse learners in terms of race, abilities, and culture. On this day, Ms Kay is exploring the different types of foods with learners. She has listed examples of different types of food on the chalkboard, and has asked the learners to identify and choose three types, and then draw them in their workbooks. About 15 minutes into the activity she discovers that six of the learners have only written the types of foods, but have not started to draw them. The majority of learners have not only drawn the types of the foods, but have also written explanations about each of the foods. Ms Kay seems only to concentrate on the majority of the learners, and seems unable to respond to the few who appear to struggle with the task.

 Stop and reflect

1   What do you think is happening in the classroom depicted in Case study 2?
2   If you were Ms Kay, how would you respond to the situation reflected in the scenario you have just read about?

 CASE STUDY 3

Varyenen (2005:7) provides this example from a Grade 6 lesson on the theme of 'Family':

Educator: Who is the head of the family?
Learners: Father.
Educator: Correct.

 Stop and reflect

1   Which dimension/s of multiculturalism has the teacher in Case study 3 not paid attention to?
2   How would you have responded to the answer that the learners provided about who the head of the family is? Why?

Teachers sometimes also use hidden curriculum to implement multicultural education.

Hidden curriculum

Hidden curriculum refers to the rules that teachers think learners know without being taught (Myles, Trautman & Shelvan, 2004). In other words, these are the values, principles, and practices that learners are supposed to follow or learn intuitively. Hidden curriculum is about attitudes and beliefs teachers attach to learning and teaching, and the power relations linked with these. These could include how desks are arranged in the classroom (the physical environment) and the social environment (how walls are decorated, the posters and the pictures, and the languages in such posters). In most cases, classroom physical layout reflects the powerful dominant culture, and may also reflect some stereotypes about certain cultural groups. Yet planning the classroom physical and social environment (such as classroom walls decorated with pictures and posters reflecting the cultures of all learners in the class (Arendse, 2012) should also be approached sensitively so that they do not perpetuate stereotypes of any race, culture, gender, religion, or group of people.

 Stop and reflect

1   As a new teacher, how would you ensure that the classroom social environment reflects the diverse nature of the learners?
2   What would guide you in the arrangement of the classroom physical space?

 CASE STUDY 4

Varyenen (2005:7) provides this example:

In Grade 5 learners are writing an assignment of 'girls' jobs and boys' jobs'. Towards the end of the period the learners report back on what they have written. The following interaction takes place between the educator and the learners:

Educator. Why don't we ask boys to make tea for the class educator?
Learners. Boys are careless.
Educator. Correct. Boys are careless.

 Stop and reflect

1   Which dimension of multiculturalism has the teacher not paid attention to, in Case sudy 4? Motivate your answer.
2   What does the teacher's response tell about his/her attitude towards gender equality?

The hidden curriculum is also determined by the language/s used inside and outside the classroom.

The use of language in the classroom

Language is used as the main vehicle for learning in the classroom. Learners in a diverse society such as South Africa bring to school their own languages, which may not necessarily be English, the language that most schools now use as the language of learning and teaching. Learners are prohibited from speaking their indigenous languages in the classroom as a strategy to promote cohesion. Giselbrecht (2009) and Mpisi (2010) perceive this as a sign that some languages and cultures are still perceived as of 'low prestige'.

CASE STUDY 5

Kathy teaches Mathematics and English in a former Model C school in East London, Eastern Cape. She is a bilingual teacher (English and Afrikaans) and her learners are 80% Afrikaans home language speakers, and 20% isiXhosa-speaking learners. In the staff complement of 20 educators, only two are isiXhosa speakers. The medium of instruction in this school is strictly English. Kathy's class has 26 learners and is characterised by many current teaching and learning technologies that include iPads, whiteboards, and data projectors. The teacher is satisfied that 70% of the learners perform well in all the assessment tasks. Her main concern is the 'few misbehaving elements in the classroom whose names I cannot even pronounce'. This misbehaviour is characterised by 'leaving at home class work, staying in the toilets during class time, disruption of other learners, etc.'. She further reports that the culprits are generally from the isiXhosa-speaking group. She shares with her fellow teacher (one of the two isiXhosa-speaking teachers in the school) that even though she is doing everything in her power to reach out to 'these isiXhosa-speaking children', they still fail most of the assessment tasks. As a result, most of the misbehaving learners have been identified for a remedial programme the following term.

Stop and reflect

1 What is going well/not going well in this class? Support your response with examples.
2 Which dimension of multiculturalism has the teacher not paid attention to?
3 If you were a teacher in this classroom, what would you do differently and why?

Pluralistic co-existence: Celebrating national heritage and civic days

In some multicultural schools in South Africa, social cohesion is promoted, variously, by the singing of the national anthem (in all four languages), and the recognition of the South Africa flag. There is, however, evidence that black South Africans identify more with the new national flag than non-blacks. Also, different groups understand and are more vocal in singing the lyrics in their own language (Bornman, 2005). Do you think that all learners understand why they have to sing in different languages? Do they all understand the lyrics?

In the South African calendar, the following dates are observed and celebrated:

- 27 April: Freedom Day
- 16 June: Youth Day
- 9 August: National Women's Day
- 24 September: Heritage Day

Another example is when, in celebration of Heritage Day on 24 September, schools might require learners from different cultural groups to display their traditional clothing and articles. Each culture gets a turn to tell the whole school something about their culture. The curriculum also requires that learners are taught about the history and importance of these public holidays.

Stop and reflect

How would you lead a discussion about the events of 16 June 1976:
- Without making white learners experience generational guilt?
- To minimise any anger or resentment from black learners for the racism and discrimination experienced by black South Africans pre-1994?

Reviewing what we know

In our discussions so far we have:
- Presented multicultural education from the perspectives of the proponents of multiculturalism.
- Presented case studies depicting teacher practice in multicultural classrooms, and interrogated each practice: Teachers' practice presented in the case studies reveal, amongst other things, the following issues:
  - Working in multicultural classrooms is a challenge.
  - South African teachers in multicultural contexts are still grappling with their own social identities and fears, as their school population transforms.
  - Multiculturalism therefore poses particular pedagogical and support challenges to professionals in the education system.
  - Most teachers' practice is underpinned by the assimilationist approach, which has a potential to disempower some learners.
- However, one example presented practices that reveal that some schools have realised the limitations of the assimilationist approach and, fuelled by the 'rainbow nation' concept, have begun to espouse a multicultural perspective. The trend in this type of school suggests that these schools recognise and celebrate cultural diversity (Vally and Dalamba, 1999).

The next section of this chapter will briefly present the criticisms of multicultural education.

Criticisms of multiculturalism

Stop and reflect

For you to ascertain whether the criticisms of multiculturalism are valid or not, refer to the section where we dealt with the goals, features and dimensions of multicultural education (page 20–22). Then, as you read the criticisms, identify the aspect of ME that is being interrogated (questioned). Also examine the relevance of the criticism in the current South African education context. Write your analysis in the form of a table, with columns for the relevant sections.

What do the theorists say about multiculturalism?

The following represents a summary of various perspectives by theorists who are critical of multiculturalist approaches:

- D'Souza and Williams (1996:383): Multicultural education is based on cultural relativism which is "the doctrine that all cultures are considered equal; no culture is regarded as superior or inferior to the any other. This doctrine that all cultures are equal does not square with our everyday observation of the world."
- Vally and Dalamba (1999): Multiculturalism is based on the premise that racism is a result of prejudice and ignorance which can be eradicated by merely promoting personal contact, educational goals, cultural exchange, understanding and the exchange of information.
- Morrow (1998, 2007): Apartheid and multiculturalism are similar to each other as they both highlight differences rather than commonalities. Alluding to this issue, Shumba and Brown (2011:537) say: "One of the dangers of multiculturalism, if mishandled, is that it promotes the idea that a nation-state consists of groups, rather than one common citizenship". In this sense, multiculturalism is often viewed as a force that disunites rather than unites people. Moreover, Glazer (1997:34) fears that "an emphasis on multiculturalism will teach our children untruths that will threaten national unity, that will undermine civic harmony, and that will do nothing to raise the achievement of the groups expected to benefit from it."
- Soudien and Sayed (2004) argue that multicultural education defined as 'respect for other cultures' fails to engage with the complex ways in which individuals and groups develop attitudes to one another.

Taking into consideration the issues highlighted in the discussion on the criticisms of multicultural education and teachers' practice, McKinney and Soudien (2011), in their report on multicultural education in South Africa, examine what it might mean to work within a multicultural framework within South Africa. This is a highlight from their report, quoted verbatim to emphasise the importance of their whole statement:

> The meaning of multicultural education in South Africa should be determined by its specific socio-historical context, both post-colonial and post-apartheid. At the most general level, multicultural education needs to be understood within a broader national context of racial redress following apartheid, and thus of the struggle to achieve access to quality education for the majority of to whom this was previously denied. But as an educational intervention, it is also about enabling all young South Africans, as the post-apartheid generations, to understand the past from which the country is still emerging, as well as the values and principles which are non-racism and non- sexism, Ubuntu (human dignity), an open society, accountability, the rule of law, respect and reconciliation (RSA, 2006). Applying a multicultural framework to South African schooling thus entails a dual focus on who is included and excluded in the current system as well as how they are included and excluded. (McKinney & Soudien, 2011:1)

McKinney and Soudien thus caution that discussions around social differences in South Africa (as is the case with multiculturalism), should consider the structural realities of South Africa and its racially determined policies, which emanate from apartheid. In their report, they also reveal how hard it is in a context like South Africa to develop and implement approaches to and systems of education that are, on one hand, inclusive in so far as they seek to bring into the ambit of teaching and learning those who had been marginalised; and, on the other hand, also just and equitable, in respect of what kinds of **cultural capital** enjoy respect and recognition (2011:17).

However much literature highlights the complexities of multicultural education in a context like South Africa, the reality is that most South African teachers face diverse classrooms every day, and they need to find ways to manage such environments. They also need to find strategies for achieving the goals of multiculturalism. As discussed earlier in this chapter, the pathway towards achieving the current goal of ME incorporates three strands of transformation, which you will remember are:

- Transformation of self
- Transformation of schools and schooling
- Transformation of society.

The next section of this chapter will argue for Ubuntu to be used as a strategy to achieve the goals of ME, and thereby help teachers manage the challenges of multiculturalism. This next section proceeds in two parts. The discussions in the first part offer a brief debate about Ubuntu, which leads into a discussion on the elements of Ubuntu. The second part features a discussion on how the elements of Ubuntu can be used to manage the challenges of multiculturalism.

cultural capital: non-financial assets like intellect and education that enable one to advance in society and in life

Examining Ubuntu

The concept of Ubuntu is found in diverse forms in many societies throughout Africa. Swanson (2001) claims that Ubuntu is short for an isiXhosa proverb in Southern Africa, which comes from *Umuntu ngumuntu ngabantu*: a person is a person through their relationship with others. Alluding to this, Khoza (2004) says that Ubuntu can be seen as the key to all African values, and involves collective personhood and collective morality. It is a social ethic, a unifying vision enshrined in the Nguni maxim, *Umuntu ngumuntu ngabantu*: a human being finds genuine human expression in human relationships with other humans – 'I am because we are'. Ubuntu is thus recognised as the African philosophy of humanism, linking the individual to the collective. Tutu (1999:34) says of Ubuntu that: "... It speaks to the very essence of being human ... When you want to give high praise to someone, we say '*Yu u nobuntu*': he or she has Ubuntu." Kunene (2009) refers to Ubuntu as a way of life, ways of treating others, and ways of behaving. When discussing Ubuntu, Brown and Shumba (2011:535) use Nelson Mandela as an example. They say: "Madiba's humanism [...] is reflected in the qualities of Ubuntu. We can infer from this that when others are tortured or treated as if they are less than who they are, Madiba feels equally diminished, humiliated, and undervalued."

In South Africa, Ubuntu is legislated in the Constitution of the Republic of South Africa (1996). South Africa, a country still emerging the apartheid era, has the following values and principles enshrined in its constitution and post-apartheid education policies. These are: non-racism and non-sexism, Ubuntu (human dignity), an open society, accountability, the rule of law, respect and reconciliation (RSA, 2006). Moreover, the South African Schools Act (No. 84 of 1996) also promotes human rights and human dignity by, amongst others, the prohibition of corporal punishment, and through the Language in Education policy.

Elements of Ubuntu

* **Values humanness**
  Generally, Ubuntu translates as humanness, justice, personhood, and morality (Kunene 2009; Khoza, 2009; Letseka, 2012; Swanson 2001; Tutu, 1999). If Ubuntu is translated through issues of justice and personhood, then we can also use Ubuntu since we are implementing multicultural education that promotes diversity, respect for human dignity, and celebration of diversity (Letseka, 2012).

* **Interdependence and dependence**
  Khoza (2004) says that Ubuntu values humanity and consultation as a value orientation, and interdependence as a value to dependence. In explaining such virtues, Mbigi (2002) refers to the African Collective Fingers Theory. According to this theory, the thumb, in order to work efficiently, will need the collective cooperation of the other fingers. This theory thus advocates open forms of communication that are inclusive. the theory embraces the old African expression 'It takes a village to raise a child'. The question that teachers could endeavour to respond to creatively could be: How do teachers embrace the expression 'it takes the village to raise a child?' According to Khoza (2004): 'Ubuntu is a concept that brings to the fore images of supportiveness, cooperation, and solidarity. It is the basis of a social contract that stems from, but transcends the narrow confines of the nuclear family to be extended kinship network, the community.'

* **Spirit of interconnectedness and social cohesion**
  Principles of interconnectedness, respect and dignity, collectivism and solidarity, communal enterprise, and leadership legitimacy are the cornerstone of Ubuntu. '[Ubuntu] speaks to the very essence of being human. We belong in a bundle of life [...] Harmony, friendliness, community, are great goods. Social harmony is for us [...] the greatest good. Anything that subverts or undermines this sought-after good is to be avoided like the plague' (Tutu, 1999:34-35). Letseka (2012) notes that South Africa, which was left

fractured with no shared moral discourse, by apartheid, needs Ubuntu. And perhaps the challenge for teachers is what teaching methods and values, which aspects of the curriculum they can use to promote these shared values, of harmony and friendliness in the classroom. How do we instil a sense of human dignity that shifts from confrontation to reconciliation, in the classroom? (Letseka, 2012). Following this theme, Msila (2009:1) suggests that, amongst others, the Ubuntu model, together with other 'universal philosophies', may help in curbing or minimising violence in educational institutions such as schools.

Littrell (2011:6) also notes that self-protection, in-group collectivism, consensus building, and a 'being your brother's keeper-type' of humane orientations need consideration. Khoza (2004) has configured Ubuntu as a leadership theory: "Ubuntu is a concept that brings to the fore images of supportiveness, cooperation, and solidarity. It is the basis of a social contract that stems from, but transcends, the narrow confines of the nuclear family to be extended into kinship network, the community. With diligent cultivation it should be extendable to the business cooperation". Mbigi, an entrepreneur, philosopher and academic, claims to be the founder of the Ubuntu philosophy for business practices (Mbigi, 2002). Mbigi, in Kunene (2009), insists that Ubuntu management philosophy unites both cooperativeness and competitiveness within an **iterative** and openly communicative model. Also exploring Ubuntu as a leadership model, Broodryk (2011) notes that Sir Richard Branson, the international entrepreneur, shocked the business world by adopting a new human philosophy and style based on a family-type business, where happiness and even fun in the workplace are encouraged. However, Blunt and Jones (1997) in Sigger, Polak and Pennink (2010) define African leadership more specifically as authoritative, paternalistic, conservative, and change-resistant. The research of Blunt and Jones conducted in Botswana (1997) shows that individual achievements are less important than interpersonal relations in Africa. Yet Broodryk (2011) explains Ubuntu as a lifestyle which is a natural response flowing from a happy approach to life. Oppenheim (2012), however, notes that Ubuntu is a spiritual ideal which, as humans, we need to aspire to continuously.

iterative: describes something that is done or stated repeatedly

- **Spirit of compassion, hospitality and sharing**
  Compassion and hospitality are also the celebrated virtues which are to be particularly shown to strangers (Broodryk, 2006). Alluding to this issue, Teffo (1999) says that compassion and hospitality are important values in the lives of African people, and are especially prevalent in rural communities. Compassion is about a deep caring and understanding of one another. Through this caring and understanding, community or team members can strive towards a shared vision. During hard times for the community or organisation, all the members share the burden (Sigger, Polak & Pennink, 2010).

They care during both the times of joy and the times of sorrow, hence 'Your joy is my joy, and your sorrow is my sorrow.'

Sharing is also one of the greatest virtues of Ubuntu. Ubuntu acknowledges that people have different qualities, talents, and resources, and these should be shared in a spirit of cooperativeness for positive living. This is indicative of the living of values like open-handedness and supportiveness in accordance with needs. In explaining the inherent spirit of sharing and caring in the spirit of Ubuntu, Desmond Tutu once noted "We Africans share everything and share nothing", meaning that people share whatever they have, even when they have nothing. Also making a case for sharing and compassion as an attribute of Ubuntu, Broodryk (2006) notes that if a person is progressing materially and receiving more than others, the extras will be shared with the under-privileged brothers and sisters. "Africa does not allow that some eat whilst others go hungry, or some sleep warm whilst others are left out in the cold." Nelson Mandela is quoted by Oppenheim (2012) who notes that in an Ubuntu spirit, a traveller through the country who stops at a village does not have to ask for food, or for water. Wherever he stops, the people give him food, entertain him, share their hospitality. However, Mandela says that sharing is not only limited to material things, but may also be linked to knowledge, skills, and other human capital. Through the sharing of knowledge, human capital, and skills, a spirit of harmony may be achieved (Nussbaum and Weichel, 2010). This may indicate that Ubuntu is a spirit of respectful win-win, cooperation in action. They refer to an African saying that "when there is peace in an individual, there is peace in a family. When there is peace in the family, there is peace in the community. When there is peace in the community, there is peace in the nation and ultimately in the world."

In the notion of sharing material things, one outstanding example is that of Mandela's donating 30 per cent of his presidential salary towards the establishment of the Mandela Children's Fund for the benefit of children's welfare (Nussbaum, 2003). This is surely indicative of the true spirit of caring, sharing, and collective personhood.

 Stop and reflect

Now that you have read about the elements of Ubuntu, synthesise the information that has been presented to you. Think back to when you were a learner and reflect on your teachers' and classmates' actions. Then copy and complete the table opposite. Try to think of at least one example from your experience to offer in each of the categories.

Elements of Ubuntu and their characteristics	Practices in my school life that were contrary to the identified elements of Ubuntu	Practices in my school life that were compatible with the identified elements of Ubuntu	The impact/effect of the practices
Spirit of compassion, hospitality and sharing Deep caring; understanding of one another; supportiveness according to needs; sharing – material goods, knowledge, skills and human capital.			
Spirit of interconnectedness and social cohesion Social harmony; interpersonal relations; shared moral discourse; friendliness; consensus building; solidarity; open forms of communication; 'it takes a village to raise a child'.			
Interdependence and dependence Solidarity; collective co-operation; I am because you are – *Umuntu ngumuntu ngabantu*; 'it takes a village to raise a child'; what is fair and just.			
Values humanness Respect for human dignity; celebrate diversity; justice and fairness			

Using elements of Ubuntu to manage challenges posed by multiculturalism

To examine how the elements of Ubuntu might be used as a tool to manage the challenges posed by multiculturalism, we are going to use Pam's dilemma (Case study 1 on page 16) as a point of reference. Do you still remember how Pam, a beginner teacher, drew the following mind map after reading her learners' narratives?

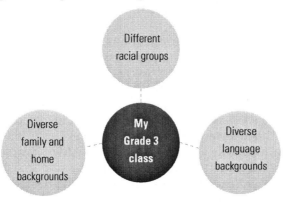

Stop and reflect

In the last activity you reflected on your own experiences as a learner, and examined the impact or effect of practices that did not reflect the elements of Ubuntu. Now help Pam to manage her classroom practice. Use the table to help her infuse elements of Ubuntu as she manages teaching and learning in her classroom. Copy and complete it as before.

Elements of Ubuntu and their characteristics	Pam's practice in response to her learners' diverse language backgrounds	Pam's practice in response to her learners' diverse home backgrounds	Pam's practice in response to her learners' racial diversity
Spirit of compassion, hospitality and sharing Deep caring; understanding of one another; supportiveness according to needs; sharing – material goods, knowledge, skills and human capital.			
Spirit of interconnectedness and social cohesion Social harmony; interpersonal relations; shared moral discourse; friendliness; consensus building; solidarity; open forms of communication; 'it takes a village to raise a child'.			
Interdependence and dependence Solidarity; collective co-operation; I am because you are – *Umuntu ngumuntu ngabantu*; 'it takes a village to raise a child'; what is fair and just.			
Values humanness Respect for human dignity; celebrate diversity; justice and fairness			

Summary of discussion

Most teachers find themselves teaching in multicultural classrooms in contemporary South Africa. In many cases, the teachers have little or nothing in common with their learners. As a result, multiculturalism poses a challenge in their daily interactions with learners. Teachers therefore need to find strategies to make sure that all learners are insiders in such classrooms, and are empowered to perform to their abilities. This chapter examined the complexities of multicultural education, especially in a context like South Africa, it explored some criticisms of approaches to multiculturalism, introduced the concept of Ubuntu, and examined how the elements of Ubuntu might be used to manage the complexities of multiculturalism. How would infusing the elements of Ubuntu in their interactions with learners benefit multicultural educators to transform their teaching and learning contexts into realistic multicultural contexts? We suggested that the pathway towards achieving the goals of ME incorporates three strands of transformation: *Transformation of self*: teachers' dual responsibility to examine their own attitudes, beliefs, and practice, and to change themselves; *Transformation of schools and schooling*: a critical examination of all aspects of schooling, from teaching methodologies to school climate, and governance; *Transformation of society*: to contribute to the application and maintenance of social justice and equity.

Closing activities

The following are two case studies designed to raise teachers' awareness of how Ubuntu can be used in the classroom to manage multicultural education. Use the questions to raise your own awareness of this approach, and to test your understanding of the issues of this chapter.

 CASE STUDY 6

More-Blessings, originally from Zimbabwe, is a 30-something Grade 6 teacher in a rural KwaZulu-Natal rural school. He is responsible for teaching Mathematics and English. The class size is typically between 45 and 65 learners. More-Blessings is very strict and learners know that they only speak in class when they are spoken to. Nonetheless, learners have been doing their work diligently until he tells them that because of the class size, he does not know all the learners by name and really doesn't care to learn all their names. He is concerned that the 'learners are sluggish, compared to what I am used to back home'. He also complains to the learners about the abolition of corporal punishment in South Africa, the overcrowded classrooms and xenophobic tendencies by some of the local villagers. He tells learners that only half the class is going to pass at the end of the year. After this comment, the majority of learners become demotivated, some even start skipping classes. As corporal punishment has been outlawed in South Africa, More-Blessings cannot use it to punish children and instead he calls in the parents to discuss learner truancy. During the meeting the parents instruct the teacher to apply corporal punishment as a corrective measure, despite the policy. More-Blessings is, however, adamant that 'as a foreigner I do not want to break any South African law'. Instead he suggests that the learners also be called into the meeting. When the learners join the meeting and tell both the teacher and the parents of their grievances, the parents change their tune and beg More-Blessings to 'treat our children like you would your own'. Some parents even promise to assist More-Blessings in any way they can.

1 What do you think are the challenges experienced by More-Blessings?
2 Identify the Ubuntu principles that were violated by More-Blessings.
3 Identify the Ubuntu principles that More-Blessings embraced.
4 What made the parents change their attitude towards corporal punishment?
5 What is the meaning of the phrase 'treat our children like you would your own'?

CASE STUDY 7

Nomsa (isiXhosa speaking) and Sara-Leigh (English speaking) are two third-year B Ed students, specialising in Foundation Phase, who are studying at the University of Eastern Cape. As part of their training, they undertake a 10-week school experience (SE) programme in one of the local informal settlements. The school is a 'forced' multi-grade school, with no electricity, no formal staffroom, and no library. Nomsa and Sara-Leigh undertake SE for four weeks during the first semester, and six weeks during the second semester. During the first semester, while other students are complaining about the cold treatment they receive from teachers in some more affluent schools, Nomsa and Sara-Leigh report a very different experience. They tell their colleagues that they 'have experienced Ubuntu' at the school. This was in relation to the teachers' commitment in mentoring and 'going an extra mile' for them. At the end of the first semester SE, Sara-Leigh has learned basic isiXhosa from both the learners and the teachers. At the end of the SE, both students feel they have to give something back to the school. Together with other university students, they raise funds for the building of a resource centre, and the installation of electricity. Nomsa's father, a professional builder, joins in the building over weekends, while Sara-Leigh's mother, a librarian, together with some volunteers from the local library, assists with cataloguing and shelving the books that have been donated. The parents on the school governing body together with other parents (all unemployed) paint the school without expecting any payment. To Nomsa and Sara-Leigh this school is their 'home'. On completion of her studies, Nomsa goes back to the school as a volunteer teacher while waiting for appointment.

1   What do the experiences of the two B Ed students tell you about the form and dimensions of Ubuntu?
2   If you were one of the two students, how would you have responded to the experience of Ubuntu, and why?

References and further reading

Aboud, F.E. 2009. Modifying children's racial attitudes. In James A. Banks (Ed). *Routledge International Companion to Multicultural Education*. Abingdon, Oxford: Taylor & Francis Group.

Arendse, A.M. 2012. The challenges of effective management of a multicultural teaching environment in Gauteng primary schools. Unpublished MEd thesis. University of South Africa.

Banks, J.A. 2006. *Cultural diversity and education: Foundations, curriculum and teaching*. Boston: Pearson.

Baruth, L.G. & Manning, M. Lee. 2000. *Multicultural education of children and adolescents*. Boston: Allyn & Bacon.

Blunt, P. & Jones, M. 1997. Exploring the limits of Western leadership theory in East Asia and Africa. *Personnel Review* 26. 6–23.

Bornman, J. 2005. Augmentative and Alternative Communication. In E. Landsberg, D. Kruger & N. Nel (Eds). *Addressing barriers to learning: A Southern African Perspective*. Pretoria: Van Schaik

Broodryk, J. 2006. *uBuntu African life coping skills: Theory and practice*. Paper delivered at CCEAM Conference, 12–17 October 2006, Lefkosia, Cyprus.

Brown, B. & Shumba, A. 2011. Managing Africa's multiculturalism: Bringing the "Madiba Magic" into the African school curriculum. In A. Bame Nsamenang & T.M.S. Tchombe (Eds). *Handbook of African Theories and Practices: A Generative Teacher Education Curriculum*. Addis Ababa: Presses Universitaires d'Afrique.

Cox, C.P. 2002. *Tolerance in Multicultural education: Developing of intervention strategies for educators.* Unpublished Master's dissertation. Pretoria: University of South Africa.

Department of Education. 1996a. *South African Schools Act.* Government Gazette Notice No. 84 of 1996. Pretoria: Government Printers.

D'Souza, D. & Williams, W. 1996. Deliberations on the end of racism. *Academic Questions.* 9(4).

Giselbrecht, M. 2009. Pluralistic approaches: A long overdue paradigm shift in education. *Scottish Languages Review.* 20:11–20. Autumn.

Glazer, N. 1997. *We are all multiculturalists now.* Cambridge, MA: Harvard University Press.

Grant, C.A. & Sleeter, C.E. 2007. *Doing Multicultural Education for Achievement and Equity.* New York: Taylor & Francis Group.

Hall, S. 1996a. When was the 'Post-Colonial'? Thinking at the limit. In I. Chambers & L. Curtis (Eds). *The Post-colonial Question: Common skies divided horizons.* London: Routledge.

Hall, S. 1996b. Introduction: Who needs 'Identity'? In S. Hall & P. Du Gay (Eds). *Questions of cultural identity.* London: SAGE Publications.

Hofstede, G. 1991. *Cultures and organisations: Software of the mind.* London: McGraw-Hill.

Jansen, J.D. 2004. Race and education after ten years. *Perspectives in Education.* 22(4):117–128.

Khoza, R. 2004. *African leadership: People solutions for African challenges?* Pretoria: University of Pretoria.

Kunene, Z. 2009. *Ubuntu.* Keynote address on behalf of Zandile Kunene in the Gauteng Department of Education Conference in September 2009.

Lemmer, E.M., Meier, C. & Van Wyk, N.J. 2012. *Multicultural Education: A manual for the South African Teacher* 2nd ed. Pretoria: Van Schaik.

Letseka, M. 2013. Educating for *Ubuntu/Botho:* Lessons from Basotho indigenous education. *Open Journal of Philosophy.* 3(2):337–344.

Littrell, R.F. 2011. Contemporary Sub-Saharan African managerial leadership research: some recent empirical studies. *Asia Pacific Journal of Business and Management,* 2(1):65–91.

McKinney, C. & Soudien, C. 2011. *2010 IALEI Country report: Multicultural education in South Africa.* Cape Town: University of Cape Town.

Meier, C. & Hartell, C. 2009. Handling cultural diversity in education in South Africa. *SA-eDUC Journal.* 6(2):180–192. November.

Mbigi, L. 2002. 'Spirit of African leadership: A comparative African perspective'. *Journal for Convergence.* 3(4):18–23.

Morrow, W. 1998. Multicultural education in South Africa. In W. Morrow & K. King (Eds). *Vision and Reality: Changing Education and Training in South Africa.* Cape Town: University of Cape Town Press.

Morrow, W. 2007. *Learning to teach in South Africa.* Cape Town: HSRC Press.

Mpisi, A.S. 2010. *The scholastic experience of black learners in Multicultural FET schools in the Northern Cape*. Unpublished doctoral thesis. Bloemfontein: University of the Free State.

Myles, B.S., Trautman, M. & Shelvan, R. 2004. *Asperger Syndrome and the Hidden Curriculum*. Shawnee Mission, KS: Autism Asperger Publishing Company.

Nkomo, S.M. 2011. A post-colonial *and* anti-colonial reading of 'African' leadership and management in organization studies: Tensions, contradictions and possibilities. *Organization*, 18(3):365–386.

Ntsebeza, L. 2006. *Democracy compromised: Chiefs and the politics of land in South Africa*. Pretoria: Human Sciences Research Council.

Nyamnjoh, F.B. 2002. *Might and right: Chieftaincy and democracy in Cameroon and Botswana*. Paper presented at the CODESRIA's 10th General Assembly on "Africa in the New Millennium", Kampala, Uganda, 8–12 December 2002. Retrieved from: http://www.codesria.org/Archives/ga10/ on 19 May 2013.

Nussbaum, B. 2003. African culture and Ubuntu: Reflections of a South African in America. *Perspectives*. 4(4):22–26.

Nussbaum, B. & Weichel, K. 2010. *The Spirit of Ubuntu*. Online article. 29 July. Retrieved from: http://www.peacexpeace.org/2010/07/the-spirit-of-ubuntu/ on 2 April 2013.

Oppenheim, C.E. 2012. Nelson Mandela and the power of uBuntu. *Religion*. 3:369–388.

Sigger, D.S., Polak, B.M. & Pennink, B.J.W. 2010. *'Ubuntu' or 'Humanness' as a Management Concept*. CDS Research Report No. 29. July.

Soudien, C. & Sayed, Y. 2004. A new racial state? Exclusion and inclusion in education policy and practice in South Africa. *Perspectives in Education*. 22(4):101–115.

Swanson, D.M. 2007. Ubuntu: An African contribution to (re)search for/with a 'humble togetherness.' *Journal of Contemporary Issues in Education*. 2:53–67.

Teffo, L. 1999. Moral renewal and African experience(s). In M.W. Makgoba (Ed). *African Renaissance: The new struggle*. Cape Town: Mafube Tafelberg.

Tutu, D. 1999. *No Future Without Forgiveness*. New York, NY: Random House.

Vally, S. & Dalambo, Y. 1999. *Racial Integration, Desegregation in Public Secondary Schools in South Africa: A report of the South African Human Rights Commission*. Johannesburg: South African Human Rights Commission.

Varyenen, S. 2005. Observations from South African Classrooms: Some inclusive strategies, South African-Finnish Co-operation Programme in the Education Sector (SCOPE). National Department of Education, Republic of South Africa.

3

Towards an Afrocentric-indigenous pedagogy

Micheal van Wyk

Chapter overview

Afrocentricity is an educational, philosophical, and theoretical paradigm in the context of schooling, society, and inclusive education. Afrocentricity is a conceptually inclusive approach, underpinned by important principles or **canons** relevant to teaching and learning in an inclusive education system in Africa. In this chapter we extract the fundamental constructs underlying the Afrocentric approach for an inclusive classroom setting. We then define indigenous knowledge and reflect on the educational value and practical relevance for Afrocentric-indigenous education. We explain the eight-way framework of the Afrocentric-indigenous pedagogy, as well the advantages for an inclusive classroom. The role of the teacher in using Afrocentric-indigenous pedagogy in the inclusive classroom is explored. Finally, we reflect on the role of communities in promoting and supporting the idea of Afrocentric-indigenous education for inclusivity.

> **canon:** a general rule or principle that sets a standard, by which something can be judged

Learning outcomes

By the end of this chapter you should be able to:

* Discuss the important canons and teaching principles underpinning Afrocentric-indigenous pedagogy for inclusive education
* Explain the eight-way framework of an Afrocentric-indigenous pedagogy, as well the advantages for implementing it in an inclusive classroom
* Reflect on the role of the teacher in using Afrocentric-indigenous pedagogy in the inclusive classroom
* Describe how communities can be involved in understanding and promoting Afrocentric-indigenous education, in support of the goal of inclusivity.

We begin this chapter with a short imagined conversation between three well known Afrocentrist indigenous scholars – George J. Sefa Dei, Molefi Kete Asante, and the late Joe L. Kincheloe – which expresses their particular views about the concept of Afrocentric-indigenous knowledge.

> I am an African. My roots are in Africa. [But], because I am in North America, I am seen as an African-American. My interest was, and is still, about my roots. I see indigenous peoples in Africa, Australia, South America, the South Sea Islands, and the Bahamas. You know, indigenous knowledge is a complex accumulation of local, context-relevant knowledge that embraces the essence of ancestral knowing, as well as the legacies of diverse histories and cultures. It represents essentially a 'speaking back' to the production, categorisation, and position of cultures, identities, and histories. This is our history.

George J. Sefa Dei

Molefi Kete Asante

You see, indigenous communities are the roots and place for indigenous ways. I see indigenous knowledge as a viable tool for reclaiming our context through relevant ways of knowing that have been deliberately suppressed by Western knowledge. Indigenous knowledge should focus on systematically unravelling power relations that have ensured the dominance of particular ways of Western knowing in academic textbooks, school textbooks, and other related texts. We need, in essence, to understand that keeping indigenous knowledge alive amounts to resistance, refusal, and transformation of our perspective of knowledge here in Africa, and globally.

My view is that the dominance of Western ways of knowing in Western academies and global social relations should not undermine the value of indigenous knowledge for continual community existence in a particular indigenous context. But, to respect indigenous knowledge and ways of knowing, is to share and empower our youth.

Joe L. Kincheloe

This 'conversation' should give you an idea of where we are going with this chapter, and what wider theoretical concepts we want you to understand and share. Throughout this chapter we hope to provide a text to empower student teachers to practise and plan ways of infusing indigenous knowledge in their classrooms every day.

Afrocentricity as a conceptual inclusive approach to teaching and learning

Afrocentric philosophy: a way of thinking from an African perspective, based on the principles of inclusivity, cultural specificity, critical awareness, committedness, and political awareness

paradigm: a pattern or model of something that represents the beliefs and theories that constitute it

In this first part of the chapter we will expose you to Afrocentricity as an educational, philosophical, and theoretical **paradigm** in the context of schooling, society, and inclusive education. African scholars, in particular Asante, started questioning Westernised views about Afrocentricity as theoretical paradigm for education in his book entitled *The Afrocentric idea in education* (1991, 1998). African scholars challenged Eurocentric perspectives and paradigms of knowledge construction as the only legitimate philosophy. From this debate, a growing intellectual African scholarly voice started to emerge in the 1980s which began to oppose prevailing Eurocentric views. Asante (1998:2) contends that African centeredness defines the inspiration and identity of African ideals, which are at the core of African culture and behaviour as a people. According to Asante (1991), the ideals, aspirations, identity, and values of African people have helped to shape this phenomenon over the last three decades on the African continent. Asante (1998:124) argues that the Afrocentricity as a philosophy is against those contradictory paradigms and ideals that 'dislocate' and push Africans to the margin of critical thought, when he says: "this opposing theory is pushing Afrocentricity to the margins of human thought and experience." Asante (1998:273) further argues that "Afrocentricity can have a significant impact on the way African researchers view their identity, specifically in the way it considers the African people as centered, located, oriented, and grounded."

Adopting an Afrocentric paradigm means that in explaining or defining our experiences, whether historical or contemporary, the **discourse** must be one that places learners at the centre, thereby moving them from the margins and empowering them by making them the subjects and not the objects of the learning encounter (Reviere, 2001; Asante, 1991). In order to be considered a paradigm, Afrocentricity, as defined earlier, must prove able to activate our consciousness, to open our hearts in such a way as to include all peoples. Yet it is a regrettable truth that many scholars have tried to reduce Afrocentricity to a mere intellectual exercise, confusing it with the creation of a shallow, discursive space with no serious and real implications for one's life choices. Still, the lives of many others who have been deeply touched by Afrocentricity attest to the fact that Afrocentricity is indeed a true paradigm for African liberation towards emancipation and economic prosperity. Afrocentricity's profound impact on African lives can be detected in at least three areas. According to Asante (1998:162–176) these areas are: 1) the exhibition of educational and cultural phenomena, such as storytelling, drama, poetry, music, or dance, clearly informed by an Afrocentric consciousness; 2) the emergence of a new political discourse and **praxis** in Africa. In the spirit of this idea of a new political discourse, leaders such as Nelson Mandela, Thabo Mbeki, Kofi Annan, and Kwame Nkrumah have openly acknowledged the need for Afrocentric policies and structures; and 3) the building of institutions, such as schools and universities, business corporates, and spiritual centres, in Africa to spread Afrocentric consciousness. In other words, as Van Wyk (2014) states, Afrocentricity meets all the functional requirements identified as critical for schooling, society, and inclusive education.

> **discourse**: a formal written or spoken discussion of a subject – like the one you are reading in this chapter
>
> **praxis**: practice, or the way in which people carry out their activities

 Stop and reflect

Before you continue with the importance of Afrocentricity as a construct of the inclusive education approach, turn back to the 'conversation' between Dei, Asante and Kincheloe. What do you make of indigenous knowledge as discussed by these three indigenous scholars? Why do you think it is important to include this phenomenon in our current discussion? Explain your ideas in a short response of not more than one page.

Principles foregrounding an Afrocentric learning environment

Afrocentric educationists say that any acceptable approach to inclusive education must be sufficiently comprehensive to address questions of how knowledge is structured and used by teachers and learners (Van Wyk, 2014:292). Several principles, or canons, for effective teaching and learning in an Afrocentric learning paradigm are identified, which will be discussed in this part of the chapter. Educationists believe that employing these Afrocentric principles to teaching and learning will ultimately enhance quality education in society at large (Asante, 1991; Reviere, 2001; Van Wyk, 2014). According these scholars, this approach requires participants (teachers and learners particularly in the inclusive classroom) to go beyond questions of *what is learned, by whom*, and *how quickly it is learned*, and rather to consider questions of *how the knowledge being disseminated is structured and applied*, particularly in diverse and inclusive classrooms (Van Wyk, 2014:292). The approach we are suggesting for this chapter requires that all role players or participants in the teaching and learning process (teachers, learners, parents, school management teams, and community) be encouraged to become involved in searching for quality teaching and learning.

In the next section we will conceptualise, and contextualise the five Afrocentric principles or canons for teaching in the context of schooling, society and inclusive education (Asante, 1991; Reviere, 2001; Van Wyk, 2014).

ukweli: a Swahili (a language of East Africa) word meaning truth

The first Afrocentric principle is *ukweli*, which means 'advancing the truth in our praxis'. The concept of 'truth' in the context of this chapter refers to the ultimate authority or 'overwhelming control of power' invested in the role and responsibilities of the teacher in an inclusive environment. According to Reviere (2001), the concept originated in and was borrowed from Swahili, in which it means that the teacher is vital in executing the role of a moral builder and a pastoral caregiver in supporting, promoting and instilling good citizenship practices in his or her lesson preparation at all times. Teachers are 'custodians' of good practice, and foreground their praxis with good teaching and learning principles, always in support of the learner. They do this by acknowledging the 'lived' experiences of all group members, but particularly of the individual learner, in an inclusive setting. The teacher has the power and responsibility to determine the content and skills to be taught to accommodate the diverse needs of her class. Van Wyk (2014:293) argues that "the standards for establishing the educational needs of the learners, and the individuals in that inclusive classroom community, must be determined by the real-life experiences of the learners". It is imperative for the teacher to understand the importance and relevance of this concept when planning, preparing and applying it in her classroom. Most learners are daily bombarded by confusing media messages and possibly distorted information. The teacher has a moral as well as a pedagogical obligation to protect her learners from distorted information on a particular topic, whether in the learner support material (LSM) or through electronic media, by providing relevant information to them. Over and above this, she helps learners develop the critical skills to analyse and evaluate information.

The role of the teacher in the inclusive class cannot be underestimated in planning effective lessons on a specific topic. She is the ultimate authority in determining what, why and how teaching and learning will ultimately constructed for the purpose of quality teaching and learning. In this case, according to Van Wyk (2014:293) "one cannot ignore the real-life and historical experiences of teachers and learners or one runs the risk of making decisions that do not fit their experiences and needs." Using frequent and current learner profiles can help to avoid this. Reviere (2001:710) posits that *ukweli* raises the issue of the subjectivity of truth. She is of the view that "one could justifiably ask whether the 'truth' as experienced by a particular community or individual has more validity than that experienced by any other". Scholars have shown that learners learn effectively when involved in their own learning through different learning experiences. In every school, and especially in inclusive classrooms, learners who are actively involved in their own learning will ultimately contribute to making the truth (Van Wyk, 2014). According to Afrocentric educationists, *ukweli* therefore mandates that the creation of knowledge must be done within the context of the school community and, in particular, in the inclusive curricula and in the community's own experiences (Reviere, 2007). In the context of inclusive education, all possible stakeholders, such as learners, teachers, facilitators, the school community, and the wider society, must be provided opportunities to participate and be included in further real decision-making in the classroom, school, and society (Van Wyk, 2014).

The second principle, **utulivu**, from a Swahili linguistic perspective, means 'create harmony for the sake of peace and respect'. Scholars argue that teachers as agents of change should prevent setting up unnecessary conflicts, but instead, supply good role models for learners (Reviere, 2001; Shockley, 2011; Van Wyk, 2014). These authors insist that the teacher in his classroom should strive to create good interactions amongst learners and within group formations. The teacher should try to put in place the means to support learners with different viewpoints on sensitive topics, such as drugs, racial and sexual abuse, to prevent tensions and disharmony in the class. For example, the teacher might play a pastoral and mediation role to support especially those learners with special needs in the classroom by providing spaces and creating enabling environments with different learning opportunities in the classroom. Van Wyk (2014) and Reviere (2001) say that in an inclusive classroom, teachers must try to create and support healthy interactions amongst groups. Scholars generally concur that learners should be given many opportunities to create and enhance good relationships that promote citizenship. Further, Afrocentric educationists argue that although the interests of the individual learner must be considered, the teacher has a greater concern for the wider school community, and especially for those who are exposed to any form of conflict in the classroom (Van Wyk, 2014).

utulivu: means harmony in Swahili

The third principle, **uhaki**, requires a learning process that is fair to all learners, and a process which is applied with the wellbeing of all the participants in mind. Fairness, or justice as defined by this principle, must apply to all communities with a stake in the outcomes

uhaki: loosely translated from Swahili, means justice

of the educational process, that is, everyone (Reviere, 2011). *Uhaki* asserts that the teacher takes account of the interests and wellbeing of the community being served, to build a just society. The best interests of learners should be uppermost – this is what is meant by justice. Application of *uhaki* also means that one cannot ignore the historical and social context in interpreting and responding to any element of the learning process. In the context of this book on inclusive education, *uhaki* also teaches that all learning materials, in the interest of inclusivity, represent fairly the perspectives of all groups that make up a specific educational community. It further says that the learning material cause no harm to any group included in that community, for example, by misrepresenting them (Reviere, 2001; Van Wyk, 2014).

ujamaa: means community in Swahili

The fourth principle, ***ujamaa***, refers to community and, in the context of this chapter, reflects the classroom and school community. It requires that the teacher reject the learner–teacher separation and does not presume to be the authority on all knowledge (Reviere, 2001; Van Wyk, 2014). Reviere (2001) says that it requires that knowledge and its dissemination should be informed by the actual and aspirational interests of the school community and not those of the teacher. Afrocentric educationists maintain that the teacher is compelled, according their role and responsibilities in the service of humanity, to support and provide every learning opportunity to those learners with special needs, especially in inclusive education. Van Wyk (2014) says that the application of the *ujamaa* principle in an inclusive setting such as the school, promotes an enabling environment for the teacher to teach the learners. The school, in particular the classroom in this case, is part of greater community which includes learners, teachers, and school management teams as participants in this relationship. In the classroom community, stakeholders (learners and teachers) strive to build good relationships, with stakeholders such as parents as an important ingredient in this togetherness. Within the inclusive classroom, then, the teacher is responsible for accommodating learners with diverse learning needs in support of their own sense and beliefs about themselves, not someone else's expectations of them. In the school, as a learning community, the purpose is to build sound relationships so as to advance teaching and learning.

kujitoa: means commitment in Swahili

The final principle, ***kujitoa***, means to be committed to the ideals of Ubuntu. *Kujitoa* requires that the teacher in the inclusive classroom places ideas about how knowledge is planned, structured, and used, above maintaining an impartial distance from the knowledge being disseminated (Reviere, 2001; Van Wyk, 2014). Afrocentric educationists believe that this empowers the learners to analyse and interpret the structure and use of texts, and other discourses, and to critically uncover the hidden assumptions embedded in the learning materials and resources used in the classroom. Teachers and learners must become aware that knowledge is not impartial and value-free, but is interwoven with its social and political contexts, especially in the school at large.

Stop and reflect

Before you continue with the importance of the principles of the Afrocentric perspective as a construct for an inclusive approach, turn to the principles discussed earlier. What do you think of these principles (sometimes called canons) and how you could apply them in your lessons? Why did you think it is important to include these principles in our daily classroom dialogue or discussions?

In the next section you will learn about the underlying principles of the Afrocentric approach for teaching in an inclusive environment. These principles are very important to keep in mind when planning and implementing your inclusive lesson.

Fundamental constructs underlying the Afrocentric approach

Emanating from the conceptualisation of the Afrocentric paradigm, Afrocentric educationists identify seven fundamental constructs:

- *Identity* – the importance of identifying the African child as an African, e.g. Thabo Mbeki's speech, 'I am an African' (1996)
- *Pan-Africanism* – the idea that all black people in the world are Africans
- *African culture and heritage* – the long-standing customs of African culture, and the traditions that sustain and bring order to African people's lives and communities
- *Adoption and transmission of African values* – the inclusion of an African ethos and morals, particularly in the classroom, to infuse diversity into the educational process for all children
- *Black nationalism* – the idea that black people, regardless of their specific geographical location or origins, constitute a 'nation' (Asante, 1991)
- *Community control with institution building* – the ability to make important decisions about the institutions that exist in one's community, such as the school, the classroom, and society
- *Education as opposed to schooling* – the idea that education is the process of imparting to children all the things they need to provide leadership within their communities, and within their nation; while schooling is a training process (Shockley & Frederick, 2010; Van Wyk, 2014).

 Stop and reflect

Why do you think, when planning a lesson, it is crucial to bear in mind the above constructs? How will you implement some of these principles in your own classroom practice? And why you do think it is important for learners to know these principles in teaching and learning in an inclusive classroom?

We will now continue to conceptualise indigenous knowledge in the context of inclusiveness. Before you read the next section, make sure you have spent some time answering the questions in the *Stop and reflect* activity.

Defining 'indigenous knowledge'

Scholars define 'indigenous knowledge' as a way of life of a specific group of people, defined by ancestral territories, cultural activities, and historical locations (Dei, 2002; Akena, 2012; Van Wyk, 2014). Van Wyk (2014:294) further defines the concept as "the knowledge and skills constructed by indigenous people with the purpose of advancing and sustaining their identity, culture, and history for the next generation." Teachers can make a very important impact on learners by teaching them how this concept relates to their uniqueness, and by advancing it in teaching and learning within inclusive education. According to Kincheloe (2006), indigenous knowledge refers to a multidimensional body of understandings that have, especially since the beginnings of the European scientific revolution of the seventeenth and eighteenth centuries, been viewed by European culture as inferior, superstitious, and primitive (Akena, 2012). For indigenous people, however, indigenous knowledge is viewed as a lived world, a form of reasoning that informs and sustains people who make their homes in a local area (Asante, 1991; Van Wyk, 2014). Mkabela and Luthuli (1997) further posit that indigenous knowledge defines and links different communities of practice (situated learning spaces), and the ecology to sustain them (environmental sustainability), over many decades.

 Stop and reflect

How do you define the concept of indigenous knowledge? How can this concept relate to the uniqueness of teaching and learning in the context of inclusive education? Reflect on the discussion on indigenous knowledge by Dei, Asante and Kincheloe at the beginning of this chapter. Write your response as your own personal view, having read the information provided.

Based on the conceptualisations of indigenous knowledge, we now look at some very important tenets of IK in an inclusive teaching and learning context.

Indigenous knowledge as a unique African practice

Indigenous knowledge is often perceived as the historical and ancient practices of the African peoples, which is a challenging perspective of a Westernised viewpoint (Van Wyk, 2014:294). Indigenous knowledge is handed down from one generation to another through symbols, art, oral narratives, proverbs, and performance such as songs, storytelling, wise sayings, riddles, and dances (Dei, 2002; Akena,

2012; Van Wyk, 2014). In this context, indigenous knowledge is a dynamic and multifaceted body of knowledge, practices, and representations that are maintained and developed by people with long histories of close interaction with their local natural environment. According to Van Wyk (2012:48), the term 'indigenous', therefore, denotes that the knowledge is typical and belongs to people from specific places who have common cultural and social ties. Throughout this chapter it is argued that indigenous knowledge is a process of learning and sharing social life, histories, identities, economic and political practices, unique to each cultural group. This reflects the uniqueness of ways in which specific societies make meaning of the world, and how such forms of knowledge address local problems and find solutions that are context-specific. In this chapter indigenous knowledge is framed as the complex set of activities, values, beliefs and practices that has evolved cumulatively over time. Indigenous knowledge is active and dynamic among indigenous African communities and groups, who are its practitioners. It remains so as long as the groups and communities who are its practitioners, such as teachers and learners, are committed to sustaining, creatively developing, and extending its potential enrichment within a specific setting; IK will be relevant, will outlast, and perhaps even outperform, many Eurocentric practices (Van Wyk, 2014).

Indigenous knowledge and critical pedagogy

Relevant questions at this point are: Is there a relationship between indigenous knowledge and critical pedagogy? And, how can IK be used as a critical pedagogy to answer practical questions in education, and bring about social change? Arguably, one of the ultimate goals of critical pedagogy is to make visible those marginal cultures that have traditionally been suppressed by hearing only Eurocentric voices (Giroux & McLaren, 1990; Akena, 2012). For the Afrocentric-indigenous teacher, Afrocentricity is a commitment to a pedagogy that is also a political education which is people-driven. It is a curriculum intended to equip learners and teachers with the necessary knowledge and skills towards the eradication of poverty, and to advance the ideals of the voiceless in society. If education is to transform and liberate our society, it should be about getting learners and teachers to work collaboratively. Giroux and McLaren (1990:156) further argue that to "think critically, struggle against social injustices, and develop relations of community based on the principles of equality, freedom and justice" means that especially in the inclusive classroom, the teacher as the change agent is compelled to promote critical thinking skills in empowering learners in schools.

The adoption of an Afrocentric-indigenous pedagogy by integrating critical pedagogy as an approach to teachers' professional practice, is a logical progression as it shares the same philosophical roots as critical theory. As Giroux and McLaren (1990:156) state, "critical pedagogy argues that school practices need to be informed by a public philosophy that addresses how to construct ideological and institutional conditions in which the lived experience of empowerment for the vast majority of learners becomes the defining feature of schooling." In this chapter and throughout this book, we take the position that it essential to empower teachers and learners at school level to express critical views which raise questions about the power relationships between the learners and teachers in classrooms and schools. We are concerned about how teachers as change agents, struggle to reclaim their authority, particularly in shaping and changing misconceptions about race, gender, class, and ethnicity in a particular society, but in particular the classroom (Yunkaporta & Kirby, 2011).

 Stop and reflect

What role can teachers play in promoting a critical awareness amongst their learners in an inclusive classroom? Why is it important for teachers and learners work together, according to Giroux and McLaren? What are your own views? Hold a class discussion with your peers and then write a short piece (one page) in which you discuss the role of teachers.

The educational value of Afrocentric-indigenous pedagogy

The epistemological constructs of African people discussed in this chapter have some practical relevance for the education particularly of African youth. These constructs are ways of knowing and interacting within the African social world and environment. These constructs speak to African people's sense of the meaning and functioning of the universe and the natural context of their own existence, as well as the values, principles, and standards of ethics and morality (Banks, 1992, cited in Van Wyk, 2014). The teaching of such ideas and values can help instil a sense of pride, self-worth, and self-esteem among learners, and enable them to identify and connect with the school.

According to Afrocentric educationists, African culture and cultural values can be used to emancipate and deconstruct Westernised views of power in the curriculum in schools. Afrocentric education, however, must be more than **emancipatory** or liberatory pedagogy, imbued with self-reflection, critique, and social action (Giroux & McLaren, 1990). Afrocentricity, as an intellectual paradigm, must focus on addressing the structural impediments to the education of African students by engaging them to identify with their history, heritage, and culture. Moreover, Giroux and McLaren (1990:168) argue that "to be successful the Afrocentric pedagogue must move away from a manipulation of the victim status and exploiting white guilt", and work towards finding solutions to the pressing problems of educating learners about their African roots, especially within the South African context.

emancipatory: able to set free someone or something, especially from legal, social, or political restrictions

Afrocentric educationists are critical of the current education system, in particular the school curricula, which do not educate the youth about Africa, but perpetuate capitalist and colonial ideologies. The current schooling system supports the prevailing status quo and therefore isolates many learners and out-of-school youth. This supports and increases unemployment, unemployability, and worse, fosters civil unrest in many developing countries, especially in the sub-Saharan region. Scholars believe that the current public school system has failed to respond adequately to the needs of the African learner (Shockley, 2011; Van Wyk, 2014). Similarly, many South African educationists, curriculum developers, school governing bodies, parents and teachers have become increasingly concerned about the dropout problem and its effects on their own communities. Parents are disappointed in what they see as the schooling system's inability to educate their children (Van Wyk, 2014).

 Stop and reflect

To understand black learners' experiences in the school system, it is important to think critically through certain questions. For example, what is it about mainstream public schools that creates many disengaged learners who fail to achieve and 'fade out'? Are there perhaps school policies and practices that place some learners at risk of failing? If so, what do you think these might be? Write your response as a short report (1–2 pages) using your own experience and current sources. Be sure to cite your sources clearly and fully.

In the current local South African school system, the average black learner performs academically dismally below white learners (Van Wyk, 2014). The South African school system has gone through several changes and challenges, to its institutions, curriculum and governance (Lowry, 1998). However, there is still an urgent need for a critical analysis of the institutional school and community power structures within which learning, teaching, and the administration of education take place in (mainly rural) schools, and how these structures function to marginalise, exclude, and alienate black youth (Van Wyk, 2014). The current processes of schooling undermine black learners' sense of identity and their lived experiences whether as poor, middle class, male, female, from single- or dual-parent families, immigrant, or South African-born communities. For many learners, the marginalisation and devaluing of their individual and collective experiences all contribute to their low self-worth and poor self-esteem. This, in turn, adds to their frustration and alienation from many societal institutions and, consequently, the tendency to rebel through oppositional behaviours like non-compliance, truancy and eventually dropping out.

In an Afrocentric-indigenous context learners must see themselves represented in all aspects of the school system. This means our schools have to incorporate Africa-centered perspectives in strategies of learning and teaching. For example, an Afrocentric-indigenous curriculum can link the schooling of youth to the traditions and histories of African peoples, and provide learners with a sense of voice and relationship to others, especially in the inclusive classroom. Van Wyk (2014:296) says "Afrocentricity – as an alternative, non-exclusionary intellectual paradigm for educating black youth – requires a pedagogical approach that centres the learner in the discussion and analysis of the events that have shaped human history and development." This way, learners see themselves as the subjects rather than as objects of education. Since they can easily identify with the materials being taught and discussed in class, they would be in a stronger position to learn. Learners must be the active generators of their own knowledge. For the African youth, Afrocentricity as a discursive practice can offer a "language of possibility" (Giroux & McLaren, 1990:156) through which to:

> *deconstruct and reclaim, not only new forms of knowledge, but also new ways of reading history and cultural activities through the reconstruction of suppressed memories that offer identities with which to challenge and contest the very conditions through which history, desire, voice and place are experienced and lived.*

Reviewing what we know

In this section IK is conceptualised, and its relationship with critical pedagogy defined and argued for, as a process of learning and sharing social life, histories, identities, economic, and political practices unique to each cultural group in the context of inclusive education.

Teaching principles underpinning indigenous pedagogy

Indigenous pedagogy (IP) is a distinct phenomenon which focuses on four relevant aspects for promoting indigenous knowledge. *First*, IK pedagogy gives a special place to knowledge rooted in oral traditions (storytelling, music, praise poetry, etc.) flowing through the complex authority of elders and older generations, over so-called 'book knowledge'. Today, this is emphatically the case concerning knowledge about the sacred, especially in light of cultural dispossession and appropriation. Perhaps it is not surprising that one finds broadly in indigenous communities a **hermeneutic** of suspicion (if not dismissal) applied to many formulations of tradition in texts, even those of IKP authorship (Yunkaporta, & Kirby, 2011; Van Wyk, 2012; 2014). Knowledge of and stories about the past in live moments of oral exchange are never simply locked up in bygone eras: they become tangible realities that create a felt relationship with the past that cannot easily be rendered in histories that are written and read on

hermeneutic: to do with interpretation, especially of religious or literary texts

one's own. Moreover, IK must at all costs be preserved for the next generation to understand the importance of a first nation. To this end, the teacher could, for example, employ storytelling as an IK tool in her teaching practice.

Second, IK pedagogy couples the knowledge taught and learned about tradition with *responsibility on the part of both teacher and learner* to use that knowledge towards community wellbeing (Shockley, 2011; Yunkaporta & Kirby, 2011; Van Wyk, 2014). Here, the oral nature of the kind of cultural exchange described above ensures that the stewards of cultural knowledge can exercise considerable control over who learns it, how and in what contexts they will learn it, and what expectations accompany the passing on of knowledge. Norman (2004) views IK as a kind of structure of intellectual **sovereignty**, the value of which has been accentuated in light of challenges to political and other kinds of sovereignty preserved throughout the years.

Third, IK pedagogy engineers first-hand learning situated and implicated in a learner's experience, at the direction of, but not determined by, the authority of elders (Shockley, 2011; Van Wyk, 2014). In indigenous communities children are refreshingly present in every ceremonial and other community occasion or experience. They are taught skills of active watching and listening, not simply the content of what to look or listen for. Norman (2004) indicates that indigenous children are taught to take in cultural lessons experientially, to take them in over time, and not to expect to be spoon-fed segmented units of knowledge. Van Wyk (2014:296) points out that until we developed a more discerning appreciation of such things, we took teachers and other traditional elders to be 'passive' teachers. Although we assert this without challenge to the rich body of scholarship on educational psychology, we understand people's claim that knowledge derived experientially is deeper in some way (Van Wyk, 2012).

Finally, IK pedagogy makes room for *holistic reflection that engenders synthesis across the **putative** boundaries* (Norman, 2004) as compared with a modern Western sociology of knowledge (especially those that differentiate religion from politics, economics, medicine, art, and history, and which differentiate knowledge about 'religion' from the spiritual experience and ethical concerns that surround it). Dei (2002) says that the contextual nature of transferring cultural knowledge, as well as the link between cultural learning and community wellbeing, is an important categorisation of IK towards the differentiated fields of inquiry and practice in an African context. Van Wyk (2012) refers to the case of the Khoisan people reclaiming the rieldans as cultural knowledge, from an indigenous knowledge perspective. According to Dei (2002:13), acquiring herbal knowledge, for example, involves plant biology, ecology, physiology, psychology, and some familiarity with the historical, economic, and social causes of illness, besides appropriate spiritual prayers and the rehearsal of sacred narratives.

sovereignty: in this context, the complete authority or absolute rule

putative: generally considered, or reputed to be

Stop and reflect

Why is it important first to understand the teaching principles underpinning the indigenous pedagogy in planning a lesson? IK pedagogy makes room for learning situated in and implicated in a learner's experience. Plan a lesson with an applicable example from your own subject area, on how you could use this principle in your lesson preparation. Your lesson plan should be 2–3 pages long.

Eight-way framework strategy of Afrocentric-indigenous pedagogy

The eight-way framework of Afrocentric-indigenous pedagogy (Figure 3.1) brings indigenous ways of knowing to the inclusive classroom. It comprises eight interconnected strategies that conceptualise teaching and learning as fundamentally holistic, non-linear, visual, kinaesthetic, social, and contextualised.

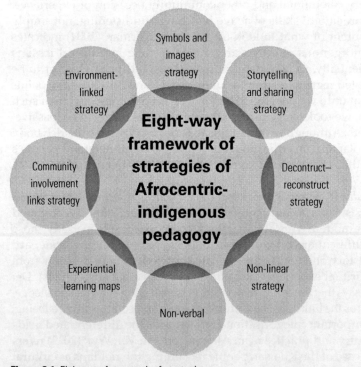

Figure 3.1: Eight-way framework of strategies

1 Storytelling and sharing of values and culture strategy

Van Wyk (2014:296) argues that storytelling is one of the key strategies of Afrocentric-indigenous pedagogy. Storytelling and sharing by elders is not only the way indigenous people keep abreast of contemporary cultural traditions but, as a way of life, they manage their dynamic but unbroken connection to nature and their environment. For example, 'yarning' or chatting is how indigenous people transmit knowledge and learn about the world (Yunkaporta & Kirby 2011; Van Wyk, 2012). In most African communities, elders teach using stories, drawing lessons from the narratives, to involve learners actively in introspection and analysis (Shockley, 2011; Van Wyk 2012). For example, the teacher in the inclusive classroom might read stories of indigenous ways of solving drought problems. In indigenous cultures, storytelling is also a way to pass down traditions, history and heritage from one generation to another (Van Wyk, 2012). It was used to pass down local customs, such as how to live off the land, and how to survive in the natural environment. Moreover, Shockley (2011) says that by exploring these oral traditions, we can learn about how important these tales are to traditional community life. As indigenous people explored their land, storytelling and sharing amongst indigenous peoples became an important tool in their cultural activities, and these ways of life are still practised in our modern society through different media.

2 Deconstruct–reconstruct strategy

This strategy is a holistic, global orientation to learning whereby the initial focus is on the whole rather than the parts. According to this strategy, the teacher designs the overall outcome of the lesson by planning, organising, and implementing the lesson with a view to achieving specific lesson objectives in the inclusive classroom. The teacher formulates purposeful lesson outcomes first and then breaks the lesson segments into manageable chunks for those learners with special needs. In this strategy, pedagogy is initially modelled by a more knowledgeable 'other' before the learner tries it independently: first watching the teacher demonstrating the lesson activities and then doing the activities themselves to see whether they have mastered the knowledge and skills taught (Norman, 2004). Scholars view this type of practice as an inclusive learning strategy in support of learning, by showing and demonstrating learning through practice (Shockley, 2011; Van Wyk, 2014).

3 Learning through associations and connections (non-linear strategy)

According Van Wyk (2014:297), indigenous pedagogy is based on learning through associations and connections as an ongoing way of making meaning by the learner. Through this strategy, problems are solved **laterally** through association and through making connections with existing knowledge. In the inclusive classroom, teachers can make use of repetition and returning to concepts for deeper understanding, a way of making meaningful connections especially to support slower learners. Indigenous people often repeat an activity to perfect it (Van Wyk, 2014). Teachers who use repetition of words (reciting poetry or singing songs) provide an effective tool

laterally: when you think laterally, you solve problems 'sideways' – indirectly and creatively; this is often contrasted with vertical thinking, which involves logical deduction only

for learners to make their own associations and connections during the learning experience.

4 Learning through field trips and environmental excursions

Afrocentric-indigenous pedagogies are intensely ecological, place-based and drawn from the living landscapes, within a framework of profound ancestral and personal relationships with place (Van Wyk, 2014). For example, teachers can plan and organise a field trip to a wildlife sanctuary or park to see animals in their environment. This is an important learning experience for those learners who are not fortunate to live in, or near, a wilderness area, or to have visited such an area. Van Wyk (2014:297) indicates that for indigenous people, learning is about linking them to land and place, as a way of life. Many wildlife parks employ local people as game rangers and field guides, who understand intuitively that the environment plays an immense role in sustaining them, and who are able to share such indigenous knowledge with learners.

5 Community involvement-linked strategy

Learning, according to indigenous pedagogy, is group-orientated, localised and connected to real-life purposes and contexts (Van Wyk, 2014:279). Teachers can, for example, invite parents of their learners to be part of an educational field trip. This strategy is effective when principals invite and involve the school community in fundraising, or the maintenance and cleaning activities of the school. These activities are a means of inclusion of the whole school community, and they also become a classroom teaching-learning strategy whereby the community is involved in supporting the school, while the school learns about community life and values.

6 Experiential learning maps

Learners learn best when the teacher uses ways to help visualise pathways of knowledge. Van Wyk (2014:297) shows how diagrams or visuals of difficult concepts can be used to map out processes explicitly for the learner. Teaching learners on how to use mind maps to plan and complete their assignments also equips them with a range of additional learning skills. In optimal indigenous pedagogy, the teacher and learner create a concrete, holistic image of the tasks to be performed which serves as a reference point for the learner (Norman, 2004; Shockley, 2011; Van Wyk, 2014).

7 Symbols and images strategy

This pedagogy uses images and metaphors to understand concepts and content. Knowledge is coded in symbols, signs, images, and metaphors and is therefore a tool for learning and memorising complex knowledge. In an Afrocentric-indigenous pedagogy, learning through strategies such as maps, symbols, and images that are naturally linked to lesson objectives to make learning meaningful, especially for learners in the Foundation Phase (Grades R to 3). Through this strategy, the teacher provides the structure of song by demonstrating to Grade 1 learners a particular sequence to be learned; or she helps learners memorise a poem by repeating the words which they learn together in the classroom.

8 Non-verbal

Perhaps also not surprisingly, Afrocentric-indigenous pedagogy is **kinaesthetic**, hands-on learning, with a strong emphasis on body language and silence (Van Wyk, 2014:297). According to this strategy, non-verbal pedagogy is more than just the idea of reduced language; learners test knowledge non-verbally through experience, introspection, and practice, thereby becoming critical thinkers who can judge the validity of new knowledge independently.

....
kinaesthetic: describes being aware of the position and movement of all parts of the body
....

 Stop and reflect

Think of ways you may have used one or some of the eight-way framework pedagogy/ies in your practice this year. How can you use the eight-way framework in your daily or future teaching practice to improve the learning outcomes of all learners? Write your response giving examples for each strategy you will use (or have used).

Benefits of Afrocentric-indigenous pedagogy for an inclusive classroom context

Several literature reviews indicate that Afrocentric-indigenous pedagogy holds advantages for the inclusive classroom (McNally, 2004; Shockley, 2011; Pellerin, 2012; Van Wyk, 2014). The following are some of the benefits that are described.

- Learners frequently return to learned knowledge

Apart from the overlaps already mentioned, which are clear advantages, the eight-way framework's strategy orientation is non-linear so learners frequently return to learned knowledge. We see this as a further advantage as it allows for deeper understanding and introspection. A criticism of Western pedagogy is that it is becoming too linear with its focus on standardised testing at the expense of other skills.

- Promotes introspection, reflection and other types of self-directed learning

According to Van Wyk (2014:295), in comparison with Afrocentric-indigenous pedagogy, Western pedagogy tends to ignore the knowledge of indigenous people that "comes from introspection, reflection and other types of self-directed learning." An important part of any learning is surely being able to reflect on what and how one learned something.

- ● **Learners are exposed to contextualised learning**

In addition, the eight-way framework strategy of place-based learning allows for more contextualised learning. This enables learners to see how education is relevant to and meaningful in their own lives.

- ● **Learners are aware of lesson outcomes and expectations**

A further advantage is the eight-way framework strategies' explicit mapping of course tasks and materials, so learners are aware of where the lesson or unit of work is going and what is expected. Before the teacher begins the lesson, he explains the outcomes to be achieved to all learners. He demonstrates the specific knowledge and skills to be learned, which will be assessed after the lesson presentation. According to scholars, the eight-way framework is easily adaptable to any lesson and can readily be integrated into the current traditional pedagogical practices, and in particular this framework therefore exposes learners to different ways and ideas within the mainstream classroom.

The eight-way framework strategies show extraordinary outcomes in terms of engagement and higher order thinking can be achieved. Learners became more focused and highly enthused by using indigenous pedagogy. In addition, the eight-way framework strategies enhance a positive shift in behaviour, attitude, relationships and quality of learners' work.

Role of the teacher in the Afrocentric-indigenous pedagogy classroom setting

In this part of the chapter, we discuss the practical implications relating to indigenous pedagogical teaching methods as best practices for an inclusive and sustainable classroom environment. In addition, a brief profile of the attitudes and behaviour of the ideal Afrocentric teacher is highlighted. Anderson (2012) views the role of the teacher to enhance learning in many innovative ways and projects that have been put into place to help African children. However, these innovations in the classroom setting often fall short of affording an educational experience that empowers members of the African community to "control the psychic and physical spaces that [Africans, in particular blacks] call their own" (Asante, 1991). Many scholars have pointed out that Africans are mis-educated because they are not the chief producers or manufacturers of any of the major goods they need for their own survival. That is, Africans are mis-educated because they have not been taught how to produce, own, and control the resources within their own communities. This remains a huge challenge for teachers in the inclusive classroom setting. Shockley (2011:1029) conducted a research study on the role of the teacher, and highlighted the following:

- Teachers must become aware of their identity, beliefs and practices; of who they are as African people.
- As teachers become ever more familiarised with the African cultural group of their choosing or belonging, they use aspects of what they themselves are learning, in the classroom.
- Teachers must be consistent in understanding their specific role as agents of change to advance African cultures.
- Teachers must be critically aware of their role as change agents and be sensitive to gender and racial issues by educating, empowering and instilling African canons in learners in the classroom. These specific canons are awareness, respect, Ubuntu, humanity, and inclusivity.
- Teachers must not marginalise or degrade other groups' perspectives, histories, cultures, and traditions in their classrooms.
- In the inclusive classroom, when a teacher gives voice and space to diverse perspectives and other legitimate interpretations of human experiences, every learner in the class gains from knowing the complete account of events that have shaped human history.

Role of communities in promoting and supporting Afrocentric-indigenous education

In line with the proverbial African saying that it takes a whole village to educate a child, Afrocentric pedagogy stresses the role and importance of the community in the education of children, and promotes the active involvement of the community in the schooling process. The emphasis on bridging the gap between the community and the school should be matched by a pedagogical style that inculcates in learners their individual responsibilities to the wider community. The community is vital and plays a significant and active role in the education of children in Africa. The focus is to establish partnerships between the school and the community, as well the involvement of the broader community in the schooling process of the child. Shockley (2011:1026) argues that the role of the community in partnership with the school can advocate for and educate youth and learners about the negative consequences of substance abuse by forming social support groupings. Moreover, Afrocentric-indigenous pedagogy as an alternative to Westernised pedagogy can play a vital role in instilling a sense of value and identity in learners and youth, as proudly African. Shockley (2011) as well Asante (1991) indicate that schools should promote the values of the cooperative individual who belongs to, and is enriched by, the group or community. Both in schooling and in education, the stress should be on group work and support as opposed to competitiveness, rugged individualism, and individual culpability (Asante, 1991; Shockley, 2011; Van Wyk, 2014)

Afrocentric teachers are always very well known in the community for their work with children and amongst the community. Such a person embraces the notion of being Afrocentric, and uses that label to describe themselves and identify with the constructs of an Afrocentric-indigenous person. The Afrocentric teacher also believes that Afrocentric-indigenous teaching is the best type of teaching for black learners and for understanding how an African-indigenous learner learns. An African-indigenous teacher is accessible for observation, consultation, and support, when approached for ideas to uplift the community at large.

Stop and reflect

Why do you think that Afrocentric-indigenous teaching is the best type of teaching for black learners? Why is it important to understand how an African learner learns? If you are working in a rural community, how would you promote the active involvement of the community in the schooling process? Outline three steps or processes in line with your argument.

Promoting an inclusive Afrocentric-indigenous classroom

In this part of the chapter we now continue to explore alternative ways to integrate Afrocentric-indigenous teachings into the school curricula in order to serve the interests of all learners. It is a challenge to think deeply about the Afrocentric teacher who now lives in an age that is radically different from the past in its celebration of difference, cultural fragmentation, and pluralism within an inclusive society. The issues raised in this chapter require that all teachers, learners, and school administrators seriously re-think some of the commonsense ideas about schooling, education, and society, in order to advance Afrocentric-indigenous ideas. The Afrocentric-indigenous pedagogical idea does not mean a complete rejection of all that mainstream education has to offer in reconstructing a clear Afrocentric identity in schooling, education, and society at large. On the contrary, it calls on all African-indigenous teachers and scholars to utilise the best of what mainstream knowledge offers through a review of its paradigms, viewpoints, and methods, as a basis to critique contemporary society on issues of social justice, racism, privilege, and to promote an inclusive encompassing education.

The Afrocentric-indigenous classroom is not only for black learners but inclusive of all learners for the advancement of quality education. While concerns about the problems of black youth in the education system may drive the school's creation, it is defined by its principles rather than by who goes there or who teaches there. It is inescapable that the current schooling system looks at the world through Western eyes. However, we want to start looking at the world through the eyes of African people – their experiences, their cultural knowledge and their history. Afrocentric-indigenous education sees schooling as a community endeavour, which means that parents, learners, administrators, educators and governments share in the responsibility to ensure success. In the existing system, learners are treated as individual students. We want them to see themselves as a community of learners with a responsibility to those who are struggling. We want all learners to help those who are not doing well. We want them to excel in life and contribute to humanity. The Afrocentric paradigm provides a space for African people to interpret their experiences on their own terms rather than through a Eurocentric lens. Of course, teachers and learners need to know about European history, but promote their African identity, cultures and values. Dei (2002) is of the view that the goal of Afrocentric-indigenous pedagogy is seeking the appropriate centrality of the African people in the classroom discourse (in contrast to their current marginality). Our view is that this pedagogy requires that teachers provide learners with the opportunity to study the world and its people, concepts, and history from an African worldview. Mazama. (2001:387) posits that "we must not deny European influences in the behaviour of African people or reject completely the intellectual validity of European culture and cultural theorists on the development of Afrocentric epistemology." Teachers must consistently and daily reflect on the practical implications relating to indigenous pedagogical teaching methods as best practice for an inclusive and sustainable classroom environment.

Alternatively, schools and teachers are often seen as contributing to educational inequality unless they are challenged to assume agency for addressing disparities through reforms that can lead to fundamental changes in schools and classrooms. Andersen (2012) provides a comprehensive overview of how culture in schools is reflected at multiple levels, whether visible or invisible, and how it has an impact on learners. The classroom is, of course, the daily lived experience of learners; thus the validation of learners' cultural identities and valuing of the cultural knowledge learners bring with them to school have the potential to make a difference.

Caring for learners as culturally located individuals within a framework of positive learner–teacher relationships is considered beneficial for all learners, but particularly so for African children. One particular issue is how Africa cares for children. We must distinguish between aesthetic caring, which involves affective expression only; and authentic caring, which entails deep reciprocity and, in the case of teachers, takes responsibility for providing an educational environment in which their learners thrive. Authentic caring entails getting to know the learner, attending to learner input about teaching and learning, respecting learners' intellectual abilities, and valuing identities learners bring into school from home. Thus, caring for learners as culturally located individuals, as understood in this context, goes beyond simple feelings of empathy, to implications for teacher pedagogy and how teachers support student learning.

The focus of this chapter is towards developing an Afrocentric-indigenous pedagogy frame for an inclusive education context as this is primarily the teacher professional development model to effect real change in classrooms. The following are specific steps for implementing this frame:

- To initiate **induction workshops** introducing the Afrocentric-indigenous pedagogy as a model of culturally responsive and inclusive pedagogies in classroom relations
- To structure **classroom observations** focused on the implementation of the Afrocentric-indigenous approach as a model, followed by feedback to teachers in individual meetings with facilitators who have inclusive and culturally responsive pedagogical expertise
- To co-construct **meetings on best practices** where teacher teams problem solve collaboratively, based on observational and learner outcomes data
- To implement specific **shadow-coaching sessions and observations** for individualised teacher professional development.

The above components incorporate sustained support for teachers over time, emphasis on specific instructional strategies and content areas, involvement of teachers collectively rather than individually, peer coaching, and active learning professional development activities.

Summary of discussion

Afrocentric educationists argue that curricula must include the achievements and knowledge of all societies, and to use the voice of the community culture itself, in order to present people's histories and struggles for affirmation. Afrocentricity as a philosophy is constructed on principles of justice, harmony, community involvement, fairness and commitment. Indigenous knowledge is a process of learning and sharing social life, histories, identities, economic, and political practices unique to each cultural group. In this chapter indigenous knowledge is expressed as the identities, values, beliefs and practices of indigenous peoples. Important teaching principles underpinning Afrocentric-indigenous pedagogy and the eight-strategy framework of Afrocentric-indigenous pedagogy as well the advantages for an inclusive classroom are discussed. Lastly, we reflect on the role of the teacher and communities in promoting and supporting the idea of Afrocentric-indigenous education for inclusivity.

Closing activities

Self-reflection

1. What do the reasons for black learners' low achievement tell us about society and individual responsibilities, accountability, and the future educational practices of our current education system? How can an Afrocentric-indigenous pedagogy support low-performing learners at school? Provide arguments for this challenge.
2. Can an Afrocentric-indigenous education make school pedagogy more effective and improve the ability of the public school system to educate all South African youth? Can the introduction of Afrocentric-indigenous education in schools help particularly black learners identify with their school system? Reflect on these issues.

Practical applications

3. In relation to the Afrocentric-indigenous pedagogy principles of teaching and learning (pages 50 to 55), plan three lessons on a topic of your particular school subject. Integrate at least one aspect of each principle in your lesson plans.
4. You have been selected to make a class presentation to your colleagues or fellow students on the Afrocentric-indigenous paradigm for an inclusive classroom setting (pages 55 to 56). What will be your main points? What applied examples would you use to illustrate your ideas? How would you prepare yourself to answer specific concerns and uncertainties that would inevitably arise? Write up your specific plan for this presentation.

Analysis and consolidation

5. Write an essay (about 3–4 pages) on the role of the teacher in promoting Afrocentric-indigenous pedagogy principles of teaching and learning in the inclusive classroom (pages 56 to 57).
6. Analyse what you see as the educational value and relevance of the Afrocentric-indigenous pedagogy for an inclusive education system. Write your analysis in the form of a report.

Further outcomes

Having completed this chapter and the activities, formulate two or more outcomes (in addition to those given under Learning outcomes at the beginning of this chapter) of what you are now able to do.

Issues for debate or further research

With a colleague or fellow student, read, reflect on, and debate the following:

The Afrocentric-indigenous paradigm provides a space for African peoples to interpret their experiences on their own terms rather than through a Eurocentric lens. Of course, learners need to know about European history. But they also need to understand that African history is central in the construction of European history. You cannot present world history in a way that leaves out a group of people or says that their history doesn't matter. For example, the 1987 British film *Cry Freedom* is ostensibly about the beliefs, struggle, and death of black activist Steve Biko in apartheid South Africa, but really turns on the story of white journalist, Donald Woods, who becomes active and fights apartheid. The questions to ask are not whether the journalist fought alone, but where were the black people, and what was their role in the struggle against apartheid? How would the story be different if told through a black person's eyes? The question to consider is: How can the school curriculum truly promote the Afrocentric-indigenous paradigm?

Currently, subjects such as Geography, History, and English can be taught from an African point of view. There is also a whole literature on ethno-mathematics and indigenous conceptions of science, mathematics, and economics. How can school subjects like Mathematics (or Mathematical Literacy), Life Sciences, and Economics be taught from an African point of view? Discuss the following example: Research and then choose textile designs used by a particular African group. What geometric forms are used? How are patterns set up and repeated? What symbolism is represented, if any, and how will you find out? And finally, how does this group use this knowledge in an entrepreneurial way?

References and further reading

Akena, F.A. 2012. Critical Analysis of the Production of Western Knowledge and Its Implications for Indigenous Knowledge and Decolonization. *Journal of Black Studies*. 43(6):599–619.

Andersen, C. 2012. Critical indigenous studies in the classroom: Exploring the local using primary evidence. *International Journal of Critical Indigenous Studies*. 5(1):67–92.

Asante, M.K. 1991. The Afrocentric idea in education. *Journal of Negro Education*. 60(2):170–179.

Asante, M.K. 1998. *The Afrocentric idea in education*. 2nd ed. Philadelphia: Temple University Press.

Banks, W.C. 1992. The theoretical and methodological crisis of Afrocentric conception. *Journal of Negro Education*. 61(3):262–272.

Dei, G.J.S. 2002. Afrocentricity: A Cornerstone of Pedagogy. *Anthropology and Education Quarterly*. 25(1):3–28. Retrieved from: http://www.academicroom.com on 26 October 2013.

Giroux, H. A. & McLaren, P. 1990. Critical pedagogy and rural education: A challenge from Poland. *Peabody Journal of Education*. 67(4):154–165.

Kincheloe, J. 2006. Critical ontology and indigenous ways of being: Forging a postcolonial curriculum. In Y. Kanu (Ed). *Curriculum as cultural practice* (pp. 181-202). Toronto, Canada: University of Toronto Press.

Lowry, R.F. 1998. Development Theory, Globalism, and the New World Order: The Need for a Postmodern, Antichrist and Multicultural Critique. *Journal of Black Studies.* (7)2:23–34.

Mazama, A. 2001. The Afrocentric Paradigm: Contours and Definitions. *Journal of Black Studies.* 31(4):387405. Retrieved from: http://www.jstor.org/page/info/about/policies/terms.jsp on 6 June 2014.

McNally, M.D. 2004. Indigenous pedagogy in the classroom: A service learning model for discussion. *The American Indian Quarterly.* Summer–Fall.

Mkabela N.Q & Luthuli P.C 1997. *Towards an African philosophy of education.* Pretoria: Kagiso Tertiary.

Norman, H. 2004. Exploring effective teaching strategies: Simulation case studies and indigenous studies at the university level. *Australian Journal of Higher Education.* 17(3): 137–143.

Pellerin M. 2012. Benefits of Afrocentricity in exploring social phenomena: Understanding Afrocentricity as a social science methodology. *Journal of Pan African Studies.* 5(4): 149–160.

Reviere, R. 2001. Towards an Afrocentric research methodology. *Journal of Black Studies.* 31(6):709–728.

Reviere, R. (n.d.). *Rethinking Open and Distance Education Practices: Unearthing Subjectivities and Barriers to Learning.* Retrieved from: http://www.col.org on 15 September 2011.

Shockley, K.G. 2011. Reaching African American students: Profile of an Afrocentric teacher. *Journal of Black Studies.* 42(7):1027–1046. Retrieved from: http://jbs.sagepub.com/content/42/7/1027 on 23 May 2013.

Shockley, K.G. & Frederick, R.M. 2010. Constructs and dimensions of Afrocentric education. *Journal of Black Studies,* 40(6):1212–1233.

Van Wyk, M.M. 2012. [Re]claiming the Riel as Khoisan indigenous cultural knowledge. *Studies on Tribes and Tribals.* 10(1):47–56.

Van Wyk, M.M. 2014. Conceptualising an Afrocentric-indigenous Pedagogy for an inclusive classroom environment. *Mediterranean Journal of Social Sciences.* 5(4):292–299

Yunkaporta, T. & Kirby, M. 2011. Yarning up Indigenous pedagogies: A dialogue about eight Aboriginal ways of learning, In R. Bell, G. Milgate & N. Purdie (Eds). *Two-Way Teaching and Learning: Toward culturally reflective and relevant education.* Camberwell Victoria: ACER Press. Retrieved from: http://vickidrozdowski.files.wordpress.com on 4 May 2013.

4

Africanisation, Ubuntu and IKS: A learner-centred approach

Muzwa Mukwambo, Kenneth Ngcoza and Charles Chikunda

Chapter overview

The first section of this chapter defines the concept of 'Africanisation of the curriculum', followed by an explanation of the concepts of Ubuntu and Indigenous knowledge, which we regard as necessary tools in the Africanisation process of the school science curriculum. The section that follows then engages the nexus of Western science and Indigenous knowledge in teaching and learning. Finally, the chapter concludes with a discussion of socio-cultural theory in order to deepen the discourse around Africanisation of the school science curriculum, focusing on situated learning and learner-centred approaches from an African theoretical perspective.

Learning outcomes

By the end of this chapter you should be able to:
*   Explain the concept of Africanisation of the school science curriculum
*   Analyse the interconnectedness of Ubuntu and Indigenous Knowledge Systems (IKS) as tools in the Africanisation of the school science curriculum
*   Integrate Ubuntu, Indigenous knowledge (IK) and Western science (WS) as a process of Africanisation of the school science curriculum
*   Explore ways of using the concept of Africanisation of the school science curriculum in your own science teaching and learning context
*   Describe the complexities and challenges related to the infusion of IK, WS and Ubuntu into a school science curriculum.

Rationale for Africanisation of the science curriculum in the context of transformation in South Africa

Since 1994 in South Africa there has been ongoing transformation in the education system. Core to such transformation has been the positioning of learners at the centre of teaching and learning processes. Learning is now perceived to be dependent on the learners making connections between existing knowledge and the content of instruction. Contemporary approaches to teaching and learning are therefore anchored in educational theories which are related to the history and culture of the communities they serve. Herein lies the importance of the concept of Africanisation of the school science curriculum. However, before we can explore the concept, a number of questions have been raised (and are still being raised) about Africanisation of the school science curriculum, which may be important to look at first.

Why is it that science always seems to refer to the experiences of people in Europe and America? Is there no science in Africa?

Well, I am not sure, but I know there is a lot of talk about Ubuntu and IKS. Any idea of what these are?

Yah, but where is the science in this? How can bringing in Ubuntu and IK make the science more local, contextual and relevant to our situation?

I am sure it's all in the teaching – how the science is presented, perhaps?

I wish someone would explain Ubuntu and IK, and how they relate to the teaching and learning of science in school.

I guess if we could do that it would make science much more accessible to most African kids, as the majority find science so alien and de-contextualised.

This chapter will respond to these questions by proposing and developing the potential for Africanising the school science curriculum.

Africanisation of the curriculum – reaching what we know with what we know

According to (Coetzee, 1999; Goduka, 1999; Luggya, 1999; Makgoba, 1998; Mbeki, 1998; Seepe, 1998), Africanisation has to do with methods and approaches in teaching and learning that can be adapted and made relevant to the African context. We share this belief that there is a need for a context-driven curriculum instead of simply transplanting ideas or policies from other countries (Viljoen & Van der Walt, 2006). Okeke (2010) also points out that sometimes such policies can be detrimental to education, especially if we fail to analyse them critically before they are implemented.

So, Africanisation of the school science curriculum is well placed to make use of the beliefs that African communities already have in particular spheres such as environmental conservation; this can be seen in the way these communities practise conservation at a communal level. The same communities, for example, practise agriculture based on knowledge and experience they have gained throughout the many years they have lived on the land. Each experience (Knowles, 1950) is used to sustain human survival and improve the communities' living conditions for each succeeding generation. The debate then is about how African communities' knowledge, and their worldviews, can be brought into and incorporated in classroom activities to enhance science teaching and learning.

Social exclusion occurs when some learners' ways of knowing are not included as worthwhile capital in the 'distribution, re-contextualisation and evaluation' of science knowledge (Bernstein, 1996). Africanisation, like any other process, requires tools. We argue here that by constructing Ubuntu, Indigenous knowledge (IK), and Western science (WS), as the 'tools' available to the science education teacher, it is possible to create a powerful point of 'pedagogical interconnectedness' in the school science curriculum. This is shown in Figure 4.1.

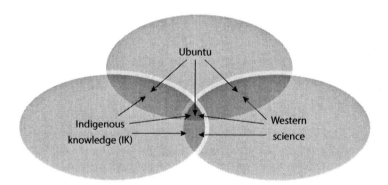

Figure 4.1: Tools in the Africanisation of the school science curriculum showing the 'point of pedagogical interconnectedness'

Let us now discuss each of these tools in detail.

The Ubuntu philosophy within the context of Africanisation

The Ubuntu philosophy is used to maintain harmony not only among community members, but also with other organisms which sustain the survival of humanity (Freris & Muitui, 2011). It is intended to sustain the whole natural ecosystem. King and Miller (2006) believe that Ubuntu is a manifestation of collective responsibility among human beings to distribute the life force for the common benefit.

Freris and Muitui (2011) reinforce this view when they say that the Ubuntu philosophy is characterised by people supporting one another within their communities. Through Ubuntu, people's conduct is regulated, and recognition and reverence of the special relationship they have with the physical environment and other non-human species is maintained. It is a view which is manifested in attitudes and practices such as respect, empathy, accountability, responsibility, fairness, justice, compassion, unity, compromise, love, caring, tolerance, and others. These attitudes and practices are a necessity in our humanity, and it follows that they should also be integrated into our education system. Essentially, the Ubuntu philosophy argues for inclusive learning environments, an aspect that enriches the possibilities for the Africanisation of the school science curriculum.

 Stop and reflect

1   Discuss the following in class or with a peer:
    The Ubuntu philosophy proclaims cooperation, respect for one another, helping others out in dire situations, common ownership of natural resources, and many other virtues, such as looking after children regardless of whether one is the biological parent or not, as central to maintaining harmony between a people (or a nation) and their environment.
    Do you agree or disagree with these ideas? Explain.
2   What implications do such ideas have in classroom practice and the day-to-day running of a school? Write your response as a one-page journal entry in which you reflect on these questions in terms of your own future teaching career.

Indigenous knowledge and Western science within the context of Africanisation

According to Semali and Kincheloe (1999:40), IK is knowledge that is produced in specific historical and cultural contexts, and is typically not "generated by a set of pre-specified procedures or rules [but] is orally passed down from one generation to the next." IK is locally specific since a given community is responsive to a particular IK which is dynamic; each community member is responsible for sharing new discoveries with other community members. Indigenous knowledge covers a range of issues, among them are those that relate to "history, education, architecture, philosophy, language, and science" (Mapara, 2009:143). Carter (2007) and Lemke (2001) posit that IK is a micro-culture of a particular community, developed in response to the culture's needs to understand, predict, and influence its environment.

In contrast, Western science is Eurocentric and manifests itself strongly and powerfully in our ideas, culture, and education. It uses the cultural background of the West – chiefly Europe and North America – to understand the environment, and even to conquer that same environment with its actions and activities. However, in teaching not only science, but other disciplines as well, we argue that IK and

WS are dialectically related, and can be used in the Africanisation of the school science curriculum. This understanding should enable teachers to consider the context of learners in the dissemination and evaluation of science curriculum knowledge. The persuasive power of WS makes science teachers move away from IK, as teachers see only its achievement and not its adverse effects on the environment, for example. One illustration of this is the replacement in 1928 of refrigerants and solvents such as ammonia, sulphur dioxide, and others, that are highly toxic to humans, with chlorofluorocarbons (CFCs), which are non-toxic organic compounds. Yet CFCs are prime contributors to stratospheric ozone depletion (Molina & Rowland, 1974); in other words, safe for humans, but toxic to the environment.

Indigenous science (IS) is embedded in WS. IS can be used as prior everyday knowledge in the classroom to offset the challenges posed by WS, since it is responsive to the environment. To mitigate potential undermining of the environment, we understand that the two knowledge systems WS and IK have to work together in a complementary way. They also have a common set, where some concepts are shared, as shown in Figure 4.2. An illustration of this is the use of barriers: WS would use lead, zinc, and other materials as a shield against radiation, whereas in IS, for example, the Himba of Namibia use *otjidje* (a mixture of ochre and animal fat) to shield themselves from the radiation of the sun. Also, in seed preservation, WS uses methods of preserving seeds in dark places after coating them with a chemical insecticide. IS, on the other hand, accepts that people from their store of IK, preserve seeds by hanging them in rafters in their kitchens where smoke from wood fires covers them naturally with soot. Soot contains creosote, which is obtained in WS through the dry distillation of coal or wood, and is used as a preservative. In this case, the argument for Africanisation of the school science curriculum is based on the assumption that scientific knowledge, as defined by WS, is embedded in most indigenous practices. Therefore, the distribution of scientific knowledge within the context of such practices has vast potential for inclusivity.

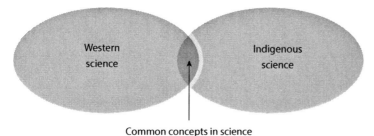

Common concepts in science

Figure 4.2: Two interacting knowledge systems

This relationship exists because WS did not emerge in a vacuum, but was influenced by many factors, such as those in other knowledge systems (algebra and astronomy from the Arab world, explosives and ceramics from the Chinese empire, road building and architecture from South and Central America, to name a few). This means that there are certain areas where the two knowledge systems coexist and overlap. With such a scenario emerging, the common concepts in the two knowledge systems can be exploited, as one needs to develop a hybrid which learners in a particular culture can understand (Thompson, 2012) to align sub-Saharan education systems to African identities. When analysing seed preservation, a teacher might start with eliciting from learners how their culture goes about seed preservation. After this, the teacher with the class might analyse how Western science achieves seed preservation, noting similarities and differences which might emerge.

However, we need to be aware that IK is not a bag of knowledge waiting to be tapped into and dispensed. Instead, there is a need to critically analyse it before it can be used, to expose any contradictions that might come with it, or be entailed by it. Currently, because of the labels that have come to be associated with IK, for example, that it is based on cultural superstitions, some have abandoned its use. This has made it impossible for the current generation of users of IK to perfect it so as to make it compatible with current science education thinking. Clearly, some communities have never abandoned IK. But since they have been interacting at community level their IK has absorbed influences through such interaction. IK as the cultural activity of a given community is porous and this makes it gather other ways of thinking and acting from other cultures. As a cultural construct of people, IK is always in a state of change.

Africanisation in teaching and learning

As shown in Figure 4.1, Africanisation as applied in education is essentially the infusion of IK, WS and Ubuntu. This is in line with the South African curriculum's quest for situated cognition and learner-centered approaches, as stated in the general aims of the national curriculum, that is, the Curriculum and Assessment Policy Statement (CAPS, 2011), which says:

> *The National Curriculum Statement Grades R-12 gives expression to the knowledge, skills and values worth learning in South African schools. This curriculum aims to ensure that children acquire and apply knowledge and skills in ways that are meaningful to their own lives. In this regard, the curriculum promotes knowledge in local contexts, while being sensitive to global imperatives.* (Department of Basic Education, 2011:4).

Furthermore, CAPS puts an emphasis on the valuing of indigenous knowledge systems, acknowledging that the rich history and heritage of South Africans is an important aspect to meaningful learning (Ibid).

Essentially, Africanisation as a curriculum philosophy resonates with the ideals of a socio-cultural approach to teaching and learning. Africanisation argues for acknowledgement of the cultural resources of learners as 'capital' for learning. Lemke (2001) argues that learning becomes effective when participants' cultural resources are harnessed in the teaching and learning scenario.

With the aid of the case study below, we show how one aspect of the Grade 10 science curriculum can be Africanised through the close links that exist between IK, WS and Ubuntu

 CASE STUDY

Nomzamo is a young Physical Science teacher in a rural school in the Eastern Cape. Guided by the curriculum that acknowledges the holistic being of the learners by valuing their life experiences as a focal point of teaching, she always tries to use local examples where appropriate to illustrate scientific issues, concepts, and processes.

Nomzamo is currently teaching her Grade 10 learners about matter and materials. To her bewilderment, the textbooks only identify mud bricks as an example that could be useful in studying ceramics from the local environment. All the other examples are foreign to her context. Nomzamo is not satisfied that this single example will fulfil the syllabus requirements of using local knowledge in teaching about materials. She wonders how she can make up her lessons around this topic so that her learners can describe the experiment to identify the physical properties of materials, as stipulated in the syllabus, with only this one local, meaningful example. None of the available textbooks are helpful besides merely listing the physical properties of materials.

It occurs to Nomzamo that, besides mud bricks, clay pots that are locally made by indigenous people could also be artefacts that she could use in her teaching of the topic. Over and above this, the curriculum requirement of "valuing indigenous knowledge systems: acknowledging the rich history and heritage of the country" (Department of Basic Education, 2011:5) motivates her to go beyond the ordinary lesson. She goes on to plan her lessons for the topic in a way that elicits learners' prior everyday knowledge and experience of traditional clay artefacts in relation to materials. She organises some field trips for learners so that they get real-life experience of making clay artefacts. As an educator, Nomzamo is convinced that the purpose of eliciting prior everyday knowledge is to make the connection between everyday and scientific concepts, about materials. In one class discussion, Nomzamo is delighted to find that her learners classify clay artefacts into two groups: clay artefacts that are heated, and those that are not. This provides her with an opportunity that she later exploits for a definition of ceramics.

Later, Nomzamo takes her class on several site visits to get first-hand experience of the indigenous practice of making ceramics. Her aim is to make matter and materials meaningful in Grade 10. To do this, she identifies two IK 'experts', older women who have been making clay artefacts for years. Site visits started with an exploration of the places where the clay soil is collected. Both women explain that most of the soil that is used to make indigenous ceramics is taken from places that hold water for long time (i.e. that do not drain easily). The following conversation captures how this local IK expert justifies choosing clay from this particular pan as good for clay artefacts.

Learners: Why did you choose to use clay soil from this particular pan? We have passed by so many pans today.

IK expert: We know this has good soil for clay pots. We were shown by our grandmothers, who also used it to make pots.

Learners: Really?

IK expert: Yes, we learned all we know about clay and how to make clay pots from our grandmothers. They told us the clay soil from this pan is the best for clay pots.

After the first visit to the site where ceramic artefacts are made, Nomzamo and her class are able to find scientific explanations in a science textbook to match the two women's indigenous knowledge of good soil for making ceramics. Among these explanations is that clay soil has small particles, making it difficult for water to drain easily; clay minerals that are formed by the process of weathering and hydrothermal activities, are eroded and transported mostly by water, and deposited at places that hold water for a long time. In subsequent visits, both the older women demonstrate traditional ways of making ceramics, and their demonstrations are very similar and consistent. They both use ground cattle hooves and ribs to process their pots. They produce pots by moulding the clay soil into shapes, allowing them to dry, and then **firing** them at a very low temperature.

Out of these visits, Nomzamo and her learners are able to follow the whole process of making, drying and firing ceramic artefacts. After each visit, the class tries to make scientific meaning of matter and materials through the processes they have observed. Despite the challenges that Nomzamo encounters, she is pleased that her teaching approach is far more fruitful than the traditional teacher talk she used to practise.

 Stop and reflect

In groups discuss the following:
1 Briefly explain the aspects of Ubuntu that you can identify in the way Nomzamo teaches this section on matter and materials in the science curriculum.
2 What do you think the benefits are of designing lessons with this Ubuntu spirit in mind? Write your answer as a one-page response supported by explanations you have read in this chapter, and in others, in this book

firing: a technique in making clay objects in which pots are dried and baked

As shown in Nomzamo's case study, Africanisation of the school science curriculum attempts to re-contextualise the learning and teaching of science. The process does not always require lengthy and rigorous steps, as in Nomzamo's case. That is, Africanisation can entail using learners' familiar knowledge to introduce or consolidate new concepts in science.

The benefits of Africanisation in teaching and learning

In proposing the Africanisation of the school science curriculum, we are promoting a teaching and learning scenario in which both teachers and learners engage in knowledge construction in the full diversity of cultural, racial, ethnic, and religious practices of all people, so as to bring about common understanding. There is already a strong body of research to support this position.

Ogunniyi (2007), for example, argues that learners are loaded with a lot of science from their home backgrounds that should be taken advantage of. Hewson, Javu and Holtman (2009) believe that IK is part of learners' prior knowledge which directly impacts their ability to accept new ideas. Based on this view, learners' new scientific ideas can be built on their everyday experiences.

Van Wyk (2002), Kibirige and Van Rooyen (2006), and Cimi (2009) make the valid point that the inclusion of everyday experiences enables adult community members to participate in education and pass on their knowledge to learners, as shown in Nomzamo's case study. O'Donoghue, Lotz-Sisitka, Asafo-Adjei, Kota and Hanisi (2007) argue that IK strengthens the community and cultural identity, and promotes the moral values of indigenous people. For this reason, when community members participate in the education discourse of their children, the curriculum becomes relevant to the lives and livelihood of learners. For example, research by O'Donoghue et al. (2007) reveals that involving learners in researching the foods preferred by indigenous people aroused learners' interest in valuing those foods.

Complexities and challenges related to Africanisation of school science curriculum

Despite the many positive reasons for Africanising the school science curriculum, and going back to our case study and many other examples in doing so, we still see complexities and challenges. To start with, science concepts are not always explicit in most indigenous practices; but Africanisation of the school science curriculum calls upon the teacher and learners to attach scientific explanation to indigenous practices, or to use indigenous practices, or even everyday knowledge, to make meaning of science. This can be observed in Nomzamo's case, when her learners ask the potter women why they choose clay from a particular pan, and are told that their grandmothers taught them where to find good clay. The women's indigenous knowledge of what makes the clay good for pottery is implicit and embedded: learners need to follow up in textbooks for explicit scientific explanations.

IK and Ubuntu are also deeply rooted in people's beliefs. Some beliefs are entrenched in myths that are hard to explain in a scientific sense. For example, most African cultures believe that lightning can be sent by individuals who have the power to do so. In South Africa the belief is widespread that *inyangas* or *sangomas* (traditional doctors) possess such superhuman powers. Some communities in Namibia believe that a rainbow is a dangerous living thing that can suck your blood. Such beliefs seem to present a barrier to learners from these cultures, when it comes to accommodating scientific principles and facts related to electrostatics and light respectively. Africanisation of the school science curriculum would therefore encourage teachers not to avoid such beliefs in the sense making of science, but instead to engage with them.

Stop and reflect

1 In a group, think of some cultural beliefs from your community that you regard as myths or non-scientific ideas. Discuss with the group what teaching and learning strategies you can put in place to teach related scientific concepts to learners who present such cultural beliefs in class.

2 Share your group's discussion and proposed strategies with other groups in class. Make notes of strategies that you would like to discuss further, and your related questions. Hand in your notes and questions for collation by your course organiser. If time allows, convene another session to discuss questions and get feedback.

Socio-cultural theory and Africanisation

Socio-cultural theory argues for situated cognition and learner-centred approaches. Knowledge is abstract or concrete, and both these forms are dialectically interwoven with culture. It follows then that IK and WS are in a dialectical relationship too. The dialectical relationship of IK, WS, and the ways of thinking and acting of indigenous communities where the Ubuntu worldview is a component, is a clear manifestation that the line of demarcation is permeable. So, Africanisation as an epistemological reconstruction is meaningless without understanding socio-cultural theory, which can uncover the kind of hybrids suitable for schools with diverse cultures.

A socio-cultural approach in teaching and learning science is based on the understanding that "human activities take place in cultural contexts, are mediated by language and other symbol systems, and can be best understood when investigated in their historical development" (John-Steiner & Mahn, 1996:2).

Socio-cultural views come with cultural resources, which can be used as learning and teaching support materials (LTSMs) (Czerniewicz, Murray & Probyn, 2000). According to Czerniewicz et al. (2000), LTSMs take on different formats and nature. For example, an earthenware pot, as a cultural artefact, can be used not only to successfully discuss the concepts of latent heat of vaporisation, and evaporation generally in Physical Sciences, but can also be used to teach the concept of semi-permeable materials in Life Sciences. An understanding of how people cool water for drinking using earthenware pots in summer when temperatures are high, enables one to execute a situated cognition lesson, and to adopt a learner-centered approach, as discussed earlier (and later) in this chapter. Such practices resonate with the perspective of Africanisation where cultural artefacts inherently 'speak science' – as in the case study of Nomzamo – and comply with the tenets of situated cognition and learner-centeredness.

leveraging: using elements in a situation to achieve other desired outcomes

Similarly, socio-cultural perspectives on learning suggest recognising the cultural elements and practices of learners, and **leveraging** these to facilitate effective learning processes. This is because within a particular community's culture is located a micro-culture of science taught at school. The micro-culture informs the practices that members use in science-related matters. The community's indigenous knowledge as a micro-culture, and a tool to Africanise sub-Saharan African countries' education systems, developed in response to the cultural needs of communities, as they use it to understand and solve issues which are related not only to the environment but also to history, education, architecture, philosophy, language, and science (Mapara, 2009).

Let us look at a scenario to illustrate this idea: teaching the concept and process of sublimation (in the science curriculum). Cultural practices can be incorporated in teaching sublimation in the following way: Instead of procuring naphthalene, (which, in most cases, is not available in the laboratory), to illustrate and demonstrate sublimation, the teacher can begin the lesson by discussing with learners how this scientific phenomenon is viewed and spoken about in the community. Teachers could ask learners what their families do when they have a urine-soaked blanket. The teacher could then explain to learners that the act of hanging the urine-soaked blanket in the sun allows sublimation of urea to occur. Similarly, sublimation can be reinforced by explaining how a urine-filled chamber pot loses the pungent smell after being put out in the sun. People's innate understanding of the phenomenon of urea sublimation allows them to have the urine-soaked blanket and chamber pot back in the bedroom at night without the pungent smell.

What is also useful to know is that these practices are carried out by both men and women, and there is an innate understanding of the reasons behind such practices. So, a proper selection of practices would also address gender issues as the education systems of sub-Saharan African countries are Africanised. An understanding of such practices which draw on indigenous knowledge, relating them to WS scientific concepts, is necessary. However, teachers need to identify IS as separate from fallacy (Kibirige & Van Rooyen, 2006).

For smooth cultural crossing to occur when teaching Western science and incorporating IK seamlessly, literacy in 'social language jargon' is fundamental (Leach & Scott, 2003; Thompson, 2012). An example of this in a science class is when the teacher asks, "What do you use to measure length?" The answer she usually gets from her learners is, "I would use a metre." Yet a metre (m) is a standard international (SI) unit, as everyone knows. However, in this local, cultural context, a one-metre stick or rod is used for measuring length, hence the way this learner answers. Understanding the social language jargon of learners is imperative in the Africanisation of the curriculum as it enables teachers to identify the kind of scientific discourse and conceptual difficulties that come from socio-cultural contexts, and language that may not fully express the scientific concepts.

The socio-cultural perspective views science as manifested by components of "the community through their actions and interactions with and through oral and written language" (Kelly, Chen & Crawford,

1998:27). Leach and Scott (2003:100) consolidate this by stating that science learning entails "internalising the social language and genres and being able to use them appropriately in various situations".

To develop this social language into the language of science, teachers need to pose questions, create arguments, and design purposeful experiments. This needs to be based on how learners view the concepts under discussion, using their IK. It might also pave the way for learning science-related concepts. This is what is exploited by those who use it since they are already "initiated into a community of practice" (Kelly et al., 1998:24). Within a community of practice (Lave & Wenger, 1991), people think in the language of science, and this thinking is like a lecture in science which then guides them in the right direction. Toulmin (1979) confirms that thinking is like talking to oneself; as humans, we set up interior conversations in which we process ideas that are then translated into outward language, giving our thoughts their social and communal dimension.

What could be achieved by bringing in the cultural setting, where language is a component, is the contextualisation of science concepts. Contextualising, according to Kelly et al. (1998:26), entails "what people are doing and where and when they are doing it." So, language and beliefs are components of culture where the Ubuntu perspective is nurtured. Some language and beliefs are related to the concepts of science and other school subjects. When these components of culture are discussed with learners, contextualisation of concepts occurs. A clear example of this is seen in Nomzamo's case, where she managed to establish connections between everyday practices and scientific concepts with her learners through discussing components of culture.

However, as we use these settings to contextualise teaching and learning, one needs especially to remember that context is not stagnant. Rather, it is dynamic and it changes with time and as we move from one locality to another. With Africanisation of the school science curriculum, teachers are urged to make full use of the local context of their learners and to incorporate it in teaching and learning. That is, we create a genuine hybrid of science concepts when we allow science teaching and learning to be incorporated with IK, and we use Ubuntu values to frame learning methodologies.

The implication of this is that we cannot learn science subjects divorced from socio-cultural settings. It is recognised, however, that for one to successfully analyse the IK which fits with WS, one needs to have a thorough understanding of WS. Western science knowledge in this instance has to be adapted in such a way that it exists in harmony with indigenous knowledge. Indigenous knowledge and practices can then be used in situated learning.

Summary of discussion

This chapter calls for the Africanisation of the school science curriculum. To this end, science teachers are urged to take advantage of the dialectical relationship between IK and WS, as well as making use of the Ubuntu philosophy in teaching and learning. We argue that indigenous knowledge and Ubuntu can be used successfully to enhance pedagogical content knowledge (PCK) in science. Shulman (1987) understands PCK as the blending of content and pedagogy into an understanding of how particular topics can be adapted to the diverse interests and abilities of learners.

The contextualising effect of Africanisation would enable teachers to be culturally inclusive of each learner's existing knowledge structures. In this way, their classrooms would become responsive to multiculturalism. It could be argued that in learners' IK there may be skills which can be exploited and used in practical activities. The skills come in the form of pedagogical technical content knowledge. In view of what has been discussed, the implication is that science teaching and learning, if modelled on Afrocentricity, offers a meaningful alternative for sub-Saharan developing countries as it is responsive to cultural differences and tolerates many modalities.

It is naïve, however, to think that Africanisation of the science curriculum will be a panacea to all educational ills related to science education. It is only one attempt to make science more meaningful to learners from different contexts. As discussed in this chapter, context is dynamic, and in response to this, we urge teachers to be on the look-out for whatever new, locally contextualised knowledge can be incorporated for the benefit of developing science education in schools. More importantly, for teachers to successfully Africanise the school science curriculum, they need to have a deep understanding and appreciation of WS concepts. This would help them to separate indigenous practices that are science-driven from those based on myth or superstition.

Closing activities

1. After reading this chapter, explain whether you are convinced (or not) that Africanisation of the science curriculum in South African schools is an imperative.
2. Think of a concept or concepts that you teach in science
    a) Suggest with reasons why you would want to use IK or indigenous practices to support the development of such concept(s) in science.
    b) Which aspect(s) of Ubuntu do you think you can use in the process of developing those concepts? Briefly explain why and how.

3. Briefly describe a policy or specific outcome from the curriculum that encourages Africanisation of the curriculum:
   a) Using informal means (discussions or observations), do you think your fellow teachers are doing enough to handle the education policy with regard to the use of Ubuntu and IK?
   b) If some other stakeholders in the system oppose it, or do not know enough about it, what measures do you think should be put in place to offset this?
4. Describe, from your own teaching context: i) a cultural practice, ii) a cultural artefact, iii) 'everyday language', which you think can be used to achieve Africanisation in the curriculum.
   a) Explain how each of these items can be used to support teaching and learning in your area of science teaching.
   b) Discuss how each of these examples can be used in a learner-centered approach and situated learning.

References and further reading

Bernstein, B. 1996. *Pedagogy, symbolic control and identity: Theory, research, critique*. London: Taylor and Francis.

Carter, L. 2007. Sociocultural influences on science education: Innovation for contemporary times. *Wiley Interscience*. 92:165–181.

Cimi, P.V. 2009. An investigation of the indigenous ways of knowing about wild food plants (imifino): A case study. Unpublished Master's dissertation. Grahamstown: Rhodes University.

Coetzee, S.A. 1999. 'n Blik op die afrikanisering van universiteite. *Suid-Afrikaanse Tydskrif vir Opvoedkunde*. 19:130–138.

Czerniewicz, L., Murray, S. & Probyn, M. 2000. *The role of learning and support materials in C2005*. Research paper for the National Centre for Curriculum Research and Development (NCCRD). Pretoria: Government Printers.

Department of Basic Education. 2011. *Curriculum and assessment policy statement: Grades 7–9 Natural Sciences*. Pretoria: Government Printers.

Freris, L. & Muitui, C. 2011.Towards harmony between African traditional religion and environmental law. In T.W. Bennett (Ed). *Traditional African religion in South African law* (pp. 200–222). Cape Town: UCT Press.

Goduka, I.N. 1996. Challenges to traditionally white universities: Affirming diversity in the curriculum. *South African Journal of Higher Education*. 10:27–39.

Hewson, M.G., Javu M.T. & Holtman, L.B. 2009. The role of African traditional health practitioners in implementing indigenous knowledge in the South African science curriculum. *African Journal of Research in Mathematics, Science, and Technology Education.* 13(2):1–10.

John-Steiner, V. & Mahn, H. 1996. *Socio-cultural approaches to learning and development: A Vygotskian framework.* Retrieved from: http://vygotsky/johnsteiner.html on 18 August 2011.

Kelly, G., Chen, C. & Crawford, T. 1998. Methodological considerations for studying science-in-the making in educational settings. *Research in Science Education.* 28(1):23–49.

Kibirige, I. & Van Rooyen, H. 2006. Enriching science teaching through the inclusion of indigenous knowledge. In J. de Beer & H. van Rooyen (Eds). *Teaching science in OBE classroom.* Braamfontein: Macmillan.

Kincheloe, J.L. & Steinberg, S.R. 2008. Indigenous knowledge in education: Complexities, dangers and profound benefits. In N.K. Denzin, Y.S. Lincoln & L.T. Smith (Eds). *Handbook of critical and indigenous methodologies.* London: Sage Publications.

King, M.C. & Miller, C.A. 2006. *Teaching model: Non-violent transformation of conflict.* Addis Ababa: University of Peace.

Knowles, S.M. 1950. *Informal adult education.* Chicago: Association Press.

Lave, J. & Wenger, E. 1991. *Situated learning: Legitimate peripheral participation.* Cambridge: Cambridge University Press.

Leach, J. & Scott, P. 2003. Individual and socio-cultural views of learning in science education. *Science and Education.* 12:91–113.

Lemke, J. 2001. Articulating communities: Sociocultural perspectives on science education. *Journal of Research in Science Education.* 38(3): 296–316.

Luggya, D. 1999. *Multicultural education: An approach to equality in education in South Africa.* Paper delivered at the Southern African Society for Education (SASE). Pretoria.

Makgoba, M.W. 1998. South African universities in transformation: An opportunity to Africanise education. In S. Seepe (Ed). *Black perspectives on tertiary institutional transformation*: Florida: Vivlia Publishers & Booksellers.

Mapara, J. 2009. Indigenous knowledge in Zimbabwe: Juxtaposing postcolonial theory. *The Journal of Pan African Studies.* 3(1):139–150.

Mbeki, T. 1998. *Statement by Deputy President Mbeki.* African Renaissance Conference. Johannesburg. 28 September.

Molina, M. & Rowland, F.S. 1974. Stratospheric sink for chlorofluoromethanes: Chlorine atom catalyzed destruction of ozone. *Nature*. 249:810–812.

O'Donoghue, R., Lotz-Sisitka, H., Asafo-Adjei, R., Kota, L. & Hanisi, N. 2007. Exploring learning interactions arising in school-community contexts of socio-ecological risk. In A.E.J. Wals (Ed). *Social learning towards a sustainable world*. Wageningen: Wageningen University Press.

Ogunniyi, M.B. 1988. Adapting Western science to African traditional culture. *International Journal of Science Education*. 10(1):1–9.

Okeke, C.I.O. 2010. A neglected Impediment to True Africanisation of African Higher Education Curricula: Same Agenda, Differential Fee Regimes. *Journal of Higher Education in Africa*. 8(2):39–52.

Seepe, S. 1998. Towards an Afrocentric understanding. In S. Seepe (Ed). *Black perspectives on tertiary institutional transformation*. Florida: Vivlia Publishers & Booksellers.

Semali, L. & Kincheloe, J. (1999). Introduction: What is indigenous knowledge and why should we study it? In L. Semali & J. Kincheloe (Eds). *What is indigenous knowledge? Voices from the academy* (pp. 3–57). London: Falmer.

Shulman, L.S. 1987. Knowledge and teaching: Foundations of the new reform. *Harvard Educational Review*. 57(1):1–22.

Thompson, P. 2012. Learner-centred and cultural translation. *International Journal of Educational Development*. 33(13):48–58.

Toulmin, S. 1979.The inwardness of mental life. *Critical Inquiry*. 6:1–16.

Van Wyk, J. 2002. Indigenous Knowledge Systems: Implications for natural science and technology teaching and learning. *South African Journal of Education*. 22(4):305–312.

Viljoen, C.T. & Van der Walt, J.L. 2006. Being and becoming: Negotiations on educational identity in (South) Africa. *South African Journal of Education*. 23(1):13–17.

5

The ecological model of human development: An African perspective

Ramodungoane Tabane

Chapter overview

This chapter will focus on Uriel Bronfenbrenner's theory of the ecological model which says that in order to understand human development, it is important to consider a person's entire ecological system. The theory has since evolved into the bio-ecological model to characterise how biological aspects in human development join with environmental forces to mould a person's development. Bronfenbrenner's theory focuses on the individual's relationship within her social contexts; human development then occurs in a set of overlapping ecological systems. In this chapter, the principles of human development will be explained and outlined as though composed of a series of five nested structures or systems (hence, multivariate systems), namely, microsystem, mesosystem, exosystem, macrosystem, and chronosystem. African perspectives on the multivariate African system in terms of cosmos, namely the micro-cosmos, meso-cosmos, exo-cosmos, macro-cosmos, and chrono-cosmos, will be outlined to explain and enrich the ecological model. Overall, each system of the ecological model is highlighted as an asset to human development, in the chapter.

Learning outcomes

By the end of this chapter you should be able to:
- Describe the central concepts of the ecological and bio-ecological models
- Describe the central concepts of the ecological model in an African perspective
- Discuss the ecological model in its application in individual, family, classroom, school, and community settings
- Explain and apply the ecological model of child development focusing on an African perspective and Bronfenbrenner's model.

 CASE STUDY 1

Jongikhaya 'Khaya', as his name suggests, is the person who takes care of his family. He is named after his paternal great-grandfather, he is told, an intelligent and great man in the community, who worked at the time as a clerk in the mines. Khaya is 14 years old and in Grade 8. He is the first of two children in the family. His younger sister is 10 years old and in Grade 4. Khaya lives with his sister, mother, and paternal grandparents in a small four-roomed house in a semi-rural township in Mpumalanga, where he also attends the local school. Khaya's father works in Rustenburg as a miner.

The family is a close one, but the situation is challenging as they have to do what they can to survive. The mother is self-employed as a street vendor but finds it is difficult to sell her goods. Often, she is unable to make enough money to buy essentials for the household. The grandparents are pensioners. In order to save money, Khaya's father only comes home during major holiday seasons like December, or when there is a big function like a funeral, during the year. As a traditionalist and a strict man, the grandfather is the head of the family. He tries to instil pride in his grandchildren about their culture and traditions, especially Khaya, who is about to enter manhood through initiation school.

Khaya's mother and grandmother are responsible for the daily running of the household: they make sure that there is food and guide Khaya's little sister. The grandfather is getting old, so before going to school, Khaya has to take the family's few cows to grazing, where the grandfather will find them later. Returning from school, Khaya must join his grandfather and together bring the livestock home. It is also expected that Khaya will help his younger sister with her homework, after he has done his own. Khaya seldom has time to play with his friends. He rarely, if ever, gets time to go to the community library to read his favourite books.

Khaya's father is not as strict as his grandfather. Khaya enjoys time with his father, but unfortunately, this is not often. When his father comes from the mines, like other men in the community, he is occupied with all the adult issues at the chief's kraal, so Khaya hardly sees him. However, problems at work have made his father grumpy and lately he is short-tempered. Khaya does not look forward to spending time with him, as he used to.

At school, Khaya's performance has dropped. He forgets instructions, seems tired, and at times falls asleep in class. His work is not as neat, it is often incomplete, and his handwriting has deteriorated. The family regularly reminds him of the person he is named after, and how neat his handwriting was. Khaya does not like this. Teachers are starting to complain, and Khaya has been called to the principal's office many times. The principal suggests that one of the teachers help Khaya by speaking to his parents to see if there are any members in the community, church, or among the neighbours, who could assist him so that he can concentrate on his school work.

The ecological model and child development

There is a famous African saying that it takes a village to raise a child, which illustrates how an individual child's development is shaped and influenced by various ecological levels in which the child finds himself. The concept of Botho or Ubuntu – the African philosophy of caring and understanding that one is because of others – is entrenched in this system. So it is that child development, as noted in earlier chapters, is influenced by theories and knowledge systems, where a social scripting about the views and expectations of the child are clearly expressed.

The ecological model of child development indicates the relationships that the child has with his environment and, in turn, the relationship that the environment has with the child. Systems theory suggests that each environment in which the child develops has its own systems, peculiarities, and influences on the growing child. The systems are overlapping and do not occur in isolation: what happens to the child, for instance, in one system, has an impact on the following overlapping system. Thus, there is interdependence between the systems which influences the fluidity of one system into and from another; and the harmonious transition from one system to the next depends on the previous system's relationships.

It is important to understand that to have a well-developed and functional child in both a Western and, most importantly, an African perspective, we need to have a child who is grounded. It is equally important to understand the value of each ecological system, in order to describe the model that the child is coming from, and where the child would like to be. This is so as to address disharmonious issues such as language challenges, learning barriers, exclusion, violence, sexual violence, and poverty, at different ecological levels.

 Getting to know Bronfenbrenner's ecological model

Urie Bronfenbrenner was a Russian-American psychologist, known for developing ecological systems theory. He also co-founded the Head Start program for disadvantaged pre-school children in the United States. He published articles and books for over 60 years on human development, and is regarded as one of the world's leading scholars in developmental psychology, child-rearing and human ecology.

In order to understand Bronfenbrenner's bio-ecological theory, it is important first to understand the historical context in which it was developed. The pioneering work of German-American social and organisational psychologist, Kurt Lewin (1890–1947), is known to have had a significant influence on Bronfenbrenner, who, in his early professional life, was a social psychologist colleague of Lewin's. Lewin, often cited as the forerunner of learning environment research (Fraser, 1994), is most renowned for his 'field theory', a proposition that human behaviour is the function of both the person and the environment (Lewin, 1935; Deaux & Wrightsman, 1988). This means that one's behaviour is related both to one's personal characteristics, and to the social situation in which one finds oneself. For Lewin, behaviour was determined by the totality of an individual's situation. In his field theory, a 'field' is defined as "the totality of coexisting facts which are conceived of as mutually interdependent" (Lewin, 1951: 240). This premise continues to be affirmed by contemporary researchers such as Harvey (2002) who proposes that individuals are a product of co-determination as a result of the **dialectic** between the individual and society. Emphasising the context-specific nature of development, Lewin asserts that individuals behave and develop differently according to the way in which tensions between perceptions of self and of the environment are worked through. Understanding the nature of this **topology** is critical to understanding the processes influencing development.

(Adapted from Lewthwaite, 2011:10).

The ecological model

The word 'ecology' derives from the Greek word, *oikos*, meaning house or environment, and *logos*, meaning knowledge. So it is as humans that we depend as living beings on knowledge and understanding of the environment for our survival.

An African perspective on the ecological model is one of the less-researched fields in current educational theory. Studies in fields like anthropology, philosophy, and theology can help us understand more about this model. The diversity of African traditions brings to the fore a wealth of information that needs to be understood as the different ethnic African groups cannot be generalised.

dialectic: the action of opposing social forces, or concepts

topology: the way in which the parts of something are arranged

According to Bronfenbrenner (1993), there are two propositions that define the properties of the ecological model. The *first proposition* states that human development takes place through processes of progressively more complex reciprocal interactions between an active, evolving bio-psychological human organism, and the persons, objects, and symbols in its immediate environment. This interaction must be regular and extend over a period of time for it to be effective. These forms of interaction in the immediate environment are referred to as proximal processes (these are explained later in this chapter). They are found, for instance, in parent–child activities; child–child activities; studying; teacher–learner activities. The *second proposition* states that the form, power, content, and direction of the proximal process affecting development, vary systematically as a joint function of the characteristics of the developing person; of the environment (both immediate and remote) in which the process is taking place, and the nature of the development outcomes expected.

Bronfenbrenner's ecological systems

Bronfenbrenner's ecological paradigm was first introduced in the 1970s. As he puts it, "the ecological environment is unique to each individual's situation and is seen as a series of nested and interconnected structures. The innermost structure is the individual." (Bronfenbrenner, 2005: 97).

After working on ecological systems for two decades, Bronfenbrenner started to refer to it as the bio-ecological systems model (Bronfenbrenner & Morris, 1998; Bronfenbrenner & Evans, 2000). He began to consider the influence that biological aspects have on the developing child, and the child's environment. Bronfenbrenner's "bio-ecological or bio-ecological systems theory considers the influences on a child's development within the context of the complex system of relationships that form his or her environment" (Lewthwaite, 2011:1). The model, however, continues to offer a conceptualisation of the child's ecology as a multi-layered set that indicates interconnectedness within the environment, where one set or layer has an influence on the next, and in return, the developing child.

Bronfenbrenner's bio-ecological theory goes beyond providing a framework for identifying and conceptualising the multi-system factors that influence development. That is, it goes beyond identifying forces within the individual and microsystem levels influencing an individual's development. It also considers an individual's topology – his or her setting, and the way in which individual and external forces interplay to influence development. It, most importantly, attempts to underscore processes and the dynamics of these processes that might influence development (Lewthwaite, 2011:10).

The understanding of Bronfenbrenner's ecological systems theory has been covered widely, and disciplines like sociology, psychology and others that are interested in child development assert related factors that explain Bronfenbrenner's theory. Dawes and Donald (1999) say that factors that influence child development can be grouped together into four interacting dimensions:

- *Person factors* include the individual biological, temperamental, intellectual, and personality characteristics of the child and significant others in the child's life – such as parents, siblings, educators, etc.
- *Process factors* include the forms of interaction that take place between individuals (supportive, destructive, informative, inclusive, power-based, etc.).
- *Contextual factors* include families, communities, societies, cultures, ideologies, etc.
- *Time variables* take into account the changes that occur over time. Context, person, and process variables change over time as a child matures and as the environment changes.

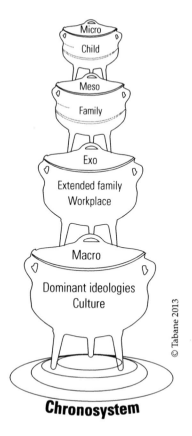

Bronfenbrenner's theory and its principles of human development can be explained and outlined as if composed of a series of five overlapping structures or systems (referred to as multivariate systems). The theory focuses on human development and follows an individual's growth into a fully competent member of society. Simultaneously, it describes socialisation in ways of becoming a member of society (Härkönen, 2007).

Bronfenbrenner's theory focuses on an individual's relationship within her social contexts: it suggests that human development occurs in a set of overlapping ecological systems. However, these systems operate together to influence what a person becomes as she develops. For this reason we see it as a constructivist model of human development.

According to Bronfenbrenner (1993), the ecological environment is based on Lewin's theory of psychological field, conceived as a set of nested structures, each inside the other, like a set of Russian dolls. Since the ecological structure moves from the inside to the outside, it is more like the set of African pots called *dipitsa tsa maoto a mararo* (three-legged pots) used mainly in large African functions like funerals and weddings, stacked together by size, with the larger one on the outside and the smaller ones inside.

Stop and reflect

Think about the important settings where the child spends time:
1   What actually happens within the settings (family, child care, school) that have an influence on the child's development?
2   What is the nature of connections between these settings that have an influence on the child's development and how regular are they?

As noted by Killian (2004), a child is in a family, the family is in a community, and the community, in turn, develops its own cultures, and then sub-cultures. These all have direct and indirect impacts on the developing child. The context in which the child is growing up is important as it will determine the kind of childhood that the developing child will experience. For instance, in South Africa with the HIV and AIDS pandemic affecting certain sectors of the community, a child growing up in that community will have a different childhood experience from one who grows up in a community where there is less preoccupation with health issues. Thus the multivariate systems continually weave influences on one another. According to the ecological model, there are five systems: the relationships between them are referred to as microsystems, mesosystems, exosystems, macrosystems, and chronosystem.

The ecological model also highlights each system as assets that can be used to the benefit of the developing child. Through an asset-based approach, the child and other role players focus on the aspects of each system that contribute positively to the child's development, rather than focusing on the negatives or deficiencies within each system.

Microsystems

A microsystem is the first system of ecological human development. It is the immediate and intimate setting in which the child finds herself (physically, socially, and psychologically). It comprises patterns of activities, roles, person-to-person interactions, and relations. It is the system that is closest to the child. As noted by Berk (2000), the microsystem encompasses the relationships and interactions a child has with her immediate surroundings. "This core entity stands as the child's [channel] for initially learning about the world" (Swick & Williams, 2006:372).

This system refers to interpersonal relations experienced by the child in a given-face-to-face setting. The setting has particular physical, social, and symbolic features that invite, permit, or inhibit engagement in sustained, progressively more complex, interactions with, and activity in, the immediate environment (Bronfenbrenner, 1993).

Härkönen (2007) asserts that it is the socialisation opportunity, or activity and interactions, that describe a microsystem and not the geographic position. So a school which is away from the home, but because of the interactions taking place there, can still be a microsystem of the child. It is about "the person´s degree of participation in [the] system. [It is] all environments, in which the developing person is an active participant, are his/her microenvironments" (Härkönen, 2007: 9). Therefore, microsystem is about a child's sense of belonging, it emphasises the child's closeness to, and where she feels most 'at home'.

During interactions in this system, the child is an active participant who **reciprocates** attention and actions with other people who are also in the system. The relationships and the interactions taking place in this level have an influence on one another, in that they are *bi-directional*.

An example of a bi-directional relationship in the microsystem might be:

| Parents' behaviour influences the child | ⟷ | Child's behaviour influences the parents |

Within the microsystem, the developing child has an influence on other people around her. It is the way the child perceives the relationships or connections that are crucial to his or her development. That is, people in the system have immediate influence on one another. For instance, adults affect children's behaviour, but children's characteristics – their physical attributes, personalities, and capacities – also affect adults' behaviour towards them. Therefore, when "these reciprocal interactions occur often over time, they have an enduring impact on development", according to Bronfenbrenner (Berk, 2003:28).

This implies that the factors that influence an individual's development cannot be generalised but, instead, are multi-system in nature, and unique to each setting. That is, in fostering development successfully, one must take into account an individual's personal attributes, the context in which the development takes place, the time at which the development process occurs, and the processes each person experiences (Lewthwaite, 2011:10).

The developing child is shaped by what he experiences in the system. Is the child experiencing love? Is there someone in the system teaching the child appropriate and acceptable behaviour? Is there anyone spending time with the child and sharing his experiences? Is there anyone reading to the child? These experiences, called proximal processes, which a child has with the people and objects in these settings, are the primary engines of human development (Bronfenbrenner & Morris, 1998; Lewthwaite, 2011). For example, a warm and patient teacher is likely to receive a warm response and attention from the child, unlike a hostile and dismissive teacher from whom the child will withdraw.

In the microsystem, we refer to close interpersonal relationships, for instance, parent–child; mother–daughter; mother–son; father–son and father–daughter relationships. It is these relationships that are close in shaping some of the attributes that the child will develop,

reciprocates: to return (e.g. love, affection, attention) to someone who gives it

for instance, a brother–sister relationship, and others like teacher–learner relationships. It includes people such as grandparents and, in the African perspective, owing to the changing socio-economic status and the HIV and AIDS pandemic, the grandparent–grandchild relationship is becoming a norm as grandparents raise their grandchildren in the absence of one or both parents. The family is like a filter which all the influences in society go through. It should guard against harmful practices and influences that might hurt the developing child. The family should protect the child as far as possible, and not expose her to harmful practices or influences.

High-risk microsystems are characterised by a lack of mutually rewarding relationships, and/or the presence of destructive interactions (Killian, 2004). For example, a child will feel neglected when attention is on another child because he is performing well at school.

Stop and reflect

Think about Khaya in Case study 1 on page 82:
1   What are the interactions in his microsystems, and what influence do they have on his development?
2   What are the assets found in Khaya's microsystem, and how can they influence his positive development?

Mesosystems

According to Bronfenbrenner (1993), mesosystems comprise the linkages and processes that take place between two or more settings containing the developing person. Mesosystem involves relationships between microsystems, such as home, school, neighbourhood, childcare centres, religious, and community gathering places. In other words, a mesosystem is a system of microsystems (Bronfenbrenner, 1993). It permeates our lives in every dimension (Swick & Williams, 2006). According to Keenan (2002:30), one can think about the mesosystem as the connection which brings together the different contexts in which a child develops.

Mesosystem, asserts Berk (2000), provides the connection between the structures of the child's microsystem. For example, a child can be taught to read and write at school. However, if there is no positive extension of this at home, or in another significant environment, the child might struggle at school; there need to be involved assets in this system, such as parents, a guardian or an older sibling, who can assist the developing child to read or write. The environment must foster the culture that is desired, so, for example, appropriate reading material should be readily available.

There should be enough stimulation and positive interaction between micro- and mesosystems. However, as noted by Killian (2004), a high-risk mesosystem would be characterised by weak or destructive associations between microsystemic contexts, including, for example, stigmatisation in the case of a family member with HIV; discrimination on religious grounds; sexism; ethnicity conflicts; where they have a negative influence on relationships between the family and the school, or the family and the community.

 Stop and reflect

In Khaya's case, what plays a role in his development?

According to Swick and Williams (2006:72) in mesosystem, there "must be loving adults beyond the parents who engage in caring ways with our children". The African perspective (or the Afrocentric view) of the extended family is important in this regard, hence the African saying, *Ngwana wa gago ke wa ka* (Your child is my child). In this view, all the adults in the community are expected to contribute positively in raising children within the community, so that if the neighbour's child is seen doing something wrong, it is incumbent on any adult noticing such behaviour to discipline that child. The parents of the child would actually agree with adult and condone the censure. This is particularly helpful in the case of orphans, where they know that all adults in the family and community are their parents. To accentuate the importance of the community in other traditions, Swick and Williams (2006:72) tell us that there is a similar practice "in the ritualistic symbols of many native American people called tiospaye, which means to be "in community with each other"'". The Afrocentric view of *motho ke motho ka batho* (a person is because of others) accentuates the importance of the mesosystem. This is what mesosystems are about: being in a relationship of ever-expanding circles or triads, and even more expansive relations, with one another.

Exosystems

Exosystems comprise the linkages and processes taking place between two or more settings. In at least one of the settings the developing child is not immediately present, but the events that occur in that system have an indirect influence in the system where the developing child lives (Bronfenbrenner, 1993). It refers to "social settings that do not have a developing child living in it or functioning directly in, but can have an impact on and influence on the child's development and influences the setting in an indirect manner" (Bronfenbrenner 1989; Lewthwaite, 2011). They include formal settings such as community health services, parks, recreation centres, sports clubs, and informal groups, social support networks, and the workplace (Keenan, 2002:31). The community lies at this level. Some examples that comprise exosystems layers are extended family, family networks, mass media, workplaces, neighbours, family friends, extended family, community health systems, legal services, social welfare services, psychological services. Swick and Williams (2006:372) emphasise that, "we all live in systems psychologically and not physically; these are exosystems." For example, a child experiencing stress, discomfort or even feeling unhappy at home because of what is happening in the parent's workplace experiences the influence of the exosystem.

Stop and reflect

The workplace (of both the mother and the father), where Khaya is not immediately involved, still impacts on him as a developing child. The events at his father's work (exosystem) influence his immediate system (microsystem). What influence does this have on Khaya's development?

Macrosystems

According to Bronfenbrenner (1993), macrosystems consist of the overarching pattern of micro, meso, and exosystems characteristic of a given culture or sub-culture, with particular reference to the belief systems, bodies of knowledge, material resources, customs, lifestyles, opportunity structures, hazards, and life course options that are embedded in each of these broader systems.

Macrosystem is the structure most removed from the individual; it is the outermost layer in the child's environment: "It refers to societal and cultural ideologies and laws that impinge on the individual" (Lewthwaite, 2011:10). The macrosystem's influence "penetrates through all other layers" (Härkönen, 2007:13).

This is the system that consists of values, laws, beliefs, religion, customs, ethnic identity of the family, traditions, and culture, that regulates the interactions and connections of the systems. According to Berk (2000), macrosystem is the outermost layer for the child. It has no distinct framework but it holds inside it the cultural values, traditions, and laws.

From an African perspective, this system influences belief systems: in, for example, the relationship between the person, values, customs, community, and ancestors. It also influences the connection with religion and such belief systems. So, according to Killian (2004), beliefs about, for example, what happens to sick people, the way people behave at funerals and during mourning periods, and what happens once someone has died, ar all part of this system.

Stop and reflect

What are the macrosystem influences on Khaya's development as a young, growing boy, according to Bronfenbrenner?

According to Kamerman (2000), the priority which the macrosystem gives to children's needs affects the support they receive at inner levels of the environment. Thus, if the environment in which the developing child grows up values life, the child will grow up respecting and valuing other people. The fundamental Afrocentric view or philosophy of *Botho* or Ubuntu is cultivated at early developmental stages in the child. This system can have powerful influence on how the developing child relates to other people within all systems, and as an adult.

In thinking of a macrosystem, one can see it as a map or a design of society as it indicates how the three systems interrelate. Bronfenbrenner (1989; 1994; 1997) refers to macrosystem as a societal blueprint for a particular culture or sub-culture.

Chronosystems

Chronosystem explains the passage of time and how time influences the systems. According to Bronfenbrenner (1993), a chronosystem encompasses change or consistency over time, not only in the characteristics of the person, but also of the person's environment. Thus "the environment is not a static force that affects children in a uniform way. Instead, it is ever changing" (Bronfenbrenner in Berk, 2003:29).

The chronosystem is a "description of the evolution, development or stream of development of the external systems in time. The chronosystem can cover either a short or long period of time" (Bronfenbrenner, 1989:201).

Culture, life, and the environment are forever changing, and are experienced differently by different individuals. Life events, such as marriage, birth of a child, death of a loved one, have an impact and influence on the developing child, and also on how this child relates or connects with other people in whatever systems she finds herself. The changes in life do not only happen outside the child; they can also arise within the child: for instance, in the transition from toddler-to-adolescent-to-teenager, each stage brings with it different attributes, characteristics, and personalities, in any given situation.

 Stop and reflect

Reflect on all the systems in relation to Khaya's case. What influence will his childhood system have on him as an adult, with his own family, as a father, a husband, and a community member?

African ecological perspectives

According to Meyer, Moore and Viljoen (1997:617) the "African views of human development and humankind are founded on a worldview where humans form a whole with the cosmos and where they are the point of departure and the centre of the universe." It is therefore from this centre that everything is understood and explained. The Afrocentric view of *Botho* or Ubuntu, where people respect one another and are cognisant that they are linked to one another within individual systems and extended systems, resonates deeply in this perspective.

According to Sow (1980), there are three realities or *mafelo/dibaka/izindawo* (spaces) ascribed spiritually that describe African ecological perspectives – the macro-, meso-, and micro-cosmos. A cosmos is an orderly or harmonious system. The word derives from the Greek term *κόσμος* (*kosmos*), literally meaning 'order', and metaphorically, 'world'; and is **antithetical** to the concept of chaos. Today, the word is generally used as a synonym for the Latin loan word 'universe'.

However, as in Bronfenbrenner's ecological systems theory, the exo- and chronosystems form part of the African ecological perspective because there are linkages between the macro-, meso- and micro-cosmos. These take place over the chrono-cosmos, that is, *nako/isikhathi/ixesha* (over time). The relationship between different systems that takes place over time is very important in the African ecological perspective, as you will read later in this chapter.

> ....
> **antithetical:**
> when two
> things are not
> compatible with
> one another
> ....

Micro-cosmos

According to Sow (1980), the micro-cosmos is the domain of the individual person in his or her everyday, collective existence, which is wholly influenced by the macro-cosmos and the meso-cosmos. This is the cosmos where the child is directly involved, and physically, socially, and psychologically affected. It is the child's immediate setting where relationships and interactions with significant others, that is, parents and extended family, are fostered.

It refers to close interpersonal relationships, for instance, parent–child; mother–daughter; mother–son; father–son; and father–daughter relationships. It is about the relationships that are close in the shaping of some of the attributes that the child will develop.

The family belief system has an influence on the developing child. In the African perspective, a child born into the family is usually given the name of a revered family member. It is believed that that child will live up to that name. This child immediately has ties to the family, and all interactions with the child proceed from here, as the family socialises the child. For instance, if the child is given the name of a successful family member, he will be treated and expected to be like that person: this may encourage him to study further, and he will be stimulated accordingly, and so forth.

As in the micro-cosmos, Härkönen (2007) notes that Bronfenbrenner, in the microsystem, pays attention to the belief systems of the people around the child because these can have a stimulating effect on the child's development. He "actually places the belief systems in both the micro- and the macrosystems. In the macrosystem definition, he additionally reveals that belief systems can be found inside each system, contained by the macrosystem, i.e. the micro-, meso-, and exosystems" (Härkönen, 2007:8).

Stop and reflect

Think about Khaya again:
1   What are the interactions in his micro-cosmos and what influence do they have on his development?
2   What are the assets found in Khaya's micro-cosmos and how can they influence his positive development?

Meso-cosmos

The meso-cosmos is the spiritual domain and is the place where all conflict, as well as events such as sickness and death, are explained. According to Sow (1980), this is the domain of traditional health practitioners (THPs), spiritual leaders and priests. This is the level from which the dynamics of behaviour of African people should be understood. That is, behaviour is not just the outcome of the actions of an individual, but is wholly attributed to external agents outside the person. For example, after a funeral, the immediate family members are cleansed to protect them from any harmful influences, including sickness. Meso-cosmos involves relationships between microsystems such as home, school, neighbourhood, child care centres, religious and community common places. It permeates our lives in every dimension (Swick & Williams, 2006).

 Stop and reflect

In Khaya's case, what plays a role in his development?

Exo-cosmos

The exo-cosmos, like the Bronfenbrenner's exosystems, represents the linkages and processes taking place between two or more settings. In this setting the child is not directly involved. However, the events in this space have an indirect influence on the child. They include formal settings such as community, extended family, family networks, workplaces, and neighbours.

The occurrences in the cosmos have an indirect influence on the child's development: for example, in rural villages, events at the chief's kraal will have an impact on the child. The extended family system in African cultures also impacts the child. In most cases, however, extended families in the African perspective are part of the family especially in a situation where brothers, sisters, aunts and uncles live with the parents and grandparents, and even great-grandparents. Even so, the face of the African family in the past century has been changing from an extended to a nuclear family arrangement.

Stop and reflect

Khaya is not involved with issues that happen at the chief's kraal (exo-cosmos).Yet what happens in the community and his father's participation in those events affect his immediate system (micro-cosmos). What influence does this have on his development?

Macro-cosmos

According to Sow (1980), the macro-cosmos is the domain in which God (*Modimo/uNkulunkulu/ uThixo/Mudzimu/Xikwembu*) is encountered, together with the ancestors (*badimo/amdlozi/izinyanya/vhadzimu*). This is the domain of dominant attitudes, beliefs, customs, values, religion, and cultural ideologies. The developing child's wellbeing is noticed and entrusted in this domain, where certain activities will take place for the child. For example, there are different ceremonies for a child in the family throughout his life, from birth, welcoming the child (*go bega/ukubikiwa/imbeleko*), to initiation when the child reaches a certain age (*koma/lebollo/ukweluka*), to marriage (*lenyalo/umshado/umtshato/ vhuhadzi*), and finally, to death.

Botho or Ubuntu is an asset in the child's development. It will be taught and transmitted so that the child understands that he does not live alone, but coexists with other people. It follows that he must be considerate so that others are considerate of him, in turn.

Stop and reflect

What are the macro-cosmos influences on Khaya's development as a young, growing boy, owing to his family's strong belief in African traditions, value, and customs?

Chrono-cosmos

This section explains the dimension of time and its influence throughout the child's development. The child grows within the system, and her role, participation, and expectations within the community increases. The child develops from toddler-to-teenager-to-adult and will be expected to instil the values and norms that she has learned, in her own children, and in other children, within the community.

In an African perspective, the passage through time is regarded as one of the most important systems. The rite of passage, from a boy to a man, symbolised by going through initiation school (*lebollo/ koma/ukweluka*), and graduating from such, is one of the important milestones in the communities that practise them. A similar rite of passage for girls growing into womanhood (*bokgarabe/umemulo*) is when they learn to prepare themselves for marriage, guided by their mothers, or older women in the community. In religions there are many stages and rituals that are observed to mark the passage from youth to adulthood; from being a child in a family to having a family with children of one's own; from learning through life to achieving the wisdom of age; to eventually become an elder. In the end, becoming an elder and teaching those that come after ensures the preservation of customs and traditions over time.

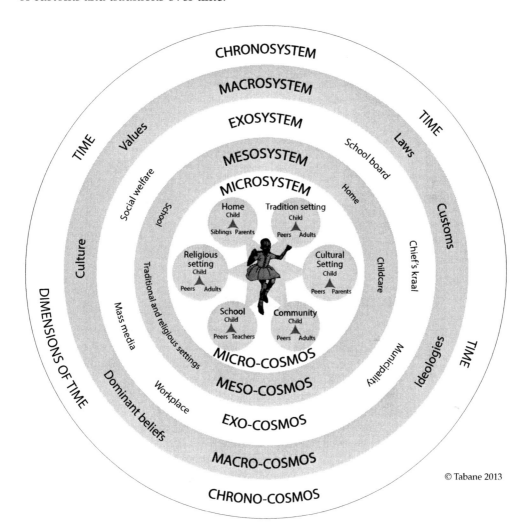

© Tabane 2013

Figure 5.1: The ecological approach and the African perspective approach

Figure 5.1 represents the conceptual integration of the ecological approach with the African perspective approach, showing a complete system around the child.

CASE STUDY 2

Khaya's family expects a lot from him. At times, Khaya thinks that he will not be able to meet their expectations. In his immediate family, Khaya has his parents, sibling, and grandparents, who can support him and make sure that he develops into a responsible man in the community. His school, and the neighbourhood where he lives offer different opportunities for him to develop and extend himself. The community in which Khaya lives, represents another asset in that the principal has asked one of the teachers to intervene when Khaya's performance starts dropping. The family's belief in their traditions will ground Khaya and teach him to learn and live harmoniously with other people in the community. Khaya will understand that his father's work environment might be contributing to his recent changed mood, and so Khaya will learn to accept that his own situation can also be affected by issues that are remote from him. Khaya is able to find positive influences in each of the five ecological systems (micro-, meso-, exo-, macro- and chronosystems) and is encouraged to draw strength from them as they assist in his development throughout his life.

Stop and reflect

Reflect on all the systems and consider Khaya's case. What influence will his childhood system have on him as an adult, with his own family, as a father, husband and community member?

Summary of discussion

It is important in addressing child development, that the child be viewed holistically and considered a developing person within and across the ecological or bio-ecological models. It is equally important that the child's development is seen from the African perspective as influenced by her environment in the micro-; meso-; exo-; macro-; and chronosystems.

According to Bee and Boyd (2007), the developing child must not only be viewed in small separate pieces of the total ecological system because this leads to a piecemeal rather than a systemic consideration. Bronfenbrenner´s ecological systems theory (later called the bio-ecological systems theory) is the theory of human development used in this chapter. It articulates the process of human socialisation and it has been a key to understanding education (Härkönen, 2007).

The systems give an opportunity to focus on positive developmental aspects, rather than negative aspects. In an inclusive society and education system, Bronfenbrenner's ecological or bio-ecological model is highly relevant as it focuses on assets that each system has, rather than only dwelling on the deficiencies within the system.

Closing activities

Self-reflection and personal development

1. Think about your own situation and life course, as we have done with Khaya's case. Take each system/cosmos and think of examples from your own life.
2. Think of your own family. How is each system/cosmos represented?
3. Think of the school you attended. In which system/cosmos would you place it? How did this system influence your own development?

Practical application

4. Consider influences of exosystem/exo-cosmos. How would you explain them to a family member or a neighbour, taking into consideration their own situations?
5. In terms of Bronfenbrenner's ecological or bio-ecological model, what makes up Khaya's mesosystem? Identify and explain the possible assets in that system.
6. In terms of the African perspective, what makes up Khaya's meso-cosmos? Identify and explain the possible assets in it.

Advocacy

7. What issues would you consider when dealing with a learner at school who might be experiencing challenges, now that you have learned about the ecological or bio-ecological model?
8. With your understanding of the African perspective of ecological development, what issues would you consider when dealing with a learner at school who might be experiencing challenges in your neighbourhood because of his or her family belief system?

References and further reading

Bee, H. & Boyd, B. 2007. *The developing child*. 11th ed. Boston: Pearson/Allyn and Bacon.

Berk, L.E. 2000. *Child development*. 5th ed. Boston: Allyn and Bacon.

Berk, L.E. 2003. *Child development*. 6th ed. Boston: Allyn and Bacon.

Bronfenbrenner, U. 1989. Ecological systems theory. *Annals of Child Development*. 6:187–249.

Bronfenbrenner, U. 1993. Ecological models of human development. *International Encyclopaedia of Education*. Vol. 3. 2nd ed. Oxford: Elsevier. Reprinted in: M. Gauvain & M. Cole (Eds). 1994. *Readings on the development of children*. 2nd ed. New York, NY: Freeman.

Bronfenbrenner, U. & Morris, P.A. 1998. The ecology of developmental processes. In W. Damon & R.M. Lerner (Eds). *Handbook of child psychology: Theoretical models of human development*. New York: Wiley.

Bronfenbrenner, U. 2005. *Making human beings human: Bio-ecological perspectives on human development*. Thousand Oaks, CA: Sage.

Dawes, A. & Donald, D. 1999. Improving children's chances: Developmental theory and effective interventions in community contexts. In D. Donald, A. Dawes & J. Louw (Eds). *Addressing childhood adversity*. Cape Town: David Phillip Publishers.

Donald, D., Lazarus, S. & Lolwana, P. 2012. *Educational psychology in social context: Ecosystemic applications in Southern Africa*. Cape Town: Oxford University Press.

Härkönen, U. 2007. *The Bronfenbrenner ecological systems theory of human development*. Paper presented at the Scientific Articles of 5th International Conference on PERSON.COLOR.NATURE.MUSIC. Daugavpils University, Saule, Republic of Latvia, 17–21 October 2007.

Keenan, T. 2002. *An introduction to child development*. London: Sage.

Killian, B. 2004. Risk and resilience. In R. Pharaoh (Ed). *A generation at risk? HIV/AIDS-vulnerable children and security in southern Africa*. Cape Town: Institute for Security Studies monograph series. 109:33–63.

Lewthwaite, B. (Ed). 2011. *Applications and utility of Urie Bronfenbrenner's bio-ecological theory*. Manitoba Education Research Network (MERN). Monograph Series Issue 4.

Meyer, W.F., Moore, C. & Viljoen, H.G. 1997. *Personology: From individual to ecosystem*. Johannesburg: Heinemann Higher and Further Education.

Sow, I. 1980. *Anthropological structures of madness in Black Africa*. New York: International Universities Press.

Swick, K.J. & Williams, R.D. 2006. An analysis of Bronfenbrenner's bio-ecological perspective for early childhood educators: Implications for working with families experiencing stress. *Early Childhood Education Journal*. 33(5):371–378.

6

Violence in educational institutions: Cyber bullying

Ellen Lombard

Chapter overview

The aim of this chapter is to gain a better understanding and to provide an overview of cyber bullying in educational institutions, the psychological impact of cyber bullying on learners, existing awareness initiatives, cyber bullying and the law, and cyber collaboration (models for critical legal pluralism in teacher education programmes). The chapter concludes with possible prevention and intervention strategies. The author ultimately aims to illustrate that synergy between different entities can contribute to effective cyber security awareness.

Learning outcomes

By the end of this chapter you should be able to:
- Describe the difference between traditional bullying and cyber bullying
- Summarise the intervention–prevention strategies
- Identify the various types and roles of cyber bullying
- Outline the different cyber-bullying environments
- Describe the educational–psychological impact of cyber bullying.

 CASE STUDY

In 2009 an 18-year-old teenager was convicted of harassment and sentenced to juvenile prison for three months. Keeley Houghton was the first person in the United Kingdom to be jailed for bullying on a social networking site. She had posted a message on Facebook in which she said that she would kill Emily Moore, a girl Houghton knew from school.

The evidence against the **defendant** established that Houghton had waged a four-year bullying campaign against Moore in which she had threatened and victimised Moore, had physically assaulted her, and had damaged her home. Two days before she made the death threat on her personal Facebook page, Houghton had approached Moore in The Vaults pub and asked her, "Are you Emily Moore? Can I have a huggle?" Moore told Houghton to leave her alone or she would call the police. Houghton replied: "I'll give you something to ring the police about." Houghton later went home and wrote on her Facebook page, "Keeley is going to murder the bitch," also naming Moore in obscene language. Houghton had two previous convictions in connection with Moore. In 2005 she assaulted Moore as she walked home from school, for which she was expelled from school. Two years later, Houghton was convicted of causing criminal damage after she kicked Moore's front door.

Bruce Morgan, the judge at Houghton's trial, said in sentencing her: "'Since Emily Moore was 14 you have waged compelling threats and violent abuse towards her. [...] Bullies are by nature cowards, in school, and society. The evil, odious effects of being bullied stay with you for life. On this day you did an act of **gratuitous** nastiness to satisfy your own twisted nature."

defendant: a person who is accused of a crime and has to appear in a law court

gratuitous: unasked for; describes something that is done for no good reason

After serving her sentence, Houghton was still banned from using social network media until the following year. She said in an interview that she didn't know why she had made the threat against Emily Moore, but had just wanted her friends to see it. She didn't think this was bullying.

"The internet is a sinister, silent enemy: you simply don't know where to start to tackle the problem," Moore's mother said later, "But faceless as a computer may be, it is every bit as threatening as a physical bully, if not more so because the audience reading these horrible messages can be enormous."

Finding new ways of hurting – the age of cyber bulling

Technology has transformed the lives of learners, including the ways they bully one another. Seven major routes that cyber bullying might take, or places it might occur, are the following: e-mail, instant messaging (IM), text messaging, websites, voting/polling booths, chat rooms, and blogs. The scourge of cyber bullying has assumed alarming proportions with an ever-increasing number of adolescents admitting to having dealt with it either as a victim or as a bystander. Social scientists describe four aspects of the world wide web (www) that change the dynamics of bullying and take it to new levels: persistence, searchability, **replicability**, and invisible audiences (Dinakar, Reichart & Lieberman, 2011:11). Cyber bullying is a more persistent version of traditional forms of bullying, extending beyond the physical confines of a learning institution, with the victim often experiencing no **respite** from it. It is a form of bullying that provides the intimidator with the power to embarrass or hurt a victim before an entire online community, effectively, the whole world.

Anonymity and the lack of meaningful supervision in the electronic media are two factors that have intensified this social menace. Although technology enhances unbridled communication, it also provides a screen behind which people may hide their mean-spiritedness. Communicators, believing that they are free from **attribution**, are less inhibited about saying things that they would not, or could not, say in a face-to-face situation. Cyber bullies engage in vindictive practices that embarrass, demean, and harm their victims, seemingly without the fear of facing the consequences of their actions (Keith & Martin, 2005; Sparling, 2004; Willard, 2005). This twenty-first century form of bullying occurs in the hidden online world of learners and students, and it reaches beyond the educational institution, and into the homes and lives of the victims. Educational institutions have generally failed to confront this cruel practice head on because they have turned their collective back on the necessary provision of a learning environment that is free from intimidation and harassment. It is therefore imperative that educators, administrators, and community representatives work together to eradicate this most insidious aspect of modern technology. To develop interventions aimed at preventing cyber bullying, and to assist the victims, educators

replicability: ability to be copied exactly, or repeated over and over in the same way

respite: relief from something unpleasant

attribution: when something is seen as belonging to, or caused by someone

need to better understand its nature; they also need to be informed about the actions they can take to combat it in their educational institutions.

Defining cyber bullying

What exactly is cyber bullying and how does it differ from traditional bullying? It is firstly important to mention that it is not the impulse behind bullying that has changed, but rather the vehicle and the name. A unique difference between traditional bullying and cyber bullying is that the perpetrator, in the case of cyber bullying, can stay anonymous by using technological media. Cyber bullying does not occur face to face, and bullies can therefore inflict pain without having to witness the consequences. The secretive nature of cyber bullying makes it so insidious.

Cyber bullying has furthermore grown into a virtual menace with the mobile web, which allows the fast distribution of information with just the touch of a button – adolescents can now, for example, take photos or videos of their peers (at any time and any place) and post them on websites, or even tag them on social networks (Raskauskas & Stoltz, 2007; Li, 2007). The dangerous nature of cyber bullying allows the tormentor to enter the victim's home, harassing him or her while the victim's parents or relatives sit comfortably in the next room (Keith & Martin 2005; Willard, 2005).

Bill Belsey, a nationally recognised educator from Alberta, Canada, first coined the term, and defines cyber bullying as follows:

> Cyber bullying involves the use of information and communication technologies such as e-mail, cell phone and pager text messages, instant messaging (IM) defamatory personal websites, and defamatory online personal polling websites, to support deliberate, repeated, and hostile behaviour by an individual or group, that is intended to harm others (Belsey 2004:7).

This definition will be accepted for the purpose of the current chapter.

Various types of cyber bullying

Burton and Mutongwizo (2009) identify various types of cyber bullying, including the following:

Harassment

Harassment occurs when a cruel or intimidating message is frequently sent via technology to a specific person with the intention to annoy, distress, or cause substantial emotional stress to the receiver. It includes threats, spreading rumours about the victim, subscribing the victim to unwanted online services, and posting information about the victim on online dating or sex services. This form of cyber bullying is usually persistent, repeated, and focused on a specific person.

Identity theft

Identity theft or impersonation occurs when a cyber bully deliberately hacks or clones another person's networking account, e.g. e-mail or personal profile. The hacker impersonates the victim by sending online messages, information or photos in an attempt to harm the victim's character, friendships, and reputation.

Denigration

Denigration involves the sending or posting of mean and belittling rumours or malicious gossip. The cyber bully's aim is to damage the victim's friendships or reputation. Denigration is often achieved by the posting or sending of digitally altered photographs of the victim to others, to portray the victim in a harmful or humiliating way.

Cyber stalking

Cyber stalking is characterised by repeated online threats of harm or intimidation.

Outing

Outing occurs when a victim's secrets or embarrassing information or photos shared online with others.

Happy slapping

Happy slapping refers to an unpleasant incident where a person walks up to someone and slaps him or her, while another person captures the episode with a mobile phone camera, and then sends the photo to a wide audience.

Cyber-bullying environments

Seven major channels or locations for cyber bullying might be e-mail, instant messaging (IM), text messages, websites, voting/polling booths, chat rooms, and blogs. The following definitions of these terms are provided by *Webopedia* (www.webopedia.com) – an online computer and internet dictionary.

 Webopedia definitions

- **E-mail:** Short for electronic mail, it is the transmission of messages over communication networks. The messages can be notes entered from the keyboard, or electronic files stored on disk. Most mainframes, minicomputers, and computer networks have an e-mail system. Some electronic mail systems are confined to a single computer system or local network, but others have gateways to other computer systems, enabling users to send electronic mail anywhere in the world. Companies that are fully computerised make extensive use of e-mail because it is fast, flexible, and reliable.

- **Instant messaging (IM):** a type of communications service that enables you to create a kind of private chat room with another individual in order to communicate in real time over the internet, analogous to a telephone conversation but using text-based, not voice-based, communication. Typically, the instant messaging system alerts you whenever somebody on your private list is online. You can then initiate a chat session with that particular individual.
- **Text messages:** Sending short text messages to a device such as a cellular phone, PDA (personal digital assistant) or pager. Text messaging is used for messages that are no longer than a few hundred characters. The term is usually applied to messaging that takes place between two or more mobile devices.
- **Websites:** Websites are found on the world wide web (www) – a system of internet servers that support specially formatted documents. The documents are formatted in a markup language called HTML (hypertext markup language) that supports links to other documents, as well as graphics, audio, and video files. This means you can jump from one document to another simply by clicking on hot spots. Not all internet servers are part of the world wide web.
- **Voting/polling booths:** Some websites enable users to create online (social, not political) voting or polling booths.
- **Chat rooms:** Real-time communication between two users via computer. Once a chat has been initiated, either user can enter text by typing on the keyboard and the entered text will appear on the other user's monitor immediately. Most networks and online services offer a chat feature. A virtual room [is] where a chat session takes place. Technically, a chat room is really a channel, but the term 'room' is used to promote the chat metaphor.
- **Blogs:** Short for web log, a blog is a web page that serves as a publicly accessible personal journal for an individual. Typically updated daily, blogs often reflect the personality of the author.

Different roles in cyber bullying

Willard (2005:4) focuses attention on the different roles in cyber bullying, and the fact that many students who actively socialise online have had some involvement in cyber bullying in one or more of the following roles:

- *Bully:* Bullies harass and humiliate others. They target those they think are inferior, weaker, or just different. Bullies might also be 'get-backers', who have themselves been bullied, and are now using technology to express their anger.
- *Target:* The target can either be the object of the cyber bully's harassment, or the bully himself or herself at the educational institution that can become the target.
- *Harmful bystander:* The harmful bystander watches and even supports the bully from the sidelines and does nothing to intervene or help the target.
- *Helpful bystander:* The helpful bystander attempts to stop the bullying by protesting against it, providing support to the target, or informing someone in authority.

Stop and reflect

Consider the different roles in cyber bullying in relation to your own online behaviour. Evaluate your own technological activities and the different roles that apply to your online presence as objectively as possible. You might have been part of cyber bullying in the past without even realising it, for example, as a harmful bystander. How will knowledge about the different roles of cyber bullying influence your future online presence?

The impact of cyber bullying

The educational–psychological impacts of bullying (O'Moore & Kirkham, 2001) include:

- loss of self-esteem
- increase in anxiety and fear
- damage to ego functioning
- enhancement of feelings of loss, helplessness, and humiliation
- enhancement of feelings of aggression, and destructive and self-destructive behaviour
- shortened attention span
- attention-deficit order
- post-traumatic stress disorder
- impaired academic achievement.

The psychological impact of cyber bullying is often more distressing than physical bullying because of the extremely public nature of cyber bullying. Victims may feel exposed to the whole world – 24 hours a day – and that there is no way that they can escape. Victims of cyber bullying are often reluctant to report the bullying for fear that their mobile phones may be confiscated or their internet access limited or suspended. Cyber bullying may cause depression, anxiety and, in extreme cases, result in suicide.

Cases showing the detrimental effects of cyber bullying

The following are only a few examples of the vast number of cases of cyber bullying showing the detrimental effects of cyber bullying:

- In 2003, Ghyslain Raza from Quebec, Canada, took a video of himself pretending to be Darth Maul, the *Star Wars* character. The unflattering video portraying Ghyslain, using a golf ball retriever as a light sabre, revealed his lack of athletic skill, and his overweight figure became one of the most viewed video clips ever. Classmates found the video and posted it online. Ghyslain was so traumatised that he dropped out of school and had to be admitted to psychiatric care (Maclean's, 2013).
- In February and March 2006 three high school boys (aged 15 to 17 years) from Pretoria, South Africa, were charged with *crimen iniuria*.

They were accused of publishing an allegedly defamatory image of the deputy principal of their school. One of the boys created this image electronically by attaching the heads and faces of the principal and the deputy principal to a sexually suggestive and intimate picture of two naked men sitting next to each other. The school badge from the school website was used to obscure the men's genitals. This image was then forwarded to other learners at the school, and one of the accused also printed it and placed it on the school's noticeboard. The school authorities disciplined the three boys by prohibiting them from assuming leadership positions at the school and from wearing honours colours for the rest of the academic year. The boys, furthermore, had to attend three hours' detention at their school for five consecutive Fridays. All three boys were criminally charged. However, since they acknowledged responsibility for their actions, the case was diverted from the criminal justice system. As a result of the diversion order, the boys had to clean cages at the local zoo for 56 hours as community service (Centre for Child Law, 2011).

- In October 2006, Megan Meier from Missouri, USA, killed herself after being rejected by a fake MySpace persona she thought she was having a relationship with. Megan died thinking that Josh Evans, who contacted her through her page on MySpace.com, the social networking website, was a real boy, and that he hated her. At first, Megan thought that Josh was the sweetest boyfriend ever, but then on 15 October 2006, Josh turned nasty. In his final message to Megan on 16 October 2006 Josh wrote, "The world would be a better place without you." Megan's mother found her daughter in her bedroom cupboard, where she had hanged herself with a belt. She was 13 years old. Six weeks after Megan's death, her parents discovered that Josh Evans had never existed. He was an online figure, created by Lori Drew (the 47-year-old mother of Megan's rival) who lived four houses down the street.

- In April 2008, a father in Gauteng, South Africa, obtained an interdict against an adult KwaZulu-Natal woman, M, who had been harassing his daughter. The woman was obsessed with his 16-year-old daughter whom she had met in a MXit chat room. The father told the court that the number and frequency of telephone and online conversations between the girl and M had got out of control. He said that M's manipulative behaviour towards his daughter was affecting her life so badly that she had stopped going to school. Copies of SMSs between M and the daughter were presented in evidence of the woman's obsessive behaviour. They said things like: "I love u more than my Life"; "Come away with me. Ur family dnt love u like i do"; "U r destroying my life"; and many more increasingly urgent and emotional statements and threats. The court subsequently prohibited the woman from having any contact (either by telephone or electronically) with the man, his daughter, or any other member of his family.

interdict: a legal order that prohibits certain actions

- In January 2009, 15-year-old Megan Gillian from Macclesfield, United Kingdom, died after taking an overdose of painkillers. She had been teased and harassed online. Fellow pupils at her school posted nasty comments on Bebo about Megan having 'scabby' belongings. A friend said in a statement, "Megan was a happy and nice girl, but had recently gone quieter. She got easily upset about things and there was one time, just before Christmas, when a girl went right up to Megan's face, shouting at her." Megan's father told the court "Her education was being disrupted by a group of girls and she was put in the same classroom as these disruptive pupils. The system is wrong." Megan's school coordinator testified that "Megan said to me: 'If you make me go back to school I'll kill myself' and there was concern about that." Megan's parents found her dead in her bed after she did not come for breakfast that morning.
- On 10 September 2012, Audrie Taylor Pott committed suicide, about a week after she was allegedly sexually assaulted by three 16-year-old boys, in California, USA. When photos of the attack were posted on the internet, Audrie could not deal with this double blow. "The whole school knows ... My life is ruined," she wrote on Facebook a few days before her suicide.

The unconstitutionality of cyber bullying

The Constitution of the Republic of South Africa, 1996 deals with the issue of equality and human dignity in Section 9 and Section 10 of the Bill of Rights:

> Equality
>
> 9. (1) Everyone is equal before the law and has the right to equal protection and benefit of the law.
>
> (2) Equality includes the full and equal enjoyment of all rights and freedoms. To promote the achievement of equality, legislative and other measures designed to protect or advance persons, or categories of persons, disadvantaged by unfair discrimination may be taken.
>
> (3) The state may not unfairly discriminate directly or indirectly against anyone on one or more grounds, including race, gender, sex, pregnancy, marital status, ethnic or social origin, colour, sexual orientation, age, disability, religion, conscience, belief, culture, language and birth.
>
> (4) No person may unfairly discriminate directly or indirectly against anyone on one or more grounds in terms of subsection (3). National legislation must be enacted to prevent or prohibit unfair discrimination.

(5) Discrimination on one or more of the grounds listed in subsection (3) is unfair unless it is established that the discrimination is fair.

Human dignity

10. Everyone has inherent dignity and the right to have their dignity respected and protected.

(Source: Constitution of the Republic of South Africa, 1996).

In his research, Kobus Maree (2005:17) comments as follows: "[O]ne cannot help but wonder how the seemingly soft stance authorities often adopt towards bullying is reconciled with the lofty ideals contained in the Constitution."

What can victims do if their educational institution is not able to stop cyber bullying?

In the case where an educational institution has not been able to stop the cyber bullying, the victim can contact the Regional Manager of the Department of Education and Training. If nothing else seems to work, the law can be of assistance. The victim can also seek legal advice. Cyber bullies can, in many cases, be sued for defamation, and for inflicting emotional distress. They may also be charged with various computer offences. A letter from a lawyer or a query from the police may often bring an end to the cyber bullying. This also encourages learners and students, parents, and educational institutions to take complaints seriously, and to take charge of the activities of cyber bullies far more vigorously.

Tips for learners and students

The literature on cyber bullying provides numerous guidelines on cyber bullying for learners and students (Aftab, 2005; Australian Government, 2004; Barr, 2005; i-SAFE, 2004; Media Awareness Network, 2007; Slater, 2005; Willard, 2005; WiredKids, 2005):

- You should never have to deal with cyber bullying alone. Tell someone about it – a trusted teacher, lecturer, or adult; a parent; a friend; or a family member.
- Protect your private information online (such as passwords, names, addresses, phone and cell numbers, photos or family information, and school names) from people you do not know, or do not trust.
- Refrain from sending messages when you are irritated or angry.
- Do not reply to messages from a bully. They usually get bored and stop the bullying if you do not respond.
- Immediately leave a chat room or instant message service if you feel harassed or uncomfortable. You can also consider blocking the person or sender.

- ID blocking can be used to hide your phone or cell number when making calls. You can also consider not giving your name on your voicemail.
- Even though you never respond to them, do not delete bullying messages. These messages can be used as evidence.
- Take a stand against cyber bullying by speaking out whenever you witness someone being bullied online.

Tips for parents

Parents can curb cyber bullying by implementing the following strategies gleaned from cyber-bullying research (Barr, 2005; i-SAFE, 2004; Media Awareness Network, 2007; Slater, 2005; Willard 2005; WiredKids, 2005):

- Teach your child online safety. Inform him or her of the basics of smart web behaviour, such as never revealing passwords or personal information to strangers, or people they do not trust; never to forward harmful or cruel messages, or to comment on these messages; to delete suspicious e-mails without opening them; to stand up to those who are cyber bullying by reporting them to the institution's authorities; and to use technology to block communication with cyber bullies.
- Be aware of the signs that might indicate that your child is being cyber bullied:
  - spending a lot of time on the computer
  - having trouble sleeping, or having nightmares
  - feeling depressed, or crying without reason
  - becoming anti-social
  - falling behind in homework or academic projects
  - feeling unwell frequently
  - experiencing mood swings.
- Learn what to look for, as well as how to 'talk the talk'. Parents, for example, should familiarise themselves with common IM acronyms, such as:
  - MIRL – Meet In Real Life
  - MYOB – Mind Your Own Business
  - NP – No Problem (*or* Nosy Parents)
  - NUB – New person to a site or game
  - POS – Parent Over Shoulder
  - RBTL – Read Between The Lines
  - ROTFLMAO – Rolling On The Floor Laughing My A** Off
  - SOS – Someone Over Shoulder
  - STBY – Sucks To Be You
- Be aware that the major internet service providers, such as Google, AOL, Yahoo!, and Microsoft all offer types of parental controls which parents can use to monitor their children's internet activities.
- Join or initiate parent–teacher associations, and team up with local law enforcement agencies to create anti-cyber-bullying programmes endeavouring to help parents and students recognise and deal with cyber bullying.

Tips for administrators of educational institutions

Administrators of educational institutions can start by putting the following prevention-intervention strategies derived from cyber-bullying literature into practice (Aftab, 2005; Australian Government, 2004; Hernandez & Seem, 2004; Media Awareness Network, 2007; Willard, 2005):

- Each and every educational institution should create and enforce a cyber-bullying policy. Ensure that learners or students fully understand the policy. It should be published and it should also be available on the institution's website.
- Many institutions already have a code of conduct related to internet use in their computer facilities. This should be extended to include cyber bullying, if it does not already do so. All learners and students, members of staff, and visitors should be aware of it and agree to comply with it as a condition of using the facilities.
- Do not ignore cyber bullying – this problem may already exist in your educational institution. Promote open communication, for example, by initiating a discussion on the online discussion forum, or by placing an announcement on the online learning management system in this regard. Provide potential victims with guidance on how to handle abuses and encourage them to report these abuses. These actions can be used to assure potential victims that a cyber-bullying policy, as well as a support system, is in place. It might also serve as a tool to deter culprits (or potential ones) by making them aware of the possible consequences of cyber bullying.
- Recognise the value of apology and discourage the bringing of such matters to civil court without attempts to resolve the complaints through communication and **restorative justice** methods.
- Create an awareness campaign. Initiate an outreach programme to educate the community about the dangers and consequences of cyber bullying.
- Understand how cyber bullying works. It is important to have an understanding of how to use different technologies and social networking tools (Australian Government, 2004).
- As much as the victims of cyber bullying should be supported through various strategies, administrators and institutions should direct attention to the perpetrators (bullies) of cyber bullying for counselling and rehabilitation.
- Demonstrate the relatedness of approaches such as Ubuntu (drawing on the ideals of community, respect, and human dignity) that may be used as a possible prevention strategy.
- One of the most important strategies to deal with cyber bullying is to encourage students to become helpful bystanders by protesting against the bullying, providing support to the target, or by informing a person in authority (Willard, 2005: 4).

restorative justice: when perpetrators offer victims acceptable apology and compensation (in the form of action, service or money) either within a legal context, or with the help of an arbitrator

Practical advice from a survivor of cyber bullying

Examples of cases of cyber bullying from around the world are provided earlier in this chapter. A number of cyber-bullying survivors – often only after many years – have shared their experiences and useful advice to overcome this hideous form of bullying. Here is one:

Ghyslain Raza, the so-called 'Star Wars Kid', spoke out after 10 years: "What I saw [online] was mean. It was violent. It was a very dark period. No matter how hard I tried to ignore people telling me to commit suicide, I couldn't help but feel worthless, like my life wasn't worth living," the now 25-year-old recalls. Raza expresses the hope that his talking about his experience will help others to deal with cyber bullying. He urges other young victims to overcome their shame and seek help. "You'll survive. You'll get through it," he says. "And you're not alone. You are surrounded by people who love you" (Maclean's, 2013:1).

Summary of discussion

Cyber bullying has reached a level of seriousness that demands swift and significant action. It is imperative that this twenty-first century form of bullying be eradicated. Failing to confront cyber bullying head on means we are turning our collective back on the most insidious aspect of modern technology and the harmful behaviours associated with it, in our educational institutions.

Maree (2005:31) concludes his research on cyber bullying as follows:

> I suggest that the only lasting solution to the problem of bullying and related evils is to facilitate the Sternbergian ideal (2001) of wisdom, and specifically its supreme ideal of promoting the common good to be practised by every person everywhere.

As educators, we all need to put our minds and energy into finding ways of replacing the destructive and negative hold of cyber bullying on young people, with a concern for the common good. This will mean truly living the principles of Ubuntu.

Closing activities

Self-reflection

1. Have you been affected by cyber bullying, either directly or indirectly? How has this left you feeling about your own online activities and presence? How have you dealt with your reactions?

Practical applications

2. Plan a discussion with a group of learners/students/parents on cyber bullying as a social problem of particular concern in your local community. Your aim is for all participants to discuss this

social problem, and to think of possible effective ways of dealing with cyber bullying.
3. Plan a cooperative project involving learners/students in carrying out a significant project in collaboration with local community members, focusing on educating the community on the reality and the consequences of cyber bullying, and on developing a safe school and community. The project must be seen as relevant by both learners/students and the community, and should involve a mixed 'team' in terms of race, gender and ability.
4. Which additional tips on dealing with cyber bullying can you suggest for learners/students, parents, and your educational institution?

Analysis and consolidation
5. Draw up a mind map in which you set out the different cyber-bullying environments, as well as at least six possible major channels or locations for cyber bullying.
6. Analyse the policies of your educational institution and ensure that a cyber-bullying policy is in place. Investigate whether or not a support system is being communicated to victims or potential victims.

Further outcomes
Having worked through this chapter and the above activities, formulate two or more outcomes (excluding the examples provided at the beginning of the chapter) of what you are now able to do.

Issue for debate
Set up a debate in which one side argues the case that educational institutions should not hesitate to take cyber-bullying cases to courts of law. The other side should argue that educational institutions should attempt to resolve the complaints through communication and restorative justice methods.

References

Aftab, P. 2005. *Cyber-bullying: A problem that got in under parents' radar*. Retrieved from: http://www.aftab.com/cyberbullyingpage.htm on 8 July 2013.

Australian Government. 2004. *What are the signs that a child is being cyber bullied?* Retrieved from: http://www.netalert.net.au on 1 July 2013.

Badenhorst, C. 2011. *Legal responses to cyber bullying and sexting in South Africa*. Cape Town: Centre for Justice and Crime Prevention.

Barr, H. 2005. *Online and out of control: Internet takes teen bullying problem to whole new level*. Retrieved from: http://news.newstimes.com/ on 1 July 2013.

Beale, A.V. & Hall, K.R. 2007. Cyber-bullying: What school administrators (and parents) can do. *A Journal of Educational Strategies, Issues and Ideas.* 81(1):8–12.

Belsey, B. 2004. *Always on? Always aware!* Retrieved from: http://www.cyberbullying.ca on 7 March 2013.

Burton, P. & Mutongwizo, T. 2009. *Inescapable violence: Cyber bullying and electronic violence against young people in South Africa.* Cape Town: Centre for Justice and Crime Prevention.

Centre for Child Law. 2011. Le Roux and Others v Dey (Freedom of Expression Institute and Restorative Justice Centre as Amici Curiae) 2011 (3) SA 274 (CC). In *Report of selected cases 2004—2011.* Pretoria: Centre for Child Law, University of Pretoria. Retrieved from: http://www.centreforchildlaw.co.za/images/ on 10 July 2013.

Davies, K. 2013. If it can happen to my daughter it can happen to anyone. *Daily Mail*, 16 April. Retrieved from: http://www.dailymail.co.uk/news/ on 8 June 2013.

Dinakar, K, Reichart, R. & Lieberman, H. 2011. *Modeling the detection of textual cyber-bullying.* Paper presented at the International conference on Weblog and Social Media – Social Mobile Web Workshop, Barcelona, Spain.

Hernandez, T.J. & Seem, S.R. 2004. A safe school climate: A systematic approach and the school counsellor. *Professional School Counselling.* 7(4):256–62.

i-SAFE. 2004. *National i-SAFE survey finds over half of students are being harassed online.* Retrieved from: http://www.isafe.org on 12 February 2013.

Keith, S. & Martin, M.E. 2005. Cyber-bullying: Creating a culture or respect in a cyber world. *Reclaiming Children and Youth.* 13(4):224–228.

Li, Q. 2007. Bullying in the new playground: Research into cyber bullying and cyber victimization. *Australasian Journal of Educational Technology.* 23(4):435–454.

Maclean's. 2013. *10 years later, "Star Wars Kid" speaks out.* Retrieved from: http://www2.macleans.ca/2013/05/09/10-years-later-the-star-wars-kid-speaks-out on 15 July 2013.

Maree, K. 2005. Bending the neck to the yoke or getting up on one's hind legs? Getting to grips with bullying. *Acta Criminologica.* 18(2):15–33.

Media Awareness Network. 2007. *Challenging cyber bullying.* Retrieved from: http://www.mediaawareness.ca/english/resources/special_initiatives/wa_resources/ on 3 July 2013.

O'Moore, M. & Kirkham, C. 2001. Self-esteem and its relationship to bullying behaviour. *Aggressive Behaviour.* 27:269–283.

Raskauskas, J. & Stoltz, A.D. 2007. Involvement in traditional and electronic bullying among adolescents. *Developmental Psychology.* 43(3):564.

Republic of South Africa. 1996. *Constitution of the Republic of South Africa, 1996.* Pretoria: Government Printers.

Slater, S. 2005. *Cyber-bullying targeted.* Retrieved from: http://www. clintonnewsrecord.com/story.php?id=141028 on 7 February 2013.

Sparling, P. 2004. Mean machines: New technologies let the neighbourhood bully taunt you anywhere, anytime. But you can fight back. *Current Health.* 28(8):8–20.

Sternberg, R.J. 2001. Wisdom and education. *Perspectives in Education.* 19(4):1–16.

Vandebosch, H. & Van Cleemput, K. 2008. Defining cyber-bullying: A qualitative research in the perceptions of youngsters. *Cyber Psychology & Behaviour.* 11(4):499-503.

Webopedia. Online computer dictionary for computer and internet. [Online]. Retrieved from: www.webopedia.com on 12 January 2013.

Willard, N. 2005. *An educator's guide to cyber-bullying and cyber-threats.* Retrieved from: http://csriu.org/cyberbullying/pdf on 6 March 2013.

WiredKids. 2005. *A quick guide on the escalating levels of response to a cyber-bullying incident.* Retrieved from: http://www. stopcyberbullying.org/parents/ on 4 March 2013.

Sexual violence in special schools

Nareadi Phasha and Doris Nyokangi

Chapter overview

This chapter discusses the phenomenon of sexual violence in South African schools, and especially exposes its existence in schools for learners with intellectual disabilities. It explores the manifestations of sexual violence and its contributing factors, as well as the implications for the education of learners with intellectual disabilities. Finally, it provides schools with suggestions for addressing the problem.

Learning outcomes

By the end of this chapter you should be able to:
- Describe and explain the phenomenon of sexual violence
- Comment on the extent of the problem amongst learners with intellectual disabilities
- Analyse vulnerability factors and the implications of the problem
- Suggest and discuss strategies for overcoming the problem.

CASE STUDY

Let us look at the following clips from some South African newspapers:

8 February, 2010: A seven-year-old girl was repeatedly raped in the school toilets by three boys (one aged 9 and two aged 11) who attended the same school.

19 February, 2010: A girl in Grade 11 at Bryanston High School in Johannesburg accused a fellow learner of raping her. He allegedly coerced her into the toilet while she was waiting for a school play to start. He was suspended for seven days.

25 May, 2010: A 14-year-old girl was raped by her school friend in the Uitenhage in the Eastern Cape. She had bunked school with a friend who later offered to escort her home. Police noticed a group behaving suspiciously in nearby bushes in the area and soon found the girl lying unconscious. Two boys, aged 15 and 18, were charged with rape. The learners were under the influence of alcohol at the time.

9 June, 2010: A boy from Mondeor and a girl from John Adamson High were at a house with friends, where they drank alcohol. The two had sex in the toilet of the house, which was recorded on a cellphone. After the school holidays, the girl discovered that the video had been widely circulated and she then laid a charge of rape against the boy. This week, the Sexual Offences Court decided not to prosecute.

4 August, 2010: Two 12-year-old boys were accused of persistently raping at least three girls at the Pugishe Primary School near Bushbuckridge. Parents said the sexual conduct had been going on since April last year. The rapes came to light when one boy asked another to assist him with "manpower because his wives were becoming many by the day". Parents accused the school of trying to sweep the scandal under the carpet.

8 November, 2010: An 11-year-old girl from Katlehong was allegedly raped by a 46-year-old school caretaker at her primary school on several occasions. He would give the girl sweets and chocolates after raping her. A school teacher discovered what was happening and reported the incidents. The caretaker was arrested.

(Adapted by Lisa Steyn from reports in: *The Herald, West Cape News, The Sandton Chronicle, The Witness, News24, The Star* and *Sowetan*)

- Teens as young as 14 kidnapped, locked up

- Tradition an excuse for 'horrific' child rape

SCHOOL OF SHAME

Disabled pupils sexually abused ...

'I didn't want to marry a madala, I just wanted to go to school'

530 kid rapes a day

ONE child is raped in South Africa every three minutes, a report by trade Union Solidarity says.

A report by Solidarity Helping Hand said while there are about 60 cases of child rape in South Africa every day, more than 88% of child rapes are never reported.

"This means that about 530 child rapes take place every day – one every three minutes," said spokeswoman, Mariana Kriel.

Kriel said the report contains statistics and facts about the levels of child murder, rape and abuse in South Africa.

"Several interviews with social workers and other employees of social welfare organisations across South Africa are included in the report, providing a unique look at the experiences of people who work with child abuse on a daily basis."

Kriel said according to the report, the levels of child abuse in South Africa are increasing rapidly.

"In 2007/08, 1 410 cases of child murder were reported – 22,4% more than in the previous year. In addition, it was found that 45% of all rapes in the country are child rapes," said Danie Langner, executive director of Solidarity Helping Hand.

"The shocking reality is that these figures do not nearly reflect the true extent of the problem."

Kriel said the report also highlights the severe shortage of trained social workers and the difficult working condition they face.

– SAPA

Stop and reflect

After reading the reports, discuss and respond to these questions on your own, or in groups:
1 What is school-based violence?
2 How serious is this problem in South African schools?
3 What are the ways in which the problem manifests itself?
4 What could be the reasons for the high incidence of the problem?
5 What sorts of strategies can be put in place to combat the problem?

The growing incidence of child sexual violence: What are we doing to our children?

Sexual violence, long considered a problem worldwide, has recently received serious recognition on the international human rights agenda. It has become clear that a large number of victims of sexual violence are younger than 15 years of age, and that one in every three women and girls around the world has experienced some form of sexual violence, or has been coerced into sex, or has been raped (Garcia-Moreno, 2002). Although levels of sexual violence vary from one country to another, generally women and girls in developing countries experience higher rates of violence. Circumstances like poverty, cultural practices, and disability may even raise their levels of risk. The problem continues to be rampant in many parts of Africa, with some evidence suggesting that South Africa is a 'hub' or 'nucleus' of sexual violence against women and girls (Calitz, 2011). The problem sees no age, class, race, religion, and cultural background.

Sexual violence permeates the walls of schools and renders them unsafe learning environments. Reports of aggressive and intimidating behaviour, unsolicited physical contact such as touching, kissing and groping, assault, sexual bullying, coercive sex, and rape, are all components of the sexual violence applicable in sexual relations formed between teachers and learners, or amongst learners themselves (UNESCO, 2003). For children with intellectual disabilities, the problem continues to occur in silence, as it is commonly assumed that these learners are not affected owing to their special school status.

The persistence of the problem endangers the achievement of the global push for Education for All (EFA) and the Millennium Development Goals, particularly Goals 2 and 3, which speak to gender parity in education, and universal access for all children to primary education. For female learners with intellectual disabilities, this becomes a double disadvantage in their education because the percentage of children with intellectual disabilities attending schools in developing countries is generally low, at only an estimated 2 per cent of the 150 million school-going children (UNESCO, 2007). The South African deputy minister for Women, Children and People with Disability, Hendrietta Bogopane-Zulu, reported the number to be 467 000 in South Africa (IOL News, 2012). According to the 2001–2011 situation analysis of children with disabilities in South Africa, a total of 68 550 children with intellectual disabilities are serviced by special schools. Furthermore, the analysis alluded to their likelihood to drop out of school in large numbers, compared with their non-disabled counterparts, particularly amongst youth in the age range of 16 to 18 years.

Understanding sexual violence

Sexual violence should be understood within the context of the following factors:

- The unequal power relations that exist in society, which promote male dominance and subject women to inferior positions in which they are dominated by men (Jewkes, Penn-Kekana, Levin, Ratsaka & Schreiber, 2001). Such a culture strips women of any control over their sexuality, and ensures their conformity with behaviour patterns required by the community.
- The construction of 'hostile masculinity' and 'hyper masculinity' lead to hostile beliefs and aggression towards women by men (Murnen, Wright & Kaluzny, 2002). This comes to be perceived as **normative**, necessary, and is sometimes reinforced in the moral framework.
- An element of males communicating defeat to other males, such as when mass rape has been used as a weapon in war-stricken countries, including South Africa during the apartheid regime. Sexual violence and rape during wars and conflicts indicates a feature of militarised masculinity, and is seen as a 'measure of victory' or a 'strategy to dominate or destroy the other group' (Alison, 2007).

....
normative:
relating to a
standard or norm
....

Sexual violence as a human rights violation

As the deeply violating and painful experience of a victimised person, the occurrence of sexual violence in schools denies female learners opportunities to experience educational activities on the same level as their male counterparts. For that reason, it is denounced by international bodies and national legislation as discriminatory. For example, Article 19 of the Convention on the Elimination on All Forms of Discrimination Against Women (CEDAW, 1979) proclaims women's rights to liberty and security, and not to be subjected to torture, cruel, inhuman or degrading treatment, and punishment. The rights of the child to protection from all forms of violence are clearly spelled out in Article 19 of the United Nations Convention on the Rights of the Child (1990). Furthermore, Article 36 of the same Convention (United Nations Convention on the Rights of the Child) affords children the rights to be protected from any activity that takes advantage of them, or could harm their welfare.

With regard to people with disabilities, the UN Convention on the Rights of Persons with Disabilities (2007) recognises their vulnerability to various forms of maltreatment; and thus it calls upon nations to ensure the protection of children and to put in place appropriate strategies to ensure their safety and wellbeing. Its Article 1 says that the Convention's purpose is to "promote, protect and ensure the full and equal enjoyment of all human rights and fundamental freedoms by all persons with disabilities, and to promote respect for their inherent dignity." Of particular note is Article 6, on 'women and disabilities'; and Article 34, which encourages the establishment of a committee on the rights of persons with disabilities.

South African legislation also criminalises all forms of sexual abuse and exploitation. It further clarifies activities which constitute sexual violence in the Sexual Offences and Related Matters Amendment Act (No. 32 of 2007) (RSA, 2007). Section 32 of the Act states categorically that special measures be taken to protect vulnerable groups, including women, children, and those with disabilities. The Employment of Educators Act (No. 76 of 1998) (RSA, 1998) and the Domestic Violence Act (No. 116 of 1998) (RSA, 1998), specifically place legal obligations on educators to report all forms of maltreatment, neglect, and abuse of all learners to the relevant authorities. The principles enshrined in Section 24 of the Constitution of the Republic of South Africa, 1996 (RSA, 1996) contain a statement which protects every human being's rights to an environment which is not harmful to their health and wellbeing. It further affords all learners the rights to education and protection from any form of maltreatment which may interfere with their educational, psychological, and social wellbeing. In addition, the Constitution guarantees the protection of all children from any form of maltreatment and abuse in Section 18 of the Children's Bill of Rights (RSA, 1996). Section 9 of the Constitution states that female learners are entitled to equal opportunities and treatment in South African schools. With regard to children with disabilities, the Constitution guarantees people with disabilities the right to non-discrimination and access to basic services. The White Paper on an Integrated National Disability Strategy (RSA, 1997) stresses that disability should be integrated into government programmes, be coordinated at all levels of government, and be promoted in public education to eliminate discriminatory attitudes against people with disabilities.

Sexual violence in South Africa

The exact rates of sexual violence in South Africa are hard to establish because many incidents rarely reach law enforcement. However, young girls under the age of 18 are frequently targeted as recipients of this form of violence. Added to this, Kalichman, Simbayi, Cain, Cherry, Henda and Cloete (2007) have suggested that many young women's first experience of sex is forced and unprotected. Gang rape is a common practice, and tends to include 'streamlining', where a soon-to-be ex-boyfriend arranges for his friends to have forced sex with his girlfriend, especially if he intends to end the relationship, or when he wants to teach the girlfriend a lesson, for example, if she refuses sex with him (Jewkes, 2009). Dating violence (or date rape) also occurs amongst South African youth (Jewkes, 2005). One local newspaper revealed a common practice in which young (school-going) girls in the age range of 14 to 17 years were forced into early marriages under the age-old custom of *ukuthwalwa*, which means 'to be carried away'. The custom involves parents arranging for their daughters to be married off to older men who pay as little as three sheep as a dowry (lobola). This form of marriage prevents girls from getting an education, maturing, enjoying their youth, or giving birth to healthy babies.

Cellphone pornography is a growing phenomenon among South African youth at schools. With almost every young person aspiring to have a cellphone of their own, such forms of sexual violence are likely to increase dramatically. A study conducted by Nyokangi (2012) suggests that girls are often shown pictures, or sent pictures, on their phones, of people having sex, or naked, by their male counterparts. Male learners use small mirrors or the cameras on cellphones to spy on girls' underwear. They then send these pictures to other learners in the school to reveal what underwear the girls are wearing. Pornographic images are also widely viewed by most youth who have cellphones (Film and Publications Board of South Africa, 2006).

How long has it been going on? Sexual violence in South African schools

School-based sexual violence is not a new phenomenon, although it was not recorded in South African schools until the late 1980s. CIET Africa's (2000) study, conducted in Johannesburg high schools in 1988, pointed to the existence of sexual assault as part of girls' school life. It said that 50 per cent of the 26 000 interviewees believed that forced sex was not sexual violence, but just 'rough' sex. Furthermore, the study reported that one in three schoolgirls had experienced sexual violence at school. Similarly, an article in *The Lancet* medical journal reported on a 1998 national study on the frequency of rape among a sample of 11 735 South African girls and women (15–49 age range). The study found that of the 159 female victims of child rape (younger than 15 years), 33 per cent had been raped by a teacher in school (Jewkes, Levin, Mbananga & Bradshaw, 2002).

The problem was once more exposed in a study by Human Rights Watch (2001), which was conducted in eight schools in three provinces of South Africa: Gauteng, KwaZulu-Natal, and the Western Cape. The study pointed to both male learners and school personnel as perpetrators of school-based sexual violence against girls. The problem is so widespread that some girls had subsequently dropped out of school as a result of their experiences. This finding was in line with Madu's (2001) study conducted in Limpopo. A report presented to the National Assembly's Committee on School-based Violence also indicated that many educators believed in having sexual relationships with female learners. Disturbingly, the report also noted that male educators had assumed that having sex with female learners was "a fringe benefit for low pay" (Prinsloo, 2006). Male head teachers and other teachers reportedly rape and impregnate girls in non-disabled schools, and frequently harass female learners sexually (Insights, 2001).

Sexual violence in South African schools for learners with intellectual disabilities

Learners with intellectual disabilities are not immune to this form of violence even though such studies are limited. A ground-breaking study conducted by Phasha and Nyokangi in 2012, involved a small sample (16 participants) and revealed the extent of the problem in schools for learners with intellectual disabilities. The study pointed to sexual violence as taking forms such as: coercive sex, forceful kissing, fondling of private parts, name-calling, pulling up of skirts, and even rape. The incidents occurred in classrooms, playgrounds, vacant spaces around the schools, toilets, and most frequently, in the school buses when learners were travelling to and from school. Interestingly, male teachers were not identified as perpetrators of sexual violence in these schools. However, male learners were chiefly identified as perpetrators, and only one female learner was named as perpetrator of sexual violence against male learners. Among the other traceable studies include those by Dickman and Roux (2006), and Dickman, Roux, Manson, Douglas and Shabalala (2006). Both studies took place in Cape Town and involved an analysis of complaints reported to a mental health facility. Although the studies did not take place in the school setting, it was interesting to note that some of the complainants were from the school-going age population, a finding which suggests that they are often the target of victimisation.

Factors promoting school-based sexual violence

Factors contributing to the vulnerability of learners with intellectual disabilities vary. The following list shows that factors occur at the various levels in which an individual interacts.

- *Isolation:* Learners with intellectual disabilities lack contact with people of their own choosing because of living in over-controlled situations. Such environments deny them opportunities to learn from others about the skills to protect themselves against abuse. Also, they may find themselves limited in developing friendships. They may come to long for any expression of intimacy, and this makes them vulnerable to victimisation.

- *Dependency on others:* Dependency on others for physical care leaves an individual with a disability with limited control over their own body. It can also cause confusion about boundaries, which increases with exposure to a large number of caregivers.
- *Negative response by schools:* In some instances, sexually violent behaviours against female learners are ignored and sometimes concealed, even when reported to school authorities, thus perpetuating the occurrence of sexual violence. Teachers dismiss or downplay boys' intimidation of girls as mere 'teasing' or as 'normal boys' behaviour'. As a result, they turn a deaf ear to female learners' complaints; and many girls do not even complain due to fear of reprisals, from both male teachers and other learners (Dunne & Leach, 2003).
- *Lack of clear school rules and regulations* guiding how to identify and handle reported incidents of sexual violence also contributes to the occurrence of sexual violence in schools. The situation leaves school personnel unsure about appropriate steps to take when sexual violence has been reported, identified, or is suspected. The perpetrator often simply escapes any discipline or prosecution, and in some instances, goes on to repeat the same violence on the same victim, or another person.
- *School culture:* Gender identification and differentiation patterns at schools leave female learners vulnerable to aggressive sexual advances from their male counterparts and teachers. These include: stereotypical masculine and feminine behaviours expected by the school; seating arrangements which require girls always to sit in the front and boys at the back; males' preferences for leadership roles, and assigning responsibilities such as cleaning and catering to girls, while boys are made responsible for digging the school grounds and planting trees. Such arrangements provide affirmation to boys that they should control and dominate females (Dunne & Leach, 2003).
- *Misconceptions about disability:* Quite a number of contradictory conceptions around intellectual disability and such individuals' sexuality contribute to their vulnerability to sexual violence. Assumptions and misconceptions include those that: they promiscuous; they are at lower risk of sexual violence than their non-disabled counterparts; they are sexually inactive and therefore virgins who could be used to 'cure' sexually-transmitted diseases; they become sexualised from a young age and that discussing sexuality issues will stimulate them (Grieveo, MacLaren & Lindsay, 2006).
- *Legal response:* The way in which reported cases are handled by the legal system discourages women and girls, particularly those with disabilities, from reporting sexual violence. These include high case dismissal rates by police and prosecutors, a low prosecution and conviction rate, and general insensitivity by police and the legal system.

- *Poverty:* Some parents in low socio-economic status families take a compromising attitude to sexual violence on their female learners because they depend on their state disability grant for the family survival. In this case, such learners are seen as a source of income to their families.

Educational implications for learners with intellectual disabilities

Beside the health, psychological, emotional, and physical consequences, the experience of sexual violence in schools exerts a negative impact on the education of female learners, and acts as a barrier to attaining education. In particular, an individual's concentration can be hampered, and so is their ability to focus in class during lessons, or do any other school-related activities at home or anywhere else. Such individuals often find it difficult to remember and follow lessons.

Avoidance of school is also common amongst victims of sexual violence. Such a problem could increase isolation, render the person vulnerable to inappropriate activities such as drug use, prostitution, and unsuitable friends. As involvement in inappropriate activities tends to leave an individual with limited time to focus of school activities, the consequences are poor school grades and dropping out. Furthermore, sexual violence against girls manifests itself in their low enrolment in school, irregular school attendance, teenage pregnancy, early marriage, and increased rates of HIV infections, especially in the 15–24-year-old age group (Leach, Fiscian, Kadzamira, Lemani & Machakanje, 2003).

Other reported responses to sexual violence by female learners include: absenteeism, a decrease in the quality of schoolwork, missing or dropping classes, as well as mental health symptoms such as nightmares, feelings of isolation, anger, and anxiety (Winters, Cliff & Maloney, 2004). Phasha (2007) noted truancy, deterioration of grades, loss of interest in school and academic subjects, repeating classes, and general failure in matriculation exams. Dropping out of school usually results from fear of recurrent humiliation, embarrassment, and the stigma attached to the abuse experience.

Suggestions for school-based sexual violence interventions

The following are some suggestions for interventions to address school-based sexual violence which have been effective locally and abroad.

- *Peer counselling:* Having peer counsellors in schools could be of assistance in facilitating disclosure of sexual violence. Some learners may prefer to share their disturbing experience with their own peers rather than with their teachers. Peer counsellors could also help in identifying sexual violence and handling it. A study conducted in Australia by Imbesis found that when peer counsellors are appointed at school, they are able to serve as links between teachers and students, and thus reporting is increased. Peer leaders could facilitate positive behaviour and attitudes amongst learners and help in creating a friendly school environment where victims feel safe in reporting incidents. Young people are able to approach their fellow peers in a friendly way to discourage inappropriate behaviours, and to act as role models. The loveLife youth programme is an example of initiatives in which youth are involved in the fight against HIV and AIDS, and the promotion of healthy sexual lifestyles. The programme is broadly youth participatory, involving young people in both the community and at schools. A study conducted amongst youth in Brazil (Pulerwitz, Barker, Nascimento & Segundo, 2006) suggests that peer counselling is effective in promoting change in norms of masculinity and lifestyle, improved relations in intimate relationships, and has led to lower rates of sexual violence.

- *School supervision:* Proper and intensive supervision on and around the school premises and other facilities linked to it could assist in the prevention of school-based sexual violence. Particular spots that should be targeted include: playgrounds, buses, and vacant lots, or unused buildings, around schools. Such a strategy becomes effective when the school has enough staff members getting involved in assisting in this effort. When high-risk areas are closely monitored, the results pay off in increasing all learners' genuine sense of safety and being 'looked out for'.

- *Teacher training:* Teacher training rarely equips teachers with the skills and knowledge to address sexuality-related matters. When such programmes become part of teacher training, teachers' prompt support of learners could be facilitated. Teachers become more understanding and sensitive to the implications of the problem. Sexual violence reporting increases and schools become safe for all learners, and their wellbeing is improved. Teachers could also come to confront their own gendered experiences and attitudes (Chege, 2006).

- *Clear policies:* Clear school policies and rules on sexual violence and other inappropriate behaviours could encourage reporting, especially if everybody at school is aware of the rules. The effectiveness of such a strategy is maximised if school policies state specific punishments of perpetrators, and there is a specially appointed person to whom learners can open up. If all stakeholders at schools are aware of such policies and rules, the school environment becomes healthy and friendly because everybody plays a role in ensuring that the rules and policies are taken seriously and enforced.

- *Sexuality education:* Sexuality education should be strengthened and incorporate issues of rights and respect for one another. Young people learn through such education that males and females have different needs, and both deserve respect (Khumalo & Garbus, 2002). Males need to regard females as their equals and treat them with respect. This will help to overcome negative attitudes towards girls, and ultimately stop the sexually violent behaviours that are currently exhibited by male learners. Berkowitz (2006) suggests that sexuality education promotes a positive approach with regard to gender norms so that healthy relationships are fostered. There would be a shift away from negative male norms that demean women, to positive ones that show them respect. Similarly, young males could be empowered to resist peer-influenced practices that shape their behaviours negatively.

Summary of discussion

Sexual violence is a serious problem in South African schools, and learners with intellectual disabilities are often among the victims. It is a violation of human rights which should be tackled head on by the school to ensure that learning takes place in safe environments. Not only do schools have the responsibility of safeguarding all learners from sexual violence, and of taking timeous action when it occurs, but they also need to have clearly stated policies for promoting healthy gender relationships. In addition, teachers and learners need to involve themselves in interventions that inform and empower them to counter and deal with sexual violence.

Closing activities

Self-reflection
1. Think back to your own high school years and recall behaviours which you or your friends experienced as unpleasant or unwanted but, at the time, you simply dismissed as 'stupid boys' behaviour'. Which of those behaviours now fits your definition of sexual violence? Could it be that such behaviours still exist in some of our schools? What factors do you regard as contributing to such behaviours?
2. What measures would you put in place to ensure that learners with intellectual disabilities are educated and sensitised about such behaviours? What strategies should be put in place to ensure that reports of such behaviours are brought to the attention of relevant authorities? What measures do you think need to be in place to make authorities respond appropriately to reports of abuse?

Practical applications
3. Learners with intellectual disabilities are certainly not immune to school-based sexual violence and its negative consequences. Considering the prevalence of this problem in our schools, work out a school policy for promoting sexual violence-free environments which are conducive for learning for all. Present your policy as a one-page proposal.
4. Pay a visit to a school for learners with intellectual disabilities to observe how learners interact with one another. Make a list of behaviours which you think might be classified as sexual

violence. Note your impression of how the school personnel handle reports of such behaviour. Also note general attitudes towards sexual violence by school staff. Write up your notes as a report (3–4 pages) with any points of concern noted for action.

References

Alison, M. 2007. "Wartime sexual violence: Women's human rights and questions of masculinity". *Review of International Studies.* 33(1):75–90.

Berkowitz, A. 2006. *Healthy norms to prevent violence and abuse: The social norms approach.* Washington, DC: Wood & Barnes Publishers.

Calitz, F.J.W. 2011. Psycho-legal challenges facing the mentally retarded rape victim. *South African Journal of Psychology.* 17(3):66–72.

Chege, F. 2007. Educational and empowerment of girls against gender-based violence. *Journal of International Cooperation in Education.* 10(1):53–70.

CEDAW. 1979. *Convention on the Elimination of All Forms of Discrimination Against Women.* Office of the United Nations High Commissioner for Human Rights.

Dahlberg, L.L. & Krug, E.G. 2002. Violence – A global public health problem. In E.G. Krug, L.L. Dahlberg, J.A. Mercy, A.B. Zwi & R. Lozano (Eds). *World Report on Violence and Health.* (pp. 3–21). Geneva: WHO.

Department of Education. 2001. *White Paper 6: Building an inclusive education and training system.* Pretoria: Government Press.

Dickman, J., & Roux, J. A. 2006. Complainants with learning disabilities in sexual abuse cases: A 10-year review of a psycho-legal project in Cape Town, South Africa. *British Journal of Learning Disabilities.* 33:138–144.

Dickman, B., Roux, A., Manson, S., Douglas, G. & Shabalala, N. 2006. How could she possibly manage in court? An intervention programme assisting complainants with intellectual disability in sexual assault cases. *Sexuality and Disability.* 24:77–88.

Dunne, M. & Leach, F. 2003. *Institutional sexism: Contexts and texts in Botswana and Ghana.* Paper presented at 7th Oxford International Conference on Educational Development, 9–11 September 2003.

Film and Publications Board. 2006. *Internet usage and the exposure of pornography to learners in South African schools.* A research report on child pornography, prepared for the Department of Home Affairs.

Garcia-Moreno, C. 2002. Violence against women: International perspectives. *American Journal of Preventive Medicine.* 19(4):330–333.

Grieveo, A., McLaren, S. & Lindsay, W.R. 2006. An evaluation of research and training resources for sex education of people with moderate to severe learning disabilities. *British Journal of Learning Disabilities.* 37(1):30–37.

Human Rights Watch. 2001. *Scared at school: Sexual violence against girls in South African schools.* New York: Human Rights Watch.

Insights. 2001. *Conspiracy of silence? Stamping out abuse in African schools.* A special issue of the Institute of Development Studies, Sussex. Retrieved from www.eldis.org on 19 April 2013.

IOL News. 2012. *Call for better attitude towards people with disabilities.* November. Retrieved from http://www.iol.co.za/news/crime-courts/ on 19 April 2013.

Jewkes, R., Penn-Kekana, L., Levin, J., Ratsaka, M. & Schreiber, M. 2001. Prevalence of emotional, physical and sexual abuse of women in three provinces. *South African Medical Journal.* 91:421–428.

Jewkes, R., Levin, J., Mbananga, N. & Bradshaw, D. 2002. Rape of girls in South Africa. *The Lancet.* 359: 319–320.

Jewkes, R. 2005. Non-consensual sex among South African youth: Prevalence of coercive sex and discourse of control and desire. In S.J. Jejeebhoy, I. Shah & S. Thapa (Eds). *Sex without consent: Young people in developing countries.* London: Zed Books.

Jewkes, R. 2009. *Understanding men's health and use of violence: Interface of rape and HIV in South Africa.* Pretoria: South African Medical Research Council.

Kalichman, S.C., Simbayi, L.C., Cain, D., Cherry, C., Henda, N. & Cloete, A. 2007. Sexual assault, sexual risks and gender attitudes in a community sample of South African men. *AIDS CARE.* 19(1):20–27.

Khumalo, G. & Garbus, L. 2002. *HIV/AIDS in Zimbabwe.* AIDS Policy Research Centre. San Francisco (CA): University of California.

Leach, F. & Machakanje, P. 2000. A preliminary investigation into the abuse of girls in Zimbabwean junior secondary schools. *Education Research* (39). London: DFID.

Leach, F., Fiscian, V., Kadzamira, E., Lemani, E. & Machakanje, L. 2003. An investigative study of the abuse of girls in African schools. *Educational Papers* (54). London: DFID.

Madu, S.N. 2001. Childhood forcible sexual abuse and victim-perpetrator relationship among a sample of secondary school students in the Northern Province (SA). *Crime Research in SA.* 291:21–25.

Murnen, S., Wright, C. & Kaluzny, G. 2002. If "Boys Will Be Boys", Then Girls Will Be Victims? A Meta-analytic Review of the Research that Relates Masculine Ideology to Sexual Aggression. *Sex Roles.* 46(11):359–375

Nyokangi, D. 2012. School-based sexual violence at selected special schools for learners with intellectual disability in Gauteng South Africa. Unpublished doctoral thesis. Pretoria: University of South Africa.

Phasha T.N. & Nyokangi, D. 2012. School-based sexual violence in schools for learners with mild intellectual disability. *Sexuality and Disability.* 18(3):309–321.

Prinsloo, S. 2006. Sexual harassment and violence in South African schools. *South African Journal of Education.* 26(2):305–318.

Pulerwitz, J., Barker, G., Segundo, M. & Nascimento, M. 2006. Promoting more gender-equitable norms and behaviors among young men as an HIV/AIDS prevention strategy. *Horizons Final Report.* Washington DC: Population Council.

Republic of South Africa. 1997. *Integrated National Disability Strategy (INDS): The White Paper.* Pretoria: Government Press.

Republic of South Africa. 1996. *Constitution of the Republic of South Africa, 1996.* Pretoria: Government Printers.

Republic of South Africa. 2007. *Sexual Offences and Related Matters Amendment Act (No. 32 of 2007).* Pretoria: Government Printers.

Republic of South Africa. 1998. *Employment of Educators Act (No. 76 of 1988).* Pretoria: Government Printers.

Republic of South Africa. 1998. *Domestic Violence Act (No. 116 of 1998).* Pretoria: Government Printers

UNESCO. 2003. The Leap to Equality: Gender and Education for All. *EFA Global Monitoring Report.* Paris: UNESCO.

UNESCO. 2007. *Stopping violence in schools: What works?* Experts Meeting. Paris: UNESCO.

United Nations. 1990. *Convention on the rights of the child.* New York: United Nations.

Winters, J., Clift, R.J.W. & Maloney, A. 2004. Adult-student sexual harassment in British Columbia High Schools. In R. Geffer, M. Braverman, J. Galasso & J. Marsh (Eds). *Aggression in organizations: Violence, abuse and harassment at work and in schools.* New York: Haworth Press.

8 Managing school violence

Matshidiso Taole

Chapter overview

Learners have the right to learn in a safe environment that is conducive to teaching and learning. However, the prevalence of violence deprives most learners of this right. Schools are supposed to be centres of excellence and to promote responsible citizenship. This chapter discusses factors that contribute to school violence, and the effects of school violence. Although it recognises that school violence is the result of multiple factors, this chapter attempts to suggest strategies that could be used to manage and prevent violence in schools.

Learning outcomes

By the end of this chapter you should be able to:
- Define school violence
- Discuss factors that contribute to school violence
- Describe the manifestations of school violence
- Outline the effects of school violence
- State the strategies to address and prevent violence in the school.

 CASE STUDY

Tshego's story
Going to school has always been an exciting thing for me; I looked forward to learning. I never once felt unsafe or in danger, until one day a boy came up to me and told me that I must give him my lunch money or else face the consequences. I was afraid, in fact, terrified; I didn't know what to do. But I gave him what he wanted. If that was not enough, he told me that from that day onwards I must give him money if I want to be happy at school. I didn't know what to do: I was afraid to report him to my class teacher because everybody was afraid of him, even my teachers. I did not even tell my parents or friends. I suffered in silence for months, and school was not fun anymore until I decided to do something. I've always told myself that if I was faced with a situation like this I'd back down, walk away, and be a bigger person. Although my parents always told me that problems are not solved through fighting, I had no option, I felt I must do something about my situation. I woke up one morning filled with anger, and suddenly nice Tshego was now this vicious teenager who wanted revenge. My mum has a very sharp knife in her kitchen drawer, which I was not allowed to use. I took it, put it in my bag, and went to school. As I walked to school I was scared, but at the same time I felt a sense of relief and security. I was determined to teach that boy a lesson. As usual, that boy came to me during lunch and demanded that I give him money. Not this time, boy. I quickly took out my knife and stabbed him in his hand. That made him angry and he started beating me. I still had the knife in my hand and stabbed him again in his thigh. Everybody was watching, even my friends, and I was hoping they would come to my rescue. No one did. On that day I decided that I am my own protector. Unfortunately, I had to learn this the hard way. You have to do something to survive in this cruel world.

Stop and reflect

Work with a partner to answer the following questions based on the case study:
1   Name the type of violence Tshego endured and describe it.
2   If you see violence in your school, what do you do about it?
3   Do you think Tshego's school has a climate that allows teacher and learner interaction?
4   If you were Tshego, what would you do in her situation?
5   Is Tshego's solution to violence the best solution? Substantiate your answer.

Schools as battlegrounds, where violence is winning

The phenomenon of the prevalence of school violence dominates current discussions among various researchers in the education sector across the world, and South Africa is no exception. The concerns are based on the seriousness and frequency of violent behaviours that tarnish learners' integrity and schools' reputations. Schools are no longer regarded as centres of learning since they have been transformed into battlegrounds. School violence has become a part of everyday life in some schools, and learners' safety cannot be guaranteed. Learners are supposed to be safe on the school premises but, because of the increasing rate of violence, schools have become highly volatile and unpredictable places where violence in schools is the norm rather than an exception.

Research conducted by Burton and Leoschut (2012:12), Unisa (2012), Zulu, Urbani and Van der Merwe (2004:70), and Le Roux and Mokhele (2011) reiterate that violence and crime in South African schools is a critical problem. The destructive and anti-social behaviours of some learners, as we have seen in the case study, results in learners becoming violent as a way of protecting themselves against their aggressors. Tshego decides to bring a weapon to school, although carrying weapons to school compromises the school as a safe place for learning and teaching. Learners will resort to carrying weapons and fighting back to protect themselves, thus perpetuating violence in schools. Violence associated with school often results in truancy as learners become too scared to go to school, or sometimes they skip classes as a way of avoiding confrontation with bullies, who are either their fellow learners, or even their teachers.

A safe school is that one that is free of danger and where there is an absence of possible harm, a place in which non-educators, educators and learners may work, teach and learn without fear of ridicule, intimidation, harassment, humiliation or violence (Prinsloo, 2005:5).

What is school violence?

The complexity of the phenomenon of school violence makes it difficult to define the concept 'school violence' in a succinct way. According to Estévez, Jiménez and Musitu (2008:3), coming up with a single definition of school violence is very problematic since this aspect of human behaviour has been studied from many different approaches; and each of them focuses on a specific part. Efforts which are directed at school violence prevention must focus on a broader definition and understanding of what constitutes school violence. This means that school violence needs to be studied deeply; what causes violence in the school should be determined before devising strategies that could be used address violence in schools. For example, locking the school gates during school hours will not be sufficient because school violence takes different forms: it often happens within the school premises, so locking the gates will not keep it out, or solve the problem.

Another example is that while a code of conduct for learners ensures that learners are clear about the rules, this alone cannot prevent school violence because learners' behaviour is a result of different elements. This means that a whole range of measures must be employed to address issues of school violence. In some instances, initiatives focus more on dealing with violence when it happens, or on providing fewer opportunities for incidents of violence to occur. Countries such as Austria, Spain, and the United Kingdom use telephone helplines so that learners can seek advice anonymously. We in South Africa need to focus more on prevention measures and not on reacting to violent incidents in schools once they have occurred.

Violence in schools is recognised as a major problem that not only affects the wellbeing and educational achievement of learners, but can undermine democratic values as set forth in South Africa's Constitution.

 Stop and reflect

Let us stop right here and look at what we have just said so far about school violence. Learners often learn violent behaviour at school as a way of protecting themselves. Now that you have read Tshego's story, you have seen that her views about school were influenced by her experiences at school. What did she learn? Did this change any of her values? How and why?

De Wet (2006:64) emphasises that every child is entitled to a safe environment, and schools have the responsibility to ensure that safety. Asbeh (2010:2) argues that the school must be responsible and accountable for the extent to which each learner makes personal progress in educational achievement and social development. This is because children spend approximately half of their waking hours at school. Schools can serve as the second most important socialising mechanism after the home (South African Council of Educators, 2011:4).

Schools are important environments in which children not only gain knowledge but also learn about themselves, how to behave, as well as how to interact with other children (Burton, 2008).

Let us now look at some of the characteristics of a safe school:

* *Good discipline.* State rules positively by telling learners what to do instead of what not to do. In addition, rules need to be applied consistently and fairly.
* *Well-maintained buildings.* School buildings reflect the general caring attitude of the school. Clean and well cared-for buildings say to the learner "you are important and we care about you."
* *Professional teacher conduct.* Legislation in the form of the Constitution of the Republic of South Africa, 1996, the Employment of Educators Act (No. 76 of 1998), and the South African Schools Act (SASA) (No. 84 of 1996) protects the rights of children. Teachers' social responsibilities are embodied in the SASA. In addition, teachers are guided by the Code of Professional Ethics of the South African Council for Educators (SACE). Teachers have an important duty to protect the safety of the learners who are placed in their care, not only in terms of the Constitution and other legislation mentioned earlier, but also in terms of their ***in loco parentis*** status.
* *Good governance and management practices.* Stakeholders, such as teachers and learners, among others, need to be involved in decision-making about school improvement, the drafting of the school mission, and its vision.

....
in loco parentis:
Latin for 'in the place of the parent'; or standing in for the parent
....

Stop and reflect

With a partner, discuss some of the other characteristics of a safe school. Before you do this, read about teachers' professional conduct below.

Why do teachers have a part to play in school violence?

School violence is a kind of behaviour that includes the general characteristics of violent behaviour, with the difference that the actors are children and adolescents and that it takes place in primary and secondary schools: in places where they are together for several hours a day, all year round (Estévez, Jiménez & Musitu, 2008:3).

SACE is a professional council that is established in terms of the SACE Act (No. 31 of 2000). SACE aims to enhance the status of the teaching profession, and to promote the development of educators and their professional conduct. The SACE Act mandates the following in terms of teachers' professional conduct: it states that the teacher shall:

* promote, develop, and maintain the image of the profession.
* behave in a way that enhances the dignity and status of the teaching profession, and that does not bring the profession into disrepute.
* keep abreast of educational trends and developments.
* promote the ongoing development of teaching as a profession.
* accept that he or she has a professional obligation towards the education and induction into the profession of new members of the teaching profession.

Violence is a result of the behaviour patterns of learners, teachers, and other role players. Let us look at the different types of school violence:

- *Direct violence.* Many different violent behaviours take place in the school context, including those directed towards objects or school property, and those directed towards individuals. Violence that is directed towards objects or school property includes: breaking desks, chairs, windows or doors, and painting names, messages, and graffiti on the school walls. The perpetrators' intention is to cause damage. Violence can also be directed towards individuals such as teachers and peers in the form of verbal and physical aggression, such as shoving, beating up, threatening, or insulting, and any other serious breach of discipline in the class, such as disobeying a teacher, or the school's internal regulations.
- *Indirect or relational violence.* In this form of violence, there is no direct physical confrontation between the aggressor and the victim. Indirect violence is defined as an act directed towards provoking damage to the learner's social group, or in her perception of belonging to that group (e.g. social exclusion, social rejection, and spreading rumours). This violence not only affects learners who are directly victimised, but also those who witness the violence occurring at school. For example, a learner witnessing his peer being bullied is affected as a spectator, and this could have serious consequences for that learner. It could create a feeling of fear, apprehension, and even shame, which would interfere with the learner's academic progress.
- *Reactive violence.* This refers to behaviours that entail a defensive response to provocation. This violence tends to be related to impulsivity and self-control problems, as well as problems in dealing with social relations. It is often based on a tendency to attribute hostile motives to other people's behaviour.
- *Proactive violence.* This refers to behaviours that entail an anticipation of some kind of benefit or outcome. For example, a female learner goes up to another girl and slaps her, as a warning to stay away from her boyfriend. It is deliberate, and controlled by external reinforcement. This kind of violence has been related to subsequent anti-social and criminal problems, and, antithetically, with high levels of social competence and leadership skills.

The extent of violence in South African schools

Media reports repeatedly confirm the current prevalence of violence in schools. Schools are no longer places conducive to teaching and learning, as both teachers and learners live in fear while on the school premises. Violence in schools can demotivate learners in their studies, and teachers from their profession as teachers. A study by the Centre for the Study of Violence and Reconciliation (CSVR, 2010) in South Africa, found that children who became persistent offenders after school were often affected by adverse family and school experiences.

Media reports further attest to school violence as a grave concern in South African schools. A recent media report recounts how a seven-year-old boy was battered by his Grade 1 classmates (*Sunday Times*, 2012:3).The Grade 1 learners were reported to have beaten him so badly that he may never walk again. These are always shocking news stories as schools are supposed to be safe places. However, the age of the learners in this case makes the news all the more shocking.

It is clear that learners are traumatised by their experiences at the school. Learners fear intimidation from fellow learners, and they even fear being attacked by other learners outside the school premises. The report of the CJCP's (Centre for Justice and Crime Prevention) National School Violence Study 2013, which involved 12 794 learners from primary and secondary schools in South Africa, shows that 15.3 per cent of children at primary and secondary schools have experienced some form of violence while at school: most commonly, threats of violence, assault, and robbery. Learners also have easy access to alcohol, drugs, and weapons at school. However, it is the responsibility of the school to protect the rights of children as articulated in the South African Constitution (1996). Learners, along with all South African citizens, have the right to, among others: a) an environment free from racial and gender discrimination; b) human dignity; c) life; d) freedom and security of person; e) protection from maltreatment; f) neglect and abuse or degradation; and, g) basic education. In addition, the Constitution gives to children specific additional rights, among which is the right to be protected from maltreatment and abuse. These rights are, or have the potential to be, infringed by both the perpetuation of school-based violence as well as the tangible threat of such violence. Unfortunately, for many children, educational settings expose them to violence, and may even teach them how to be violent, as in Tshego's case.

 Stop and reflect

1 Write a brief explanation of each of the constitutional values above, including the specific children's right mentioned.
2 How do you think these rights should protect learners from school violence?

 Why do schools need to be safe environments?

It may seem obvious, but here are some further reasons to consider about why schools need to be safe places for learners especially, and their teachers:

Schools are important environments in which children not only gain knowledge, but also learn about themselves, how to behave, as well as how to interact with other children (Burton, 2008).

Schools are supposed to be safe places where all learners have equal access to equal educational opportunities, and are treated equally (Taole, 2013:249).

Every child is entitled to a safe environment and schools have the responsibility to ensure that safety (De Wet, 2006:64).

Children spend approximately half of their waking hours at school; schools can serve as the second most important socialising mechanism after the home (South African Council of Educators, 2011:4).

Manifestations of school violence

Violence in schools, like other types of victimisation, manifests itself in various forms. Let us now look at the different forms of violence that occur in schools, which are:

Learner to learner

In most cases, violence in schools happens in playgrounds, toilets, at bus and taxi stops, and even in classrooms. Violence in these places usually takes place when the teacher is not present. This type of violence often happens because of a lack of tolerance among learners, and their inability to control their emotions, e.g. losing their temper, or retaliating physically or verbally. Learner-to-learner violence takes the form of: a) fighting; b) bullying (this can take the form of physical violence between learners, or when learners verbally abuse one another); c) use of weapons; and d) teasing.

Teacher to learner

Teachers are supposed to care for and protect learners at school. However, teachers are sometimes seen as perpetrators of violence. Teachers contribute to school violence by not honouring their teaching commitments and being in classrooms at the right time. More often than not, learners find themselves idle and unsupervised, and get involved in violent activities. This is confirmed by research conducted by the University of South Africa (2012) which frequently indicates that teachers' absenteeism from their classes contributes to violence in schools. Jacobs, Vakalisa and Gawe (2011:23) maintain that teachers must have a positive work ethic, display appropriate values, and conduct themselves in a manner which benefits, enhances, and develops the teaching profession. Violence perpetrated directly by teachers includes: a) corporal punishment (which is outlawed by Section 10 of the South African Schools Act No. 84 of 1996); b) cruel and humiliating forms of psychological punishment; c) sexual violence; d) gender-based violence; e) bullying; f) verbal degradation; and g) name calling.

Learner to teacher

Learners are sometimes violent towards their teachers. As a result, teachers do not feel safe in schools. Feeling unsafe at the school can compromise the quality of teaching and can lower teachers' morale. Teachers should feel happy in their jobs so as to be effective in their delivery of the learning experience. Some examples of learner-to-teacher violence are: a) teachers being physically attacked by learners;

b) incidents of psychological violence against teachers, such as learners acting disrespectfully; c) learners swearing at and taunting teachers; d) learners ignoring teachers or disrupting classes; e) learners intimidating or bullying teachers; and, f) incidents with discriminatory racist and sexist undertones.

People from outside, or community members

Schools do not operate in a vacuum. They form an integral part of the community, so school violence should be looked at in relation to the community in which these schools belong. Violent behaviour in the broader community usually spills over into schools. This is because learners know about criminality in the community, as well as how to get access to alcohol, drugs, and weapons in the community. Schools are also affected by events in the wider community, such as: a) the prevalence of gang culture; b) gang-related criminal activity; c) use and abuse of drugs and alcohol; d) sexual abuse; and, e) gender-based violence. Examples of the common types of violence that take place in schools are shown in Figure 8.1.

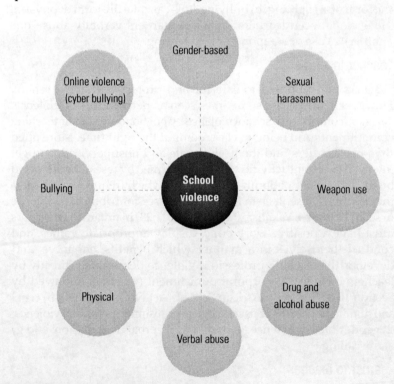

Figure 8.1: Examples of violence occurring in schools

What do we know about bullying and gangsterism?

Bullying can be defined as intentional, repeated, hurtful acts, words, or other behaviour, such as name-calling, or shunning, committed by an individual or individuals against another individual or individuals (De Wet 2006:62). Bullying infringes the learners' rights to dignity, freedom, security, and social and emotional fulfilment. There are three types of bullying, namely:
- Physical: pushing, shoving, kicking, slapping, and punching.
- Verbal: calling names, teasing, threatening, insulting, and humiliating.
- Relational: gossiping or spreading rumours about someone, telling others to stop liking or associating with someone, ignoring or stopping talking to someone

Gangs are a widespread problem in urban and rural communities across the country. They are criminal organisations that create many problems in communities, often recruiting young members, controlling, intimidating, and even terrorising communities. Gang members often wear the same colour clothing, have specific body tattoos, use hand signals known as gang signs or codes, and adorn personal belongings or public property with graffiti.

Factors contributing to school violence

School violence is a multifaceted phenomenon and no single explanation is sufficient to explain why learners behave the way they do. Therefore, any attempt to prevent school violence needs to consider the multifaceted nature of school violence. Learners' behaviour could be the result of what they have experienced at home, in the media, or at school. Flores (2005:82) argues that children's behaviours are the product of multiple interactions that take place in multiple settings. This is true for school violence; it takes place in different ways, in a wide range of contexts. Therefore, it is important to consider a comprehensive view of interrelated factors influencing both the perpetrator and the victim of violence. While it can be random, school violence does not take place in isolation: it is always influenced and shaped by contextual factors (SACE 2011:7).

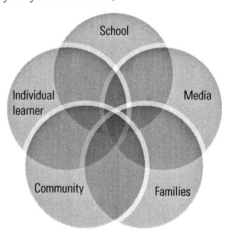

Figure 8.2: Factors contributing to school violence

School

Learners no longer feel safe on the school premises because of the high level of violence in their schools. There are areas in the school that are characterised as high-risk zones, and these become a source of fear, but also curiosity, for learners. Children who are exposed to violence in schools tend to model the same behaviour. This is evident in the first case study, where we saw that Tshego learned violent behaviour at school. The way learners perceive the school will influence the way they feel about school (initially, for example, Tshego enjoyed her school and then came to regard it as an unsafe place when she was bullied). In addition, school experiences will influence learners' perception about going to school and education in general. Therefore, situations that learners find themselves in at school contribute significantly to the way they will behave, and to effective teaching and learning.

Feelings about the school environment relate to how comfortable or uncomfortable each learner feels about the school environment. Skiba, Simmons, Peterson, Kelvey, Forde & Gallini (2004) suggest that these feelings include teacher–learner relationships; learner–peer relationships; order of discipline; support, and fairness of rules; and learners' overall perception of the school climate. According to Cohen (2010:1), school climate is based on patterns of people's experience of school life, and reflects norms, goals, values, interpersonal relationships, teaching and learning, leadership practices, and organisational structures. Defour (2005:89) posits that school climate involves the unwritten beliefs, values, and attitudes that become the style of interaction between teachers, learners, and administrators. Welsh (2000:89) contends that the school climate sets the parameters of acceptable behaviour among all school actors, and it assigns individual and institutional responsibility for school safety. "If violence occurs at schools and is not addressed, it can destroy the school culture and school climate, as well as diminish the protective influence of the school" (Barnes, Brynard & De Wet, 2012:9). A positive school climate will enhance learning and teaching in the school, as well as positive behaviour and attitudes.

Conversely, negative feelings such as fear, bullying, and intolerance would negatively affect learning and behaviour. In addition, an unattractive or depressing school environment can also increase the negative perception of learners about their school. For example, some classrooms do not have sufficient desks, tables and chairs for learners to sit at, and learners are either crowded into insufficiently equipped spaces, or fighting over them. The school environment should promote positive feelings between learners, and reduce hostile and negative feelings among learners. If the school property is not well cared for, learners, in turn, will not feel that they have any responsibility to take care of school property. This will increase their feeling of being disregarded and neglected by those in authority.

Danger zone or learning zone – what do we know about school climate?

High-risk zones are dangerous areas in the school that increase learners' (and teachers') vulnerability of becoming victims of violence. They could be anywhere in the school – playgrounds, sports fields, toilets, parking areas, or classrooms themselves; or even the area where the school itself is located.

The school climate is a reflection of the positive or negative feelings regarding the school environment that may directly or indirectly affect a variety of learning outcomes (Peterson & Skiba, 2000:122). School climate can be defined in terms of four aspects of the school environment:

1 Physical environment: an environment that is welcoming and conducive to learning
2 Social environment: an environment that promotes communication and interaction
3 Affective environment: an environment that promotes a sense of belonging and self-esteem
4 Academic environment: an environment that promotes learning and self-fulfilment.

Stop and reflect

Look at the newspaper picture of learners in a classroom. How might this school environment influence learners' behaviour and possibly contribute to school violence? Write your response in the form of a letter to a provincial education authority explaining the risks of school violence in such situations.

Families

The attributes of a young person's family and home environment also play a key role in the child's risk of victimisation and perpetration of violence. A report of the South African Council of Educators (2011) on school-based violence found out that parents play an important role in modelling behaviour, as well as in **mediating** other factors, such as poverty, school truancy, and peer pressure, which may increase the risk of school-based violence. Parents serve as a support

Sibongile Mashaba: *Sowetan* (2013)

This picture, taken in 2010, shows learners at Matjeni Primary School in Tonga, Mpumalanga, who have no desks to sit on and have to use their laps to support their books.

base for children, and therefore should provide a solid foundation for their children. Well-supported learners tend to be less aggressive, can control their emotions, and generally do well at school, whereas neglected learners tend to be aggressive and do not do well at school.

Some learners come from **dysfunctional** families where parents or family members display violent behaviour on a daily basis. For example, the father will beat the mother if he does not get his way, or when he wants to control her and the children. In this situation, the child will learn that violence instead of communication can be used to settle issues or effect outcomes. Learners who grow up with violence in the home are more likely to display violent behaviour in

....
mediate: to play a role or have an influence in a situation, or on behaviour
dysfunctional: not working or behaving properly; being unable to deal with normal social relations
....

school. Families constitute the primary context in which young people learn about which behaviours are considered acceptable or unacceptable, in their society. These are some of the family factors that relate to violence in school:

- Problems with communication within the family
- Lack of affective cohesion
- Poor parental support
- Presence of regular conflicts
- Dysfunctional strategies of conflict resolution
- Uninvolved or authoritarian parental style
- A family history of problem behaviour.

 Stop and reflect

We have seen that families play an important role in the lives on the learners. Can you give examples to demonstrate your understanding of the listed family factors that are related to school violence? For each factor and example, explain the influence it might have on the learner.

Community

What happens in the school is usually a reflection of what is happening in the wider society. Disorganised and disorderly communities in which learners live, are communities that are found to be powerful facilitators of crime and violence. For example, community members sell drugs to learners and some adults give learners drugs to sell at school. In some instances, learners grow up in communities where violent and aggressive behaviour is modelled by significant individuals in their lives, such as their parents or close relatives. Bandura (1977) argues that violent behaviour that is modelled is more likely to be imitated and replicated when the person modelling the behaviour has a relationship with the child or young person, than when there is no relationship between the individuals. Bandura (1977) considers that violent behaviour is learned through observation and imitation of behaviours that occur in the immediate contexts of the individual. For example, bullies in the immediate community or family may influence their children to become involved in bullying. This usually takes the form of group fighting or gangs. The learner will eventually replicate this bullying act because she sees it as a normal behaviour to solve conflicts and problems. When learners passively watch the bullying activity, they are actually learning and encouraging violence, since perpetrators want to impress the spectators who are usually their peers.

What does Bandura's social learning theory say?

Albert Bandura (1925–) is a Canadian psychologist who is currently the David Starr Jordan Professor Emeritus of Social Science in Psychology at Stanford University, USA. He originated social learning theory and is considered one of the foremost social psychologists of the current era.

In social learning theory, Bandura (1977) states that behaviour is learned from the environment through a process of observational learning. Individuals who are observed are called models. In society, children are surrounded by many influential models, such as parents within the family, characters on children's TV, friends within their peer group, and teachers at school. Children consciously and unconsciously observe the behaviour of these models, especially in dealing with situations of aggression and anger. They are then likely to learn and replicate such behaviour in their own responses.

Media

The media are a powerful tool in influencing learners' behaviour. Television, cinema, and the internet are full of violent images and language, which are used by fictional characters as a regular way to achieve their aims. Some violent behaviours in real-life situations that involve children and adolescents, are inspired by films, TV series, and even cartoons. Increasingly, learners watch films that are violent in nature and, more often than not, the violent characters will be victorious. Learners will perceive violence as a 'cool' act and will want to imitate the character that they have seen. For example, if learners watch a movie and see a violent character getting his way, they will come to see violence as a solution, and regard that character as a hero. They may try to emulate that character in turn by becoming violent towards other learners.

The media can also serve as an inhibiting factor in the fight against violence in schools. Bester and Du Plessis (2010:226) argue that because of the media, teachers are reluctant to deal with or expose violence, as many schools are afraid they may end up on the front pages of newspapers. Teachers who do stand up against troublemakers are often regarded in the media as violators of children's rights. Sometimes the elevation of children's rights by the media defeats all attempts to fight school violence, since any form of discipline is regarded as abuse. Teachers have few or no alternative methods of disciplining unruly behaviour in their classrooms, and on the school premises.

Individual learners

Learners are the population most at risk in the school setting. Their actions can contribute to increasing school violence. Learners can be victims or perpetrators of school violence. If learners are not happy about their lives, either their social lives or their family lives, they will seek attention from their peers and usually become a bully or emotionally unstable. Let us look at the individual learner factors that are related to school violence:

- Irritability
- **Impulsivity**

impulsivity: prone to acting without thinking

- Low frustration tolerance
- Low empathy
- Poor satisfaction with life
- Desire to dominate others
- Negative attitude to authority.

Effects of school violence

School violence has a negative impact on learners' emotional development, social development, intellectual development, and the development of the learner as whole. Let us look at other effects of school violence on learners, according to Burton and Leoschut (2012:12):

- Both direct and indirect violence associated with school often results in truancy from school, as learners become too scared to attend, or try to avoid the school environment in an attempt to avoid the attendant violence.
- School violence often results in a decrease in educational performance as victims battle to focus on content and on their school work in general.
- Depression and fatigue, two other common results of violence, can, in turn, further impact negatively on school performance.
- Those who are victimised at a young age are at greater risk of themselves engaging in violent and anti-social behaviour as they get older.
- School violence can also erode the ability of victims to form healthy, pro-social, and trusting relationships with peers and adults.
- Exposure to violence can reinforce the message that violence is the most appropriate way of resolving conflict and instilling discipline – messages that are internalised and acted upon as the young person grows into adulthood.
- Violence at school can erode young people's sense of hope and optimism in their future and, consequently, their ability to cope with any adversity and difficulties they may face growing up in a social and economic environment that is, at best, challenging.

Let us now turn to the consequences of school-based violence, as shown in summary in the following table.

Table 8.1: Consequences of school-based violence

Psychological impact	<ul><li>depression</li><li>poor self-esteem</li><li>feelings of isolation</li><li>fear</li><li>humiliation</li><li>developing an aversion to school</li></ul>

Learning problems	• limited concentration span • serious numeracy and literacy problems • inability to handle class assignments • poor performance in the classroom • high absentee and dropout rates • being unmotivated to succeed in school, and life in general
Physical effects	• scars • unexplained bruising and wounds • ill health and pains
Emotional effects	• trauma • suicidal thoughts • overwhelming sadness • depression • fatigue
Social	• problems in adulthood, such as lack of trust • unhealthy relationships

Strategies to manage school violence

School violence can be prevented: schools are in the best position to identify violent behaviour among learners early, and to implement prevention strategies that could benefit the communities in which learners live. The old adage "prevention is better than cure" is relevant in the fight against school violence. However, prevention of school violence is not an individual effort; different stakeholders need to work together. School violence is the result of multiple factors, so multiple strategies should be used to address individual, relationship, community, and societal issues that influence the likelihood of school violence. A number of good and promising programmes have been suggested by researchers nationally and internationally about what works, and what does not work, in the prevention of school violence. For example, SACE (2011) suggested counselling services for learners, forming community structures, and teacher training programmes in dealing with school violence. However, as Burton and Leoschut (2012:104) mention, there is little rigorous evaluation, and even less dissemination of the successes and lessons learned. Let us examine how different levels and different stakeholders can integrate their contributions, and participate in preventing violence in schools, as illustrated in the following table.

Table 8.2: Involvement of different stake holders in school violence prevention

Stakeholders/ levels	Actions	Benefit
Teachers	• Model non-violent behaviour and attitudes • Show love, support and care towards learners who have experienced violence • Involvement in continuous professional development programmes that aim to assist them in dealing with school violence • Discuss children's academic progress with their parents. • Also contact parents when learners do something good, not only when there is a problem.	• Promotes youth's sense of well-being; promotes a positive school climate • Learners will feel comfortable talking to them about violence-related issues • Builds a healthy relationship between teachers and learners • Teachers will be observant and respond to learner needs before they result in unhealthy behaviours.

Stakeholders/ levels	Actions	Benefit
Parents	• Parents' are involved in their children's academic and social lives • Respond positively to meetings organised by teachers and the school • Participate in their children's sporting activities • Parents are involved in drawing up the school's mission and vision	• Improves communication between the school and parents • Leads to improved learner performance • Creates a nurturing environment that enhance participation • Fosters better classroom behaviour among learners • Increases support of schools • Improves school attendance among learners • Improves learners' emotional well-being • Parents also experience feelings of ownership and are committed to supporting the school's vision and mission
School governing bodies (SGBs)	• Ensure that the school physical environment is safe • Create a warm and welcoming school environment • Maintain school buildings • Develop violence reporting mechanisms to respond to learners' concerns and reports of violence • Draft a school safety plan	• Contributes to a positive school climate • Learners will feel safe and protected
Government officials/ Department of Education	• Support effective classroom management • Promote cooperative learning • Provide teachers with training and support to help them meet the diverse needs of their learners • Make available counselling for violence victims and perpetrators • Organise parenting classes for parents • Curriculum should include conflict management strategies	• Teachers will feel supported • Teachers will deal with school violence more efficiently and effectively • Both victims and perpetrators will feel supported • Learners will be empowered to deal with school violence • Learners will avoid fights and learn to solve problems • Promotes good personal, intrapersonal, and interpersonal skills among learners
Community	• Provide youth with more structured and supervised after-school activities such as mentoring programmes or recreational activities • Organise awareness workshops • Address social norms	• Increases monitoring and healthy skills development • Gives learners a constructive alternative to unhealthy behaviours and gang involvement • Empowers learners to deal with violence effectively • Promotes strong educational growth
Learners	• Report violence • Provide information about weapons being brought into the school • Encourage other learners to seek professional help • Support one another	• Improves learners' social and problem-solving skills • Builds positive peer and teacher relationships • Know how to appropriately and safely intervene to stop violent episodes between peers • Take responsibility for their wellbeing and actions

Stop and reflect

Think of other stakeholders, such as school managers and NGOs, and decide on their roles, and the benefit their involvement will bring in preventing and reducing violence in schools. Do some research on at least one local programme aimed at addressing school violence. Describe its aims and strategies.

It is evident that learners' experience violence in their schools, and this affects them profoundly. School violence impacts negatively on our learners and their development. As teachers, possibly parents, and community members, we have a joint responsibility to address school violence in whatever way we can. Let us look at some ideas from learners themselves.

 Stop and reflect

Meet four learners in Tshego's school who give their views on what can be done to make the school safe, and especially, prevent violence in schools.

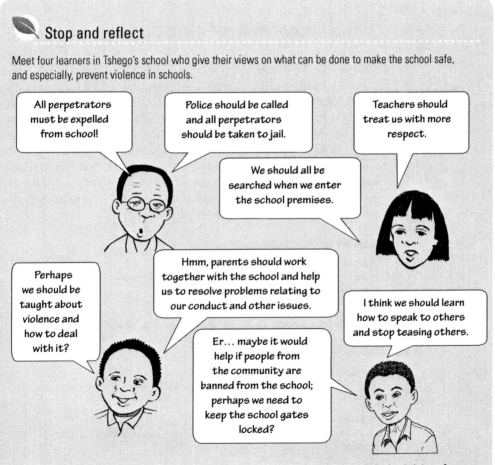

1 What do you think of their views? Do you think their ideas will solve the problem of school violence?
2 Think about what you can do to prevent violence in your school (or your future school). Suggest some measures that have not been mentioned already.

Now read the following case study about Mpho and Lerato.

 CASE STUDY 2

The learners in a Grade 3 class are painting. Mpho is using a large paintbrush, but wants a smaller one to finish her work. Lerato is also using a large paintbrush, but has a smaller one in front of her that she is not using. When Mpho asks her for the smaller brush, Lerato tells her she has to wait until she (Lerato) is finished with her painting. When she turns around, Lerato accidentally touches Mpho's skirt with her paintbrush and leaves a paint stain. Mpho gets upset and pours water on Lerato's picture.

Imagine you are the teacher in this classroom. Make notes about the following:
- How does Mpho feel?
- How does Lerato feel?
- How can this situation be resolved?
- How could this situation be prevented in future?

Conflict management and the curriculum

Conflict management is an important skill that both learners and teachers need to be taught. It is imperative that our school curriculum should include conflict management strategies. Life Orientation, as a compulsory subject that all learners take throughout their schooling in South Africa, presents many opportunities for developing life and conflict resolution skills, as well as personal and anger management skills. These will be a combination of intrapersonal and interpersonal skills. Intrapersonal skills refer to self-awareness, managing feelings, and motivation, whereas interpersonal skills include empathy and social skills. The important skills that are needed in conflict management are demonstrated in the table below.

Table 8.3: Skills for conflict management

Self-awareness
Recognising and identifying feelings; defining the problem ("I am feeling X because…"); recognising and taking responsibility where appropriate.

Empathy
Recognising and identifying feelings that other parties may be experiencing; ability to understand why the other person may have acted as they did; understanding the need for any agreed outcome to be of mutual benefit or fair to all parties

Social skills
Good listening skills; assertiveness skills when needed; knowing how to apologise, and how to accept an apology

Managing feelings
Being able to calm down when angry; waiting your turn – not interrupting (i.e. deferring gratification)

Motivation
Wanting to solve the conflict (not have an excuse to make the other person feel bad, etc.); identifying what you want to happen (goal-setting); identifying a plan to achieve this with another person; following the plan, overcoming obstacles, and so on.

Summary of discussion

School violence robs our children of their right to dignity, and the right to education. Learners are traumatised throughout their school years because of the unsafe conditions at schools. It follows most urgently that something should be done to prevent and eradicate school violence. Learners spend most of their time at school, so schools can and must play a critical role in addressing the ills of society, since learners are also members of that society. Consequently, schools need to be active in teaching moral behaviour and values. It has been established that school violence is the result of the interaction of many factors, and therefore should be addressed on multiple levels, such as school, home, and community. Prevention methods should be based on local priorities and draw on the experiences and contribution of everyone within the school body; that is, learners, parents, teachers, and other stakeholders.

The collaboration and involvement of different stakeholders will ensure that strategies and measures are relevant, appropriate, will serve the needs of the learners, and importantly, will achieve the desired outcomes. When there is a collaborative effort among different stakeholders, violence in schools can be prevented and reduced, and schools can become safer places to foster learners' development. In addition, the school curriculum can be influential in improving the ethos of non-violence in the school. This implies that the curriculum must be relevant: it must address the needs of learners and the community at large.

It is the purpose of the curriculum to prepare learners for the challenges that they currently face, and those that they may face in future. In the South African context, Life Orientation, as a compulsory subject for learners, can also be used to teach learners about conflict resolution and violence prevention. Generally, schools need to create a supportive environment that gives learners the opportunity to feel a sense of belonging and safety.

Closing activities

1. Explain 'school violence' in your own words.
2. Name and discuss three factors that contribute to school violence
3. List three forms of school violence, with examples of each (at least two to three examples).
4. Discuss the role that can be played by the following in addressing the issue of violence in schools:
   a) Community
   b) Teachers
   c) Learners
   d) Parents.

5. For the curriculum to be relevant in addressing issues of violence in schools what do you think should be included in that curriculum? Expand your response into a one-page proposal for curriculum inclusion, suggesting where and how it might be incorporated.
6. Reflect on a recent conflict situation that you have witnessed in your school. Describe the skills that you think are needed in resolving this conflict peacefully. Also suggest who the role players would be in the conflict resolution.

References

Asbeh, K.A. 2010. The phenomenon of school violence among learners in the education system. *Jadal.* 6:1–3.

Bandura, A. 1977. *Social learning theory.* Englewood Cliffs: Prentice Hall.

Barnes, K. Brynard, S. & De Wet, C. 2012. The influence of school culture and school culture on violence in schools of the Eastern Cape Province. *South African Journal of Education.* 32: 69–82.

Bester, S & Du Plessis, A. 2010.Exploring a secondary school educator's experiences of school violence: a case study. *South African Journal of Education.* 30:203–229

Burton, P. 2008. *Merchants, skollies and stones: Experiences of school violence in South Africa.* Cape Town: Centre for Justice and Crime Prevention.

Burton, P. & Leoschut, L. 2013. *School violence in South Africa: Results of the 2012 National School Violence Study.* Cape Town: Centre for Justice and Crime Prevention.

Cohen, J. 2010. *Measuring and improving school climate: A school improvement strategy that supports the whole child and the whole community.* New York (NY): The Centre for Social and Emotional Education.

Defour, D. 2005. Gender and ethnicity issues in school violence. In F. Denmark, H.H. Krauss, R.W. Wesner, E. Midlarsky & U.P. Gielen (Eds). *Violence in schools: Cross-national and cross-cultural perspectives.* New York (NY): Springer Science and Business Media.

De Wet, C. 2006. Free State educators' experiences and recognition of bullying at schools. *South African Journal of Education.* 26(1):61–73.

Estévez, E., Jiménez, T. & Musitu, G. 2008. Violence and victimization at school in adolescence. In D.H. Molina (Ed). *School psychology: 21st century issues and challenges.* New York (NY): Nova Publishers.

Flores, R.L. 2005. Developmental aspects of school violence: a contextualized approach. In F. Denmark, H.H. Krauss, R.W. Wesner, E. Midlarsky & U.P. Gielen (Eds). *Violence in schools: Cross-national and cross-cultural perspectives*. New York (NY): Springer Science and Business Media.

Jacobs, M., Vakalisa, N.C.G. & Gawe, N. 2011. *Teaching-learning dynamics*. Cape Town: Pearson.

Le Roux, C. & Mokhele, P.R. 2011. The persistence of violence South Africa's schools: In search of solutions. *Africa Education Review*. 8(2):318–335.

Mncube, V. & Harber, C. 2013. *The dynamics of violence in South African Schools: Report 2012*. Pretoria: Unisa Press.

Peterson, R.L. & Skiba, R. 2000. Creating school climate that prevent school violence. *Preventing School Failure*, 4(3):122–129.

Prinsloo, L.J. 2005. How safe are South African schools? *South African Journal of Education*. 25(1):5–10.

Republic of South Africa. 1996. *Constitution of the Republic of South Africa, 1996*. Pretoria: Government Printers.

Republic of South Africa. 1996. *South African Schools Act, No. 84 of 1996*. Pretoria: Government Printers.

Republic of South Africa. 1998. *Employment of Educators Act, No. 76 of 1998*. Pretoria: Government Printers.

Skiba, R., Simmons, A.B., Peterson, R., McKelvey, J., Forde, S. & Gallini, S. 2004. Beyond guns, drugs and gangs: The structure of student perceptions of school safety. *Journal of School Violence*. 3:149–171.

South African Council of Educators. 2011. *School-based violence report: An overview of school-based violence in South Africa*. Pretoria: Government Printers.

Sowetan. 2013. *Bad state: A chair, desk for every pupil, Motshekga*. 7 August. p. 4.

Taole, M. Joyce. 2013. School violence: Re-imagining schools as 'safe havens'. *Journal of Social Sciences*. 37(3):249–258.

The Sunday Times. 2012. *Violence in schools*. 5 September. p. 3.

Welsh, W.N. 2000. The effects of school climate on school disorder. *Annals, AAPSS*. 567:88–107.

Zulu, B.M., Urbani G. & Van der Merwe, A. 2004. Violence as an impediment to a culture of teaching and learning in some South African schools. *South African Journal of Education*. 24(2):170–175.

9

Poverty and education in post-democratic South Africa

Vussy Nkonyane

Chapter overview

The dilemma we face in South Africa is high poverty levels and the increasing gap between the haves and have-nots. Today, almost half of South Africans are living below the poverty line, surviving on just over R570 a month – an improvement from 1993, where this was the case for the majority of the population. Poverty has far-reaching effects on the physical, emotional, cognitive, psychological, and social lives of children. The educational implications of this problem on children form the main theme of this chapter. We explore and describe the origins of poverty in South Africa and Africa, particularly as a background to rural poverty. We will also define the different meanings of poverty and explain how poverty impacts children's education. In particular, we discuss how poverty excludes poor children from education in the inclusive context, in South Africa. We explore possible ways to deal with the scourge of poverty and ask you to relate each way to your own teaching context.

Learning outcomes

By the end of this chapter you should be able to:
- Describe the origins of poverty in South Africa and the African continent.
- Define the different meanings of poverty and relate each to your context.
- Reflect on the effects of poverty on the physical, emotional, cognitive, psychological and social lives of children.
- Discuss the factors of poverty and their educational implications on children, especially in rural areas.
- Discuss how poverty excludes poor children from education in the inclusive context, in South Africa and elsewhere.

Read the following short case study in which a teacher in a poverty-stricken school feels his situation is so bad that he cannot wait to leave or retire.

 CASE STUDY 3

Tebogo Mphephethe, with an Honours degree in Mathematics, teaches Natural Sciences and Mathematics in an impoverished secondary school in a rural part of the Free State. He has been teaching for 14 years and believes he is a good teacher. Yet he gets frustrated in his classes and falls into despair at least once a week. His complaints about his learners are common among many who teach economically disadvantaged learners: chronic late-coming and absenteeism, lack of motivation and low achievement, and generally inappropriate behaviour. Mr Mphephethe complains that his learners are unruly, use profanity, and disrespect others. "It's like going to war every day," he says. He also knows that many of his learners will not complete even the basic education programme, but will instead drop out. Mr Mphephethe wonders why he is wasting his time.

The recurring thought that goes through his mind is "Retirement is only six years away." To avoid taking early retirement, he has resolved to leave this school and to try and move to a better one, perhaps in an urban area.

What Mr Mphephethe is facing is the common experience of the effects of poverty in the classroom, felt by many teachers throughout South Africa, and indeed the continent. Poverty, and what can be done about it, is what this chapter seeks to explore and address.

Contextualising poverty in South Africa and Africa

Endemic and widespread poverty continues to disfigure the face of our country. It will always be impossible for us to say that we have fully restored the dignity of all our people as long as this situation persists. For this reason, the struggle to eradicate poverty has been and will continue to be a central part of the national effort to build the new South Africa (Mbeki, 2004).

Ten years after the former president of South Africa, Thabo Mbeki, said these words at his inauguration, they are even more relevant today than they were in 2004. Then, he was reflecting on immediate post-apartheid conditions in the country. Although the country is no longer segregated according to race, the effects of apartheid's race-based systems remain. Most of the poor people in the country are not white, and most middle- and upper-class people are. This means that the effects of poverty are felt by particular race groups, especially black people.

South Africa not only has high levels of poverty, but also high levels of inequality (Smith & Barrett, 2011). This means that there is extreme wealth on the one hand, and extreme poverty on the other. We see this clearly in the metropolitan areas, like Cape Town and Johannesburg. In fact, South Africa is the most unequal society in the world (Oxfam, 2013). This inequality can also be seen in our education system, where former model C schools in the cities perform far better than township or rural schools (Aliber, 2003).

The picture painted here is also true for the continent, with extremes of income distribution characterised by generally better-resourced metropolitan areas and vast, neglected, poverty-stricken rural areas. In 2009 it was reported that the population of Africa had exceeded one billion for the first time. A year later, figures claimed that numbers on the continent had reached 1,022,234,000. These statistics make Africa the second most populous continent on the planet, after Asia (World Bank, 1995). Such an increase in the population of a continent, which is mostly underdeveloped or partly developing, poses serious challenges for both the natural and financial resources of its different countries. The negative impact of this high population—low development case is exacerbated on a continent that in the main depends on international investment for its economic development. The problem is sometimes complicated by the prevalence of political instabilities and civil wars which deter investors from investing in African countries. Sometimes corruption, perceived and real, sends wrong messages to possible investors. All these factors ultimately make it difficult for our continent to generate more income to fight against poverty.

Poverty, as we have said, is most evident in rural African communities, with high unemployment and low levels of education. More than 70 per cent of the African continent's poor people live in rural areas and depend on agriculture for food and livelihood, yet development assistance to agriculture is decreasing (Morrisson, 2002; Londoño, 1996). Added to the lack of agricultural development, specific natural disasters such as long periods of drought, unexpected severe weather patterns like storms, flooding and heavy hailstorms due to global warming, and plant-destroying pests and diseases, undermine any attempt at supporting the development of subsistence farming for food production. The 2008–2009 world economic meltdown has compounded the decline of the continent's economy. As a result, most African economies have been shedding jobs instead of creating them. In addition, post-colonialism has not always brought freedom and peace as envisaged during the liberation struggles but, in most instances, has been accompanied by instability, turmoil, and economic collapse through civil wars. All this has dragged the continent further down into the abyss of poverty.

Poverty in many rural areas of Africa has its roots in the colonial system, and the policies and institutional restraints that it imposed on indigenous people (Levin, 2004). Colonialism depended on a constant supply of cheap labour for its sustainability. As towns and cities developed around industries under colonialism, especially in South Africa, the indigenous people were dispossessed of their land on which they depended for food production and cattle grazing (by e.g. the Natives Land Act, No. 27 of 1913). Many were forced to work for a pittance in the cities and mines as migrant workers. This resulted in a system with one group owning the wealth and the other living under extreme poverty. In recent post-colonial decades, economic policies and institutional structures have been modified to close the income gap. However, structural adjustments have dismantled existing rural systems, but have not always built new ones. In many transitional economies, the rural situation is marked by continuing **stagnation**, poor production, low incomes, and the increasing vulnerability of poor people. Lack of access to markets is a problem for many small-scale enterprises in Africa. The rural population is poorly organised and often isolated, beyond the reach of social safety nets and poverty programmes (Hanushek & Kimko, 2000). Increasingly, government policies and investment in poverty reduction tend to favour urban over rural areas. This state of affairs has resulted in the donor-dependent syndrome in Africa, making it difficult for all countries on the continent to do away with the 'third world' or 'underdeveloped world' status (Hanushek & Wößmann, 2007).

The problem of rural poverty in Africa has been worsened by HIV and AIDS which has ravaged stable family units and destroyed well-established support systems within these families. In the traditional

stagnation: a term in economics that describes a situation when there is no growth or development happening

African culture of communality there were no single-parent or child-headed families, something which is common now. HIV and AIDS has put an unbearable strain on poor rural households, where labour is the primary income-earning asset. It is currently estimated that about two-thirds of the 34 million people in the world with HIV and AIDS live on the African continent (Ogunbudede, 2004).

Stop and reflect

Do any of the observations made in 'contextualising poverty' strike you particularly? What are your views about poverty affecting rural people more than urban people? Why is there a difference between rural and urban poverty, if there is any? Write your own response (one page) and then swap with another student and read theirs.

The meaning of poverty

Poverty can be defined in different ways, such as a lack of income or failure to access opportunities or acquire capabilities. It "can be chronic or temporary, is sometimes closely associated with inequality, and is often correlated with vulnerabilities, underdevelopment and economic exclusion" (Mbuli, 2008:14). It is therefore not surprising to find that the question 'What does it mean to be poor?' evokes different responses from one person to another. Furthermore, O'Boyle (1999) argues that ideas about poverty evoke different responses because each person's answer is a reflection of a personal value system. According to Alcock (1997), this emphasises the fact that poverty is a contested problem. However, deciding on a definition for the purposes of this chapter is vital because such a definition serves as a platform from which poverty in South Africa can be examined, and interventions to reduce its effects determined.

According to the United Nations (1996), poverty is fundamentally a denial of choices and opportunities, a violation of human dignity. Poverty means a lack of the basic capacity to participate effectively in society. It means not having enough to food and clothing in a family; not having a school or clinic to go to; not having the land on which to grow one's food; or a job to earn one's living; and not having access to credit. It means insecurity, powerlessness, and exclusion of individuals, households, and communities. It means vulnerability to violence, and it often implies living in marginal or **fragile environments**, without access to clean water or sanitation. Poverty is pronounced deprivation in wellbeing, and comprises many dimensions. It includes low incomes and the inability to acquire the basic goods and services necessary for survival with dignity. Poverty also encompasses low levels of health and education, poor access to clean water and sanitation, inadequate physical security, lack of voice, and insufficient capacity and opportunity to better one's life.

fragile environment: in this case, a place or community that is in constant danger from, for example, the elements (rain and flooding, extreme temperatures, etc.), or fires, or even removal by local authorities; typically, it is an informal settlement, or 'squatter' camp.

So *economic aspects of poverty* focus on material needs, typically including the necessities of daily living, such as food, clothing, shelter, and safe drinking water. Poverty, in this sense, may be understood as a condition in which a person or community is lacking in the basic needs for a minimum standard of wellbeing and survival, particularly as a result of constant lack of income.

Turning to the *social aspects of poverty*, analysis links conditions of scarcity to many other things, like the distribution of resources and power in a society. Such analysis recognises that poverty may be a function of the diminished capability of people to live the kinds of lives they want to live and value. The social aspects of poverty may include lack of access to information, education, health care, or political power. Poverty may also be understood as an aspect of unequal social status and inequitable social relationships, experienced as social exclusion, dependency, and diminished capacity to participate, or to develop meaningful connections with other people in society. Such social exclusion can be reduced through strengthened connections with the **mainstream**, such as through the provision of care and support to those who are experiencing poverty. The provision of education is recognised as an especially significant means of strengthening connections with the mainstream.

> **mainstream:** the normal course of human ideas, values, activities, and developments in society

Stop and reflect

What does it mean that 'poverty is a contested problem'? Do you identify with any of the suggested meanings described earlier? Which ones, and why? Write your response to these questions as a journal entry in which you reflect your own ideas and experience.

Dimensions of poverty

According to Bourguignon & Pereira da Silva (2003), the concepts of *absolute* and *relative poverty* are not exclusive, but are aimed at describing and analysing different issues related to poverty. They simply describe different conditions and may, in some instances, call for different policies. Physical or absolute poverty is about mere survival, which is the capacity to buy food and all the goods necessary for the fulfilment of basic physical needs. Relative poverty, or social deprivation, is about not being like others, being marginalised from participation in all the normal opportunities of society, like education, health care, employment. If physical poverty is very widespread in a country, as is the case in the poorest developing countries, **growth**-enhancing policies must be given high priority. If physical poverty is less important, but if social poverty – and therefore 'social exclusion' – is found to be excessive, then **redistribution** policies, or possibly growth and redistribution policies, are called for.

> **growth:** in economics, growth is a measure of a country's economic expansion and development over a period of time, usually a year
>
> **redistribution:** a plan to address economic inequities through, for example, taxes, land ownership, social grants, etc.

Absolute poverty would correspond to a situation where an individual would remain permanently, or at least for a very long time, below some physical poverty line. This might be for two reasons: limited income mobility and slow economic growth, making it more difficult for poor people to cross the poverty line. It has been shown that such defining absolute poverty, in terms of duration – i.e. how many people are below the poverty line and for how long – is not separate from the initial importance of relative deprivation, or more generally, of inequality (Kakwani, 1993; Chen & Ravallion, 1997). In other words, when people are poor over a long period, they are also usually disempowered, and vice versa.

Reviewing what we know

Let us review the definitions of poverty:

- Relative poverty is seen as poverty that is partly determined by the society in which a person lives. Someone, who may not be regarded as poor in Bangladesh, may (with the same financial resources) be considered poor in Sweden (Van der Berg, 1999).
- Absolute poverty is the absence of financial resources required to maintain a certain minimum standard of living. For example, an absolute poverty line can be set, based on factors such as the financial resources needed for the most basic needs, or the income level required to purchase basic food needs (Fields, 2000; Deaton, 1997). Such poverty lines need to be adjusted for inflation if they are to be used at different time points. A poverty line commonly used by the World Bank for making international comparisons is US$1 per person per day, or sometimes, US$2 per person per day. This kind of absolute poverty line provides a fixed yardstick against which to measure change, for example, to see whether a country is making any progress in reducing poverty, or to compare several countries, or several regions.

Measurement of poverty

For the sake of being able to measure poverty along its many dimensions, Morrisson (2002) proposes some further operational definitions of deprivation of the basic human needs, especially for youth:

- *Food deprivation*: where body mass index (BMI) is 18.5 or below (i.e. underweight).
- *Water deprivation*: access only to unimproved water sources such as open wells, open springs, or surface water, or having to walk for more than 15 minutes to a water source (30 minutes round trip).
- *Deprivation of sanitation facilities*: access only to unimproved sanitation facilities, e.g. poor flush latrines; covered pit latrines; open pit latrines; and buckets; or no access to a toilet of any kind.
- *Health deprivation*: women who do not receive treatment for a recent serious illness, or who do not receive the minimum standard of antenatal care from a person trained in midwifery; and men and women who do not know that a healthy person can transmit HIV,

or who do not know that using a condom during sex can prevent HIV transmission.
- *Shelter deprivation*: living in dwellings with three or more people per room (overcrowding) or in a house with no flooring (e.g. a mud floor) or inadequate roofing (e.g. natural roofing materials).
- *Education deprivation*: youth who do not complete primary school, or who are illiterate.
- *Information deprivation*: no access to a radio or television (i.e. broadcast media) at home.

Stop and reflect

It is not always true that if a person suffers from one of the above deprivations of basic human needs, she is poor. But a combination of most, if not all of these, can indicate poverty. Choose an individual or community you know and use these factors as proof of the poverty of the individual or community. Write your analysis in table form, giving examples for the individual or community you have chosen.

The demographics of poverty (who, where and how?)

Having discussed how we define and measure poverty in general, in this section we now try to provide an overview of the extent and distribution of poverty in South Africa. So far, research is not unanimous on crude estimates of the extent of poverty in South Africa. According to Ntuli (2008), estimates of the prevalence of poverty in South Africa range from 45 per cent to 57 per cent, depending on the poverty line that has been used (StatsSA, 2000; UNDP, 2003; May, 2000; Woolard & Leibbrandt, 2001; Taylor Committee, 2002). What is apparent from these various studies is that poverty in South Africa includes rural, regional, race, age, gender, literacy, and unemployment dimensions. In addition, the poor tend to live in large households (with many dependents), and usually have inadequate access to basic services.

Where are the poor in South Africa?
According to Mbuli (2008), poverty in South Africa has strong rural and regional dimensions.
- *Poverty in South Africa's rural areas*. In South Africa, the majority of people living in rural areas are poor, and the majority of the poor live in rural areas. (May, 2000).
- *Poverty in South Africa's nine provinces*. A wide range of evidence shows that poverty is unevenly distributed among South Africa's nine provinces. For example, the 2003 UN Human Development Report found that, with the exception of Gauteng and the Western Cape, over half the population in all remaining provinces live in

poverty. The highest poverty rates are in the Eastern Cape and Limpopo Provinces (Mbuli, 2008:4).

Who are the poor in South Africa?

Post-apartheid South Africa continues to show a persistent correlation between poverty and the following factors:

- *Poverty and race in South Africa.* Poverty in South Africa has a strong racial dimension. Even though after democracy whites also became exposed to poverty, May (1998) argues that poverty is still concentrated mainly among blacks.
- *Poverty and age in South Africa.* Many of the people who are involved in violent service delivery demonstrations in the townships are young people, often of school-going age. Because of their reliance on adults for the provision of basic needs, the impact of poverty is greatest on youth and adolescents.
- *Poverty and gender in South Africa.* Poverty in South Africa also has a strong gender dimension. Evidence shows that the poverty rate among females tends to be considerably higher than that among males. For example, May's 1998 report showed that the poverty rate among female-headed households was 60 per cent, while it was 31 per cent among male-headed households (Mbuli, 2008).
- *Poverty and low levels of education in South Africa.* According to Van der Berg (2008) there is a very strong correlation between level of education and standard of living in South Africa (which you will read about further, later in this chapter).
- *Poverty and unemployment in South Africa.* Poverty and unemployment are also closely related in South Africa (Fleisch, 2008), forming a vicious cycle which locks people in inter-generational poverty (which you will read about further in the following chapter).

Factors contributing to low income and poverty in rural areas

Mbuli (2008) highlights a number of factors that might explain why poverty is higher in rural areas than in urban areas, and those worth mentioning include the following:

- *Lack of resources, technological development and employment opportunity.* Rural areas are heavily dependent on primary economic activities like agricultural production, forestry, and small-scale mining production. All these activities can only absorb a certain number of people for employment. While they are generally labour-intensive, no specific high-level or technological skills are needed to be employed in this area. This explains why incomes are so low in these activities, leaving the comparatively few people working in them without hope of making a decent living from their employment. This keeps them trapped in poverty even though they are employed, and without access to technological development.

- *Urban bias.* The apartheid economy was based on the ideology of separate development. Under this policy, black people were pushed away from the fertile land they had occupied and forced into semi-arid areas where it was difficult to practise productive farming. Under apartheid, towns and cities became industrialised, benefiting from infrastructural development, while the rural areas were left in desolate conditions on the periphery of the country's economy. All the best facilities were therefore located in the urban areas. Under such structural inequality, the urban centres had higher average incomes as compared with the lower income averages of rural areas. The only African people who benefited from this arrangement were those who worked in the cities and lived in urban townships.
- *Vulnerability to natural disasters.* Rural areas depend on farming for employment and survival. Natural disasters such as drought or flooding tend to affect rural areas more severely than urban areas. With the commercialisation of farming, less human labour is needed to carry out the same jobs on farms. This has resulted in a large number of people losing jobs and their livelihood. Subsistence farming and small-scale stock farming are also affected adversely by natural disasters, along with a lack of investment, and low development. This pushes rural communities further down into the pit of poverty from which it is not easy to escape.
- *Lack of access to basic services.* Government is struggling to provide basic services like piped water, sanitation, electricity, and refuse removal to poor rural communities. Many people are unemployed and cannot afford to pay for these services, as they come at a price. Generally, mainly urban areas benefit from service delivery since more people can make the required payment. But the current growing unemployment rates around the country, even in urban areas, have seen many community protests taking place in demand of service delivery. Health facilities exist but suffer from a shortage of skilled human resources. Given the choice, highly qualified doctors and nurses prefer to work in towns and bigger cities for the better quality of life and access to amenities. The rural areas remain critically under-served by adequate health care provision.

 Stop and reflect

How can you accommodate the different factors of poverty in your classroom teaching? Do you think these factors have a role in the exclusion of affected communities from education? Explain your answer by suggesting what a teacher needs to look out for as a sign of deprivation amongst her learners. Write your answer as a short set of guidelines to teachers on what to look for, and how to respond.

The link between poverty and disease

According to Van der Berg (2008), the academic achievement differential between rich and poor schools, and between those in large cities and isolated rural areas in South Africa, is extremely marked. This view is supported by Fleisch (2008), who argues that poor health in children is one of the major causes of low school achievement. Fleisch draws a relationship between poor health in children with high levels of poverty. He concludes that in South Africa poor health in children is a marker of poverty. Poverty impacts on learning through chronic and acute ill-health. This happens at three levels: 1) prior to schooling, as shown in neurological damage to the baby during pregnancy because of the lack of antenatal care available to mothers; 2) in early childhood; and finally, 3) during the normal cycle of the school year, when both life-threatening diseases and common health problems go untreated. The collapse of the public health system, especially in some rural parts of South Africa, has left children of low socio-economic status without adequate health care, like immunisation programmes and developmental health checks. Low-income children are also less likely to receive dental care (Schultz, 1999) or regular eye checks. Poor parents cannot afford the exorbitant fees of private medical facilities, nor do they have medical aid for such.

 Stop and reflect

What is the relationship between poverty and disease? How does that relationship influence the education of learners? Describe the causal relationships in the form of a flow chart or cycle.

The impact of poverty on the South African schoolchild

Research has found that there is a high risk of educational underachievement for children who are from low-income housing circumstances (Spreen & Vally, 2006). This is often a process that begins in primary school for some less fortunate children. In South Africa, like the US educational system, as well as that in most other countries, instruction tends to be geared towards those students who come from more advantaged backgrounds (Londoño, 1996). As a result, poor children are at a higher risk than other children for retention in their grade, and even not completing their high school education (Londoño, ibid). In a study on attrition of learners from schools in the North West Province of South Africa by Mahlomaholo, Mamiala and Nkonyane (2010), it was found that a high percentage of dropouts consisted of black learners who come from poor backgrounds. There are many explanations for why learners tend to drop out of school, but one is the circumstances in which they attend school. Schools in poverty-stricken areas have specific conditions that hinder children from learning in a safe environment, let alone one that is conducive to inclusive learning. Researchers internationally have developed a name for areas like this: urban war zones, that is, poor, crime-laden districts in which deteriorated, violent, even war-like conditions, and under-funded, largely ineffective and unsafe schools promote inferior academic performance, including irregular attendance (by both learners and teachers), and disruptive or non-compliant classroom behaviour (Levin, 2004). In the local study of children in poorly resourced environments by Mahlomaholo et al., the risk factors are similar, such as juvenile delinquency rates, higher levels of teenage pregnancy, and economic dependency on their low-income or unemployed parents.

According to Schultz (1999), a home background of poverty often drastically affects children's chance of success in school. A child's home activities, preferences, and behaviour should align with the world of education, and when they do not, these learners are always at a disadvantage in the school, and most importantly, in the classroom. Poor children, as we have seen, have inadequate health care and this ultimately results in many absences from the academic programme during the year. Additionally, poor children are much more likely to suffer from hunger, fatigue, irritability, headaches, ear infections, flu and colds. These illnesses could potentially restrict a child's focus and concentration (Hanushek & Zhang, 2006) ultimately impacting on their school performance.

According to experts (Drukker, Kaplan, Feron & Van Os, 2003), many poor women and girls become victims of human trafficking, the most common form of which is prostitution, as a means of survival in economic desperation. Deterioration of living conditions can often compel children, especially girls, to abandon school in order to contribute to the family income, putting them at risk of being exploited, according to ECPAT International, an NGO designed to end the commercial sexual exploitation of children. For example, in Zimbabwe, a number of girls are turning to prostitution for food to survive because of the increasing poverty in their environment (Drukker, et al., 2003).

 Stop and reflect

What does poverty mean for children? How does a chronic lack of income influence children's day-to-day lives? Is it through inadequate nutrition, fewer learning experiences, instability of residence, lower quality of schools, exposure to environmental toxins, family violence, homelessness, dangerous streets; or reduced access to friends, services, recreational facilities, and, for adolescents, after-school jobs? Draw a table in which you chart the factors of poverty and their influence on children's lives. Provide an example for each factor.

Educational consequences of poverty in South Africa

There are many success stories about children who beat the odds and rise up out of poverty to become successful. Unfortunately, the 'failure stories' are less likely to be told, but statistics show that many children who are born in poverty are far more likely to become unemployed or under-employed adults. You have already learned that children who are born into less affluent homes are more likely to suffer from health-related problems, have more difficulties with reading and learning, and have higher dropout rates than children from upper- or middle-class circumstances. Let us look at some additional factors that affect the lives of poor children.

Children who come from poor families find themselves trapped in a vicious cycle from which it is very difficult to escape. These are the children who leave school early and fall into drugs, alcohol abuse, and crime. These young people do not have skills for employment, and end up in prison in many instances.

- *Early childhood:* A high-poverty environment can have a profound effect on a child's ability to learn. Poverty often leads people to anti-social activities like drug and alcohol abuse. The participation of a mother in such behaviour can affect the unborn child negatively. Children growing up in poverty sometimes suffer from malnutrition, leading to delayed mental development. Such a child may find it difficult to cope with learning in future and, in turn, develop a negative attitude towards schooling. If that is the case, it follows that the child leaves school earlier.
- *Literacy in poverty:* In South Africa, academic performance reflects the socio-geopolitics of the country. The lowest performing provinces rank high on poverty (Limpopo, Eastern Cape and Mpumalanga), while the high economic performers also score high on academic performance (Gauteng and Western Cape). The academic success of a child is determined by a number of factors, among which is parental support. Parents in poor environments are unable to support their children in their school work meaningfully. For this reason, children from low socio-economic environments have lower reading scores than their upper- and middle-class counterparts. One reason for their struggle with literacy is because many parents who are living in poverty also have difficulty reading. As a result, they do not have books in the home, and do not read to their children.
- *Truancy:* Without proper parental care, children in poverty are more prone to absenteeism from school than other children. They have more health problems and can only access public health institutions, which usually have inadequate resources to help them. Their poor attendance at school tends to compound their learning difficulties.
- *Dropout rates:* The study by Mahlomaholo, Mamiala and Nkonyane (2010) on learner attrition in the North West Province of South Africa found that dropping out of school was rife among lower

socio-economic class black learners. Their schools have fewer resources and less opportunity for advancement than many other rural and urban schools. In the same study it emerged that most teenage girls in poverty tend to engage in more risk-taking behaviours, such as early sexual activity, with resulting high teenage pregnancies. All of these factors increased teenage dropout rates, which contributes to the cycle of poverty.

 Stop and reflect

Under poverty, children become the primary victims of a vicious cycle of poverty. How can education be used to break this cycle? What can be done in order to reduce dropout rates of poor children from school? How can the involvement of parents from poor households in their children's school work be improved? Develop a set of guidelines for involving parents and caregivers.

Strategies to address poverty in schools in South Africa

In this section we turn to steps, programmes, and strategies that are being used, and can yet be used to address poverty. We look at what is being done for the poor, especially the poorest, but focus on what is and can be done in schools in rural areas.

Government-provided comprehensive healthcare plan and school feeding

Most learners from poor households cannot afford to pay medical fees. Government must provide free primary health care in all schools. Presently, there is a national dental care programme that is running effectively as part of the National Health Plan, but this needs to be expanded particularly to children in rural areas. Adequate health care is critical in the struggle against poverty to maintain a good quality of life, ensure adults are able to work and care for their families, and that children grow up healthy. If health care is unaffordable, an illness in the family can plunge a marginal family into crisis. Moreover, providing adequate health care for all is a critical element in building social trust and solidarity (Pretorius & Currin, 2010). Government has introduced a school feeding scheme policy in which a meal is supplied to public primary school learners who come to school hungry. This is important because for some learners this is the only meal that they have for the whole day. Some schools have even found it necessary to give two meals a day to very needy children.

Access to assets

Learners from poor social environments are likely to suffer from a lack of access to facilities like libraries, sports and recreational centres, which affects their academic performance. Access to services (assets), such as electricity and running water, provides economic and social stability, as well as a stronger basis for income generation (Pretorius & Currin, 2010). Current development programmes (both government- and non-government-funded) revolve around land, housing, and community infrastructure. As will be noted later in this chapter, a critical issue is to ensure that any form of land reform is linked more coherently to the creation of livelihoods for the poor. There is also a need to support those already on the land, or working the land, to enable them to improve their access to land, and to translate such access into more sustainable incomes (Smith & Barrett, 2011). Current housing programmes, such as converting the old single-sex urban hostels into family units, and giving title deeds to township house owners, while they have transferred assets on a huge scale to poor families, have not maximised their economic impact. There needs to be far greater empowerment of communities to enhance their assets through urban and rural infrastructure, and housing development.

Social cohesion towards inclusive education

Social cohesion, in our context, can be defined as the extent to which a society holds together, is united and functional, and provides an environment within which its citizens can flourish (Soudien, 2007). Clearly, the promotion of social cohesion, nation-building, and national identity remains firmly on the agenda of the South African government. Indications are that there have been increasing levels of social cohesion among South Africans since democracy in 1994. For instance, a recent Human Sciences Research Council (HSRC) social attitudes survey shows that South Africa's inherited historical **fault-lines** are declining. According to the survey, more than 60 per cent of South Africans reported that they did not feel at all discriminated against, as opposed to 27 per cent who said they sometimes felt discriminated against. Beyond this, the survey shows that across races, pride in being a South African remains high: 94 per cent for Africans, 84 per cent for Indians, 87 per cent for coloureds, and 75 per cent for whites. In total, 93 per cent are proud to be South African, and 83 per cent would rather be a citizen of South Africa than of any other country. The main issues that need attention in South Africa are social integration and reconciliation (Soudien, 2007).

Recognising the material and spiritual nature of social cohesion issues in South Africa, initiatives for improving social cohesion could be on two levels: the human development level that seeks to improve the living conditions of all citizens; and the nation-building level that seeks to promote pride in being South African, a sense of belonging, values, caring for one another, and solidarity among South

fault-line: a geological term that means a place in rock formations where breaks or displacement occur; here, it refers to issues which divide and disconnect people

Africans. Both levels are imperative in promoting inclusive education: where all people feel included, and their sense of belonging translates into care and pride in who they are.

The state has the responsibility to provide leadership in ensuring service delivery at all levels of government responsibility by helping create an appropriate environment for development (Lam, Ardington & Leibbrandt, 2011). Government has made considerable progress in transforming the state machinery and in improving policy coordination across local, provincial and national government spheres, but these initiatives need consolidation and oversight. Strong representative democratic institutions; in particular school governing bodies (SGBs) must create a democratic culture and environment where citizens (learners, parents and teachers) articulate and pursue their political views and ideals without fear of intimidation. According to Yamauchi (2005), the achievement of government's developmental objectives will largely be determined by the appropriateness of the institutional framework created by the Constitution and related laws. It also depends on harnessing all the networks through central coordination and leadership in ways that ensures that the many separate activities and interests become complementary to the developmental effort.

Economic development in rural and poorer areas

The tendency has been that urban areas generally benefit more from government programmes than the rural areas. The National Development Plan of 2011 (NDP) is a government blueprint for a future South Africa and a direct response to the issues that still beset our economy. It lays out the way in which this country must be developed in all aspects: economically, socially, politically, and other ways. A concern is that out of the 400 pages of this document, only 13 pages are dedicated to rural communities. This needs to change by focusing more effort and resources on promoting rural economic development. The following could and should be done if the situation to redress poverty, and especially educational opportunity, is faced seriously:

- Anti-poverty work must be integrated with broader urban and rural regeneration initiatives. Poor areas that suffer from the greatest disadvantage should be prioritised in the strategy. This requires the injection and maintenance of government investment within these areas. Anti-poverty policies should ensure that all government action on poverty addresses the differing needs of rural areas (Ntshoe, 2003; Saha, 1993; Carter & May, 2001)
- Economic development requires a pro-poor pattern of public expenditure in favour of the rural poor and the agricultural sector, that will produce a sustained and shared growth process. There should be concerted efforts on the part of government to facilitate building primary assets for the poor through measures such as equitable distribution of land, extensive public provision of free education, promotion of small-scale enterprises, and development

of rural infrastructure – roads, irrigation, agricultural support outposts, health clinics, etc.

- Land reform must be linked more coherently to the creation of livelihoods for the poor. This requires increased post-settlement support as well as an understanding of how to ensure that broad-based ownership or partnerships with private managers generate sustainable improvements in income for new farm owners.

- The most available resource in South Africa is land. Support for livelihood strategies for landed households in poor areas and for peri-urban households essentially requires a step-up in extension, marketing assistance, and production. Government should therefore establish support structures to give skills training and guidance on farming and land development to rural communities. This will reduce the problem of the flight of people from rural to urban areas in search of economic opportunities. With proper support, rural communities can make farming profitable, sustainable, and overcome poverty.

- It is true that farm workers are among the lowest paid workers in the country, and it is a common perception that their employers profit hugely from their labour. Farm worker organisations should be supported through the provision of service centres, in collaboration with labour unions, community and faith organisations, and non-governmental organisations. Attending school is currently compulsory but it should be enforced by law for all children of farm workers. School transport has to be provided for farm children who live far from schools.

- Smallholder schemes and broad-based ownership schemes, in both the former Bantustans and in commercial farm areas, are critical to rural employment creation and poverty eradication. The link between land reform, agrarian development, and poverty alleviation must be strengthened. Rural communities who were forced off their land for business purposes during apartheid, must be given opportunities to return to their land and work together with the present owners to benefit from it. In addition, there needs to be an increase in funding for smallholder support in agriculture, including both survival strategies and post-settlement support.

Human resource development – education

Education eradicates poverty

Initiatives to improve skills and employment opportunities are the most sensible way to tackle the problem of persistent poverty. Hanushek & Zhang (2006) agree that education can be the tool to eradicate poverty, by giving every child an equal opportunity of fulfilling their potential. Furthermore, we argue that government should provide children with food at school (feeding schemes) and institute more non-fee-paying schools, so that that it is individuals' skills and abilities, and not their parents' life circumstances that determine educational attainment. Educational disadvantage emerges very early in life – before primary school. Therefore, to tackle poverty and inequality, early childhood development (ECD) is a top priority, and that should be reflected in decisions about spending priorities. ECD should address the health, nutrition, psycho-social, and cognitive development needs of vulnerable children. Proper nutrition is critical for all learners' ability to learn and concentrate, but poor children especially should be the target of school feeding schemes.

Education and rural poverty

The most deprived communities generally have the worst educational outcomes. As deprivation has become more concentrated, the challenges facing schools in deprived areas, particularly the rural areas which are the focus of our discussion, have grown. There is a long trail of poor performance and low aspirations, as a quarter of children leave primary school without even basic literacy and numeracy skills (Ginsburg, Richter, Fleisch & Norris, 2011).

- Extra attention should be paid to educational opportunities for the poor, for females, and for other vulnerable social groups, such as AIDS orphans.
- Closer attention should be paid to the kinds of skills required to cope with constantly changing rural and other local labour markets. Education for rural people needs to include skills for diversified rural development and sustainability.
- Vocational agricultural secondary education should adjust to current and future rural development needs.
- Higher education should also adjust to new needs in rural development, and enable graduates and others to keep abreast of advances. These include offering teaching in areas such as natural resources management, and rural development with off-farm employment.
- Training has to be provided to rural areas to complement other support related to agricultural assistance.

Education and training

People with no qualifications and low skills are at high risk of a future of unemployment, or low-paid and insecure employment, and are twice as likely to be living in poverty. Improving the educational outcomes and aspirations of children and young people is the single most important factor in breaking generational cycles of poverty. Therefore, initiatives to improve skills and employment opportunities are probably the only sensible way to tackle the problem of persistent poverty (Spaull, 2013). Interventions need to focus on the retention of learners in the school system to complete their basic education, minimising early dropping out. Over and above this, initiatives aimed at supporting poor learners in school, and fostering their aspirations for post-school education and training should be developed.

Meeting basic needs – provision of basic services

Finally, while it has been a common thread through this chapter, any strategy to address poverty, especially rural poverty, must deliver the basics.

Establish targeted support system for the poor households

South Africa has developed an exceptionally well-organised system of social assistance grants, the most important of which are the state old-age pension, the disability grant (both of which had been existence for decades) and the child support grant, which was introduced in April, 1998 (Armstrong et al., 2008). Augmenting the social grants system, many public schools (in urban, township and rural areas) have been declared 'non-fee-paying schools'. This means that no child may be excluded from education because of an inability to pay school fees. Together with feeding schemes in schools, poor children are specifically targeted for retention by the education system.

While it is well established that many people are affected by poverty, local governments and metros must make it their business to know who their poor are. Municipalities should identify households in need, their specific needs, and then coordinate and support their access to services. They should monitor the progress of these households' indigent status through an indigent register. Services like a specific amount of free electricity and water can be allocated to poor people per month. They could also be exempted from making rubbish removal payments. This is the basic safety net of poor households. As their status changes or improves, poor households can be brought into the service payment system.

 Stop and reflect

A multi-pronged approach is needed for resolving the problem of poverty. Identify any two strategies that you think are critical in the alleviation of poverty and discuss in detail how they can be used for such a purpose.

Summary of discussion

South Africa not only has high levels of poverty, but also high levels of inequality. This means that there is extreme wealth on the one hand and extreme poverty on the other. Despite significant post-apartheid reform, the education system has been failing the poor who still have to overcome many more obstacles in order to succeed. The quality and duration of education a learner receives has a significant effect on his or her chances in life.

In this chapter, poverty is framed in both relative and absolute terms. A contextualised picture of poverty has been drawn by establishing the historical causes of poverty in South Africa and on the African continent, and specifically by looking into who the poor in South Africa are, and where they are found. How we measure poverty was discussed by identifying operational definitions of the deprivation of basic human needs for youth. Since poverty affects mostly rural populations, it was necessary to highlight the factors that contribute to low income and poverty in rural areas, and to the vulnerability of the poor to illness and disease, natural disasters, and general underdevelopment. We examined in detail how poverty has a very severe effect on children. It limits the access children have to educational opportunities, especially early childhood development. It increases their risk of dropping out early. It also undermines their chances of full participation in employment, as adults. Poverty results in unstable families with disempowered parents who fail to support their children. Finally, poverty compounds and recreates the vicious cycle that locks people into inter-generational poverty.

Education is understood as the most significant factor in breaking the cycle of poverty, but it depends on many other factors and support mechanisms. A range of interventions, initiatives and systems in South Africa – both proposed and ongoing – were discussed, focusing particularly on the rural poor. While such interventions as social grants, non-fee-paying schools, and school feeding schemes are necessary, it was made clear that these cannot close the inequality gap in South Africa, nor are they sustainable by themselves. Education that is truly inclusive, that delivers appropriately to the poor, and that is supported and extended on a number of fronts, is the only viable and sustainable way to eradicate poverty and improve children's life chances.

Closing activities

Self-reflection
1. Post 1994 has seen an influx of so-called township learners into the former model C schools in towns and cities. This might be because of the good results produced by the urban schools compared to their township or village counterparts. What are the possible causes of the differential academic performance between these two groups?

Practical applications
2. You have been appointed as the principal of a very dysfunctional and poorly performing high school in an informal settlement, with a high rate of unemployment among both parents and youth. Prepare a 3–4-page presentation to be delivered at a meeting where the community will be welcoming you as the school's principal. Remember, all the education stakeholders will be present.
3. Is it important to develop a culture of teaching and learning in the school described in Question 2? Why and how?

Analysis and consolidation
4. Write an essay (3–4 pages) about how the government should be using education in the empowerment of communities affected by poverty, and in the alleviation of poverty. Provide practical suggestions, not just policy statements, although you should acknowledge and refer to current initiatives. Include a reference list of sources consulted.
5. Discuss how, as a teacher, you can assist both parents or caregivers and learners from poor backgrounds to change their attitudes and see value in education as a means to escape from poverty.

References

Alcock, P. 1997. *Understanding poverty*. Basingstoke: Macmillan Press.

Aliber, M. 2003. Chronic poverty in South Africa: Incidence, causes and policies. *World Development*. 31(3):473–490.

Armstrong, P., Lekezwa, B. & Siebrits, K. 2008. Poverty in South Africa: A profile based on household surveys. *Stellenbosch Economic Working Papers*. Retrieved from: http://scholar.google.co.za on 11 May 2014.

Bourguignon, F. & Pereira da Silva, L.A (Eds). 2003. *The Impact of Economic Policies on Poverty and Income Distribution: Evaluation Techniques and Tools*. New York: Oxford University Press.

Carter, M.R. & May, J. 2001. One kind of freedom: Poverty dynamics in post-apartheid South Africa. *World Development*. 29(12):1987–2006.

Chen, S. & Ravallion, M. 2004. *How has the world's poorest fared since the early committee of inquiry into a comprehensive social security system (CICSSS)?* Baltimore: The Johns Hopkins University Press.

Deaton, A. 1997. *The Analysis of Household Surveys: A Microeconometric Approach to Development Policy*. Baltimore: The Johns Hopkins University Press.

Drukker, M., Kaplan, C., Feron, F. & Van Os, J. 2003. Children's health-related quality of life, neighbourhood socio-economic deprivation and social capital: A contextual analysis. *Social Science & Medicine*. 57(5):825–841.

Education policy: School feeding scheme. Retrieved from: http://www.etu.org.za/toolbox/docs/government/feeding.html on 10 April 2014.

Fields, G.S. 2000. *Poverty, inequality and development*. Cambridge: Cambridge University Press.

Fleisch, B. 2008. *Primary Education in Crisis*. Cape Town: Juta.

Ginsburg, C., Richter, L.M., Fleisch, B. & Norris, S.A. 2011. An Analysis of Association between Residential and School Mobility and Educational Outcomes in South African Urban Children: The birth to twenty cohort. *International Journal of Educational Development*. 31(3):213–222

Hanushek, E.A. & Wößmann, L. 2007. *The role of school improvement in economic development*. NBER Working Paper 12832. Cambridge: National Bureau of Economic Research.

Hanushek, E.A. & Zhang, L. 2006. *Quality-consistent estimates of international returns to skills*. NBER Working Paper 12664. Paris: Organisation for Economic Cooperation and Development.

Hanushek, E. & Kimko, D.D. 2000. Schooling, labour-force quality and the growth of nations. *American Economic Review*. 90(5):1184–1208.

Inhoe, K. & Plotnick, R. 2000. Do Children from Welfare Families Obtain Less Education? In Robert D. Plotnick. Discussion papers: Do Children from Welfare Families Obtain Less Education? 0(1217). University of Wisconsin, Madison: Institute for Research on Poverty.

Kakwani, N. 1993. Performance in Living Standards: An International Comparison. *Journal of Development Economics*. 41(2):307–36.

Lam, D., Ardington, C. & Leibbrandt, M. 2011. Schooling as a lottery: Racial differences in school advancement in urban South Africa. *Journal of Development Economics*. 95(2):121–136.

Levin, B. 2004. Poverty and inner-city education. *Horizons*. 7(2):45–50.

Londoño, J.L. 1996. *Poverty, inequality, and human capital development in Latin America*. Washington, D.C: World Bank.

Mahlomaholo, M.G., Mamiala, T. & Nkonyane, V.A. 2010. Unpublished Report on Attrition and African learner underrepresentation in the Grade 12 top 20 list of the North West Education Department in South Africa.

May, J. 1998. *Poverty and Inequality in South Africa*. Report prepared for the Office of the Executive Deputy President and the Inter-Ministerial Committee for Poverty and Inequality. Durban: Praxis

May, J. 2000. *Poverty and Inequality in South Africa: Meeting the Challenge*. Cape Town: David Philip.

Mbeki, T. 2004. Address by the President of South Africa on the occasion of his inauguration and the 10th Anniversary of Freedom, Pretoria, 27 April 2004. Retrieved from: http://www.dfa.gov.za/docs/speeches/2004/mbek0427.htm on 5 February 2014.

Mbuli, N.B. 2008. Poverty reduction strategies in South Africa. Unpublished Master's dissertation in Economics. Pretoria: Unisa.

Meth, C. & Dias, R. 2004. Increase in poverty in South Africa, 1999–2002. *Development Southern Africa*. 21(1):59–85.

Morrisson, C. 2002. *Health, education and poverty reduction*. Policy Brief No. 19, OECD Development Centre. Paris: Organisation for Economic Cooperation and Development.

National Development Plan. 2011. *Vision for 2030*. South Africa. Retrieved from: http://npconline.co.za on 11 May 2014.

Ntshoe, I.M. 2003. The political economy of access and equitable allocation of resources to higher education. *International Journal of Educational Development*. 23(4):381–398.

Ntuli, T. 2008. Culture, indigenous knowledge systems and sustainable development: A critical view of education in an African context. *International Journal of Educational Development*. 29(2):140–148.

O'Boyle, E.J. 1999. Toward an improved definition of poverty. *Review of Social Economy*. 57(3): 281–307.

Ogunbudede, E.O. 2004. HIV/AIDS Situation in Africa. *International Dental Journal*. 54:352–360.

Oxfam. 2013. *The cost of inequality: how wealth and income extremes hurt us all*. Oxfam media briefing. 18 January 2013. Retrieved from: http://www.oxfam.org/sites/www.oxfam.org/files/cost-of-inequality-oxfam-mb180113.pdf on 14 April 2014.

Pretorius, E.J. & Currin, S. 2010. Do the rich get richer and the poor poorer? The effects of an intervention programme on reading in the home and school language in a high poverty multilingual context. *International Journal of Educational Development*. 30(1):67–76.

Ravallion, M. & Chen, S. 1997. What can new survey data tell us about recent changes in distribution and poverty? *World Bank Economic Review*. 11:357–82.

Saha, L.J. 1993. The effects of socio-economic development on student academic performance and life plans: A cross-national analysis. *International Journal of Educational Development*. 12(3):191–204.

SALDRU. 1995: RDP. Key Indicators of Poverty. An analysis prepared for the Ministry in the Office of the President. University of Cape Town. Cape Town.

Schultz, T.P. 1999. Health and schooling investment in Africa. *Journal of Economic Perspectives*. 13(3):67–88.

Smith, M. & Barrett, A.M. 2011. Capabilities for learning to read:

An investigation of social and economic effects for Grade 6 learners in Southern and East Africa. *International Journal of Educational Development.* 31(1) January: 23–36.

Soudien, C. 2007. The "A" factor: Coming to terms with the question of legacy in South African education. *International Journal of Educational Development.* 27(2) March:182–193.

South Africa Human Development Report. 2003. Cape Town: Oxford University Press Southern Africa.

Spaull, N. 2013. Poverty & privilege: Primary school inequality in South Africa. *International Journal of Educational Development.* 33(5):436–447.

Spreen C.A. & Vally, S. 2006. Education rights, education policies and inequality in South Africa. *International Journal of Educational Development.* 26(4):352–362.

Statistics South Africa (StatsSA). 2000. *Measuring Poverty.* Report No. 0-621-30092-6.

Taylor Committee. 2002. *Transforming the Present – Protecting the Future.* Consolidated Report of the Committee of Inquiry into a Comprehensive System of Social Security for South Africa. March. Retrieved from: http://www.sarpn.org/CountryPovertyPapers/SouthAfrica/march2002/report/Transforming_the_Present_pre.pdf on 14 March 2014.

Taylor Committee. n.d. *Committee Report No 8: Poverty, Social Assistance and the Basic Income Grant.* Retrieved from: http://www.sarpn.org/CountryPovertyPapers/South Africa/taylor/ on 11 May 2014.

The Native Land Act of 1913. South African History Online. Retrieved from: http://www.sahistory.org.za on 11 May 2014.

United Nations Development Program (UNDP). 2003. *Human Development Report: A Compact Among Nations to End Human Poverty.* Retrieved from http://ideas.repec.org/b/hdr/report/hdr2003.html on 30 March 2014.

United Nations. 1996. *Food Security for All, Food Security for Rural Women.* Geneva: International Steering Committee on Economic Advancement of Rural Women.

Van der Berg, S. 1999. *Social Policy to Address Poverty.* DPRU Working Paper 99/30.

Van der Berg, S. 2008. How effective are poor schools? Poverty and educational outcomes in South Africa. *Studies in Educational Evaluation.* 34(2008): pp. 145–154.

Whiteford, A & Van Seventer, D 1999. *Winners and Losers: South Africa's changing income distribution in the 1990s.* WEFA Southern Africa. Retrieved from: www.wefa.co.za on 20 March 2014.

Woolard, I. 2002. Income mobility and household dynamics in South Africa: The case of Africans in KwaZulu-Natal. *Labour Markets and Social Frontiers*. 2:5–11.

Woolard, I. & Leibbrandt, M. 2001. Measuring Poverty in South Africa. In M. Maziya, S., Van der Berg, & I. Woolard (Eds). *Fighting poverty: Labour markets and inequality in South Africa*. University of Cape Town: Development Policy Research Unit.

World Bank. 1993. *Implementing the World Bank's Strategy to Reduce Poverty: Progress and challenges*. Washington D.C.: World Bank.

Yamauchi, F. 2005. Race, equity, and public schools in post-apartheid South Africa: Equal opportunity for all kids. *Economics of Education Review*. 24(2):213–233.

10

Education and poverty in sub-Saharan Africa

Walter Sukati and Thembinkosi Dlamini

Literacy is a bridge from misery to hope. It is a tool for daily life in modern society. It is a bulwark against poverty, and a building block of development ...

Kofi Annan, Former Secretary-General of the United Nations

Chapter overview

The major aim of this chapter is to reveal how education in general, and inclusive education in particular, is related to poverty, and to further discuss how education can be structured to be used as a weapon to alleviate poverty. The chapter therefore forms a solid base, and further justification for why it is necessary to produce a book on inclusive education, like this one. Student teachers in sub-Saharan Africa who live and work in these poverty-stricken environments need to understand:

- What is poverty?
- What are the measurements and indicators of poverty?
- How does sub-Saharan Africa compare to other world regions in levels of poverty?
- What are the causes of poverty, and among whom and where is poverty mostly found?
- How is poverty related to education, and to inclusive education in particular?
- What education planning models and policies are necessary to address poverty in sub-Saharan Africa?

Learning outcomes

By the end of this chapter you should be able to:

- Define poverty, and the measurements and indicators of poverty that are commonly used
- Explain and compare poverty levels between world regions, and also between countries in sub-Saharan Africa
- Describe the common causes of poverty
- Explain how inclusive education is related to productivity, development and economic growth, dependency ratios, and to poverty
- Explain the relationship between education and poverty, how education affects poverty, and how poverty affects education
- Outline education planning models and policies that are necessary to alleviate poverty.

Let us start by looking at the following case from Mbabane, in the Lubombo region of Swaziland.

CASE STUDY 1

Mr Khumalo was a migrant mine worker from rural Swaziland who worked in the gold mines of Gauteng in South Africa. His parents were poor and had never attended school, and he too never went to school. Mr Khumalo had six young children to whom he desperately wanted to give an education so that they could learn to speak English, get jobs, and be better off than their parents. That is what drove him to leave his family for 18 months at a time, and go to work in the mines.

Just after his first two children started school, he lost his job in the mines and had to come home. A month after his return from Gauteng, he discovered he had tuberculosis. Four months later, he found out that he had AIDS. He had to visit the hospital frequently. This depleted any savings that he had, and he could no longer afford school fees, to buy uniforms, or pay for textbooks, etc. His children were sent away from school. The four younger children could also not go to school when they reached school-going age.

Mr Khumalo died six months later, and his wife also died soon afterwards. The children were left with no one to look after them, or pay for them to go to school. Without hope of an education, this was the beginning of their long and miserable journey to poverty.

1 In your community, are you aware of any similar stories? If so, discuss them.
2 In Mr Khumalo's perception, what were the benefits of education?
3 Do you see a cycle of poverty in this story? If so, describe it in a diagram.

Who is poor? Understanding poverty in the world today

Poverty is a threat to existence of humanity in modern times as it poses the greatest danger to peace and stability, especially in the developing world, and in particular, in sub-Saharan Africa (Mualuko, 2007). It is therefore rightly contended that there is no more crucial context in which to ask questions about the dynamics of poverty than in Africa, where poverty persists and grows deeper, despite numerous local, national, and international attempts to reduce it (Gaventa, 2004). This is partly the chief reason why reducing poverty was indicated as goal number 1 in the eight Millennium Development Goals (MDGs). Sub-Saharan Africa therefore faces significant challenges in meeting the MDGs on almost every dimension of poverty, with many countries falling behind. So it is perhaps the most important region in the fight against poverty.

Although there is general agreement on what poverty is, there are however, multitudes of definitions of this term. This chapter starts with a brief review of some of the more common definitions of poverty. It then proceeds to present the measures and indicators of poverty that are commonly used. These measures and indicators are then used to compare the poverty rates between world regions, and between countries in sub-Saharan Africa. As there are wide variations on poverty rates between regions, and also between the sub-Saharan African countries, the chapter will provide information on the common major causes of poverty, who is poor, and where the poor are likely to be found. The chapter continues by discussing the relationship between education and poverty; whether poor education leads to poverty or if it is poverty that leads to poor education. The chapter concludes with educational planning models and policies that educators and teachers have to take cognisance of in their quest to address poverty in sub-Saharan Africa.

What is poverty?

It is difficult to have a universal definition of the term 'poverty' since it is defined in many different ways. The difficulty lies in the fact that poverty is a complex problem, and is often specific to a location, country, or region (Tilak, 2007; Hemmer & Wilhelm, 2000; Republic of South Africa, 2000). Despite this difficulty, however, there is some general agreement on what it entails, and that it can be defined in terms of three distinguishable degrees. The general agreement is that poverty entails some deprivation, and a lack of the means to provide for basic needs and the essential items for survival, such as food, clothing, shelter, water, education, and health. It is further extended to mean the denial of choices and opportunities, powerlessness and exclusion, the basic capacity to effectively participate in society, and a violation of human dignity. The Asian Development Bank (2006) rightly reveals that poverty is much more complex than simply income deprivation, as it also entails lack of empowerment, of knowledge, of opportunity, and of income and capital. It should be noted, however, that it does not mean that people living in poverty are deprived of all these things. They might have some of them, e.g. water, but not enough of the others, like food, shelter, education, health, etc.

Further general agreement is that poverty can be defined in terms of three distinguishable degrees (Mualuko, 2007; Tilak, 2007). These degrees are:

Absolute or extreme poverty

Absolute poverty or destitution refers to a severe deprivation of basic human needs, and means that the individuals, families or households live in a state such that they cannot meet their basic needs of food, shelter, health care, etc., for their survival. The **Millennium Development Goals** are the world's time-bound and quantitative targets for addressing extreme poverty in its many dimensions – income poverty, hunger, disease, lack of adequate shelter, and exclusion.

Moderate poverty

Moderate poverty generally refers to conditions of life in which the basic needs of individuals, families, and households are barely met.

Relative poverty

Relative poverty sees poverty as socially defined and dependent on the social context. It occurs when people do not enjoy a certain minimum level of living standards, as determined by a government. It is taken to mean that the individual, family, or household income

The eight **Millennium Development Goals** (MDGs) are a United Nations blueprint, agreed to by all the world's countries and leading development institutions, for a range of goals to be achieved by 2015. The goals include halving extreme poverty rates; achieving universal primary education; promoting gender equality and empowering women; reducing child mortality; improving maternal health; combating HIV and AIDS, malaria, and other diseases; ensuring environmental sustainability; and forming a global partnership for development. The UN is now also working with governments, civil society, and other partners to build on the MDGs and carry on with them after 2015.

median income: refers to the income level earned by a given household, where half of the households in a particular area or region earn more, and half earn less. It is a measure used instead of the average or mean household income because it can give a more accurate picture of an area or region's actual economic status.

level is below a given proportion of the average national income. It is therefore measured as a percentage of the population with income less than some fixed proportion of **median income**.

What are the measurements and indicators of poverty?

There are several measures and indicators of poverty that are commonly used. Some of the popular ones are (Government of South Africa, 2000):

- **Poverty line:** A common method of measuring poverty is based on incomes and consumption levels. An individual, family, or household is considered poor if its income level is below the minimum level necessary to meet basic needs. This minimum level is called the poverty line. Poverty lines vary according to time and place, and each country often has its own poverty line that is appropriate to its level of development, societal norms, and values. Sample surveys are used to collect information on consumption and income levels, where households answer detailed questions on their spending patterns and habits, and also on their sources and levels of income. To complement this information, households are now also asked about their possessions and their needs. The poverty line for a certain income and consumption amount per year is based on the estimated value of a basket of goods (food, clothing, shelter, water, education, health, etc.) that they need for proper living.

  The most commonly used indicator of global poverty is the absolute poverty line set by the World Bank. For a very long time, the World Bank set the extreme poverty line at US$1 a day or less, and the poverty line at US$2 a day or less. Following extensive studies and research on the cost of living across the world, to reflect the observed higher cost of living, the World Bank revised these figures. Now extreme poverty is set at an income level of US$1.25 a day or less. This figure set by the World Bank is, however, controversial. Some scholars argue that the method used by the World Bank is fundamentally flawed in its capacity to yield results that are accurate. Some argue that it sets the figure too high, and others argue that it is too low; both say that because of this, the level of poverty remains unknown. Still others believe that the poverty line misleads as it measures everyone below this line to be the same; yet the people below this line also differ. There are those who are at US$1.2 per day, and those who are at US$0.3 per day, and so forth. Though all poor, these people are not the same, as they are at different levels of poverty. The whole population (using sample surveys) is then surveyed to see how many of them live below the poverty line and how many are above this line. Once this information is acquired, it can then be determined what percentage of the population is below this line. This, then, provides an indicator of the poverty rate in the country. The next section of this chapter will provide information on the poverty rates for each region, and for the countries in sub-Saharan Africa.

- **The Gini coefficient**: Another method used to measure poverty is the measure of inequality in income distribution. This measures the difference between the richest people in the country and the poorest. It can show who is considered poor, compared to others in the same social group or society. There are two major ways that are used to measure the inequality in incomes in a society – the Gini coefficient, and the decile dispersion ratio.

   The Gini coefficient is commonly used in conjunction with a Lorenz curve, which is a graph that evaluates a country's income inequality. The Gini coefficient usually varies between 0.2 and 0.75, and, when it is multiplied by 100, it is called a Gini index. When inequality is low in a country, the Gini index is also low; and when inequality is high, the Gini index is also high. There are wide variations in the Gini index in sub-Saharan Africa, with a number of countries, such as Niger, Togo, and Benin having a low Gini index, indicating low inequality. Others, such as Namibia, South Africa, and Swaziland, have a high Gini index, indicating high rates of inequality in these countries. The decile dispersion ratio, which is another method used to determine inequality, expresses the income of the rich as a multiple of that of the poor. To calculate this ratio, the average income of the top 10 per cent of income makers is divided by the average income of the bottom 10 per cent of income makers.

- **Human Development Index:** A further measure which is often used to determine a country's progress and as indicator of poverty is the United Nations Human Development Index (HDI). The HDI uses a number of variables, such as life expectancy, education, GDP, etc., to determine a country's development progress.

- **Gross National Product per capita:** Another indicator of poverty is GNP per capita, now known as GNI per capita. This is calculated by taking the gross national income (product) and dividing it by the mid-year population of that country. In effect, this gives the average income in each country. According to the World Bank (2013), most countries in the developed world have a high per capita income, e.g. Canada $45 550, Denmark $60 160, Belgium $45 930; while sub-Saharan African countries have a far lower per capita income, e.g. Botswana $7 470, Kenya $820, Nigeria $1 280, Senegal $1 070, South Africa $6 960.

 Stop and reflect

- What is the poverty line? Are the majority of people in your community living above or below this line? What makes you say so?
- Of the indicators of poverty discussed here, which one do you think is the best indicator? Explain why you think so.

Poverty levels between world regions, and between countries in sub-Saharan Africa

It should be noted that while there are criticisms of the way in which poverty rates are calculated by the World Bank, these rates are still widely used as there have been no other better rates that have been put forward. Poverty rates differ greatly from one world region to another. Table 10.1 shows how these rates differ, and how they have changed over time, from one region to another.

Table 10.1: Poverty rates for selected world regions

Region	People living on US$1.25 per day, or less	
	1990 %	2010 %
East Asia and Pacific	56.2	12.5
Europe and Central Asia	1.9	0.7
Latin America and the Caribbean	12.2	5.5
Middle East and North Africa	5.8	2.4
South Asia	53.8	31
Sub-Saharan Africa	56.5	48.5
World average	31.06	16.7

(Source: Adapted from http://povertydata.worldbank.org/poverty/region/, accessed 7 April 2014)

Two major findings emerge from this table. The *first finding* is that poverty rates have been going down over the years for all world regions. The decrease in poverty rates over the years is seen when the poverty line is set at US$1.25 per day. This is good news as it means that the proportion of people who live in poverty is decreasing every year, and that if this trend continues, some time in the future this rate will reach zero, i.e. when all people will be above the poverty line.

The *second finding* is that these poverty rates differ markedly between the world regions, and that the sub-Saharan Africa region has the highest rates. While sub-Saharan Africa had poverty rates over 56.5% in 1990, all the other regions had lower rates, with East Asia and Pacific being the closest, with a rate of 56.2%. By 2010, while sub-Saharan Africa had a poverty rate of 48.5%, South Asia had a rate of 31%, East Asia and Pacific had a 12.5% rate, Latin America and Caribbean had 5.5%, the Middle East and North Africa had 2.4%, and Europe and Central Asia had 0.7%. The table also shows that the poverty rates fell rapidly in much of Asia, whereas they declined only marginally in sub-Saharan Africa (United Nations, 2006; World Bank, 2012).

There are also some vast differences in the poverty rates between the countries in sub-Saharan Africa. Table 10.2 shows some of these differences.

Table 10.2: Poverty rates of selected sub-Saharan African countries between 2008 and 2010 at US$1.25 per day

Poverty rate	Country
High poverty rates – above 30%	Angola, Burkina Faso, Central African Republic, Madagascar, Malawi, Mali, Mozambique, Niger, Nigeria, Rwanda, Sierra Leone, Swaziland, Uganda, Zambia
Medium poverty rates – between 20% and 30%	Côte d'Ivoire, Mauritania, Senegal, Togo
Low poverty rates – below 20%	Gabon, South Africa, Sudan

(Adapted by the authors from http://data.worldbank.org/ indicator/SI.POV.DDAY, accessed 13 June 2013)

The table shows the vast differences in poverty rates between the sub-Saharan African countries. Arimah (2004), in his article on *Poverty reduction and human development in Africa,* discusses this variation in poverty levels between the sub-Saharan African countries. While many countries have poverty rates above 30 per cent, only a few of them have rates below 20 per cent. It can be concluded therefore that most sub-Saharan African countries are very poor.

What are the causes of poverty?

It is beneficial and interesting to look at the causes of poverty if you want to understand why so many people and countries are where they are today, and to get an idea what can be done or needs to be done to break the vicious cycle of poverty. There are several causes of poverty that have been identified, and it has now become apparent that sub-Saharan Africa is caught in a vicious cycle of poverty. In sub-Saharan Africa, it is believed that these causes originate from colonisation to industrialisation, from political institutions to geographical factors, to poor governance, to demographic transitions, to laziness and poor agricultural practices, to corruption and to neo-colonialism. In most cases, the causes and effects of poverty are related and interact, so that what makes people poor also creates conditions that keep them poor. Some of the major causes of poverty in sub-Saharan Africa, according to a number of authors (e.g. Harber, 2002; Durston & Nashire, 2001; Department for International Development, 2001) are:

Population increases

Many countries in sub-Saharan Africa have high population growth rates, averaging 2.5 per cent, and these are set to double within a generation. This becomes a problem when the increase in population numbers is not matched by a high economic rate of growth. This mismatch then means the economy, and the limited available resources, are not able to handle the large numbers and are spread thinly, so that the GDP per capita decreases. When the GDP per capita decreases, poverty increases. Hence, large population increases become one of the main causes behind the menace of poverty in sub-Saharan Africa.

Lack of employment opportunities

When the economy of sub-Saharan African countries grows at a low rate, it means that there are few employment opportunities opening up. When there are few employment opportunities available, only a few of the people of these countries can be employed and earn some income. The many who are unemployed consequently have no income and cannot provide for their basic needs, and are forced to live in poverty.

Lack of access to basic education opportunities

In sub-Saharan Africa, many people are illiterate and further, substantial numbers do not have access to schooling. Enrolment ratios are low, and this shows that people who should be attending school are not doing so, hence the projections that sub-Saharan Africa will not achieve universal primary education (the second of the MDGs) by 2015. There are several reasons why the enrolment ratios are low, such as a lack of schools, lack of the necessary school fees, culture of illiteracy, non-belief in education for girls, etc. This lack of education denies children a chance to improve themselves and on completion of schooling, to enter gainful employment that would lift them and their families out of poverty.

Lack of an appropriate quality education

The problem of poor quality education persists in sub-Saharan Africa. It springs from an education that is not relevant to people's needs and to the needs of the world of work. Poor quality education is one that does not give people the right knowledge, skills, and attitudes to secure employment, to survive, and to create jobs. So a lack of appropriate quality education means lack of employment avenues, which leads to no income in the future, low productivity and unemployment, coupled with poverty.

Poor health

Sub-Saharan Africa is heavily affected by HIV and AIDS, tuberculosis, and malaria. The onset of these diseases results in poor health and death. When people are in poor health, their productivity is reduced, and hence their income is also reduced. They incur huge medical bills which further reduce the resources they have to provide for their basic needs. They eventually die and their families have to fund their funerals, which further depletes the resources of the family. Because of these diseases, and others, and the death of parents, caregivers, and breadwinners, many sub-Saharan African countries are left with large numbers of orphans who have no one to support them, further exacerbating the scourge of poverty.

Poor governance

It is believed that many sub-Saharan African leaders have failed to practise and nurture good governance and democracy, which are the cornerstones to elevating economic performance and standards of living. Good governance also helps in reducing inequalities and corruption by putting in place a system of 'checks and balances', crucial in founding capable and effective states. Widespread corruption means that the resources aimed at helping the poor, and citizens in general, end up in the pockets of corrupt politicians and bureaucrats. The poor do not get any benefit from these national resources and so they continue to live in poverty.

Capital flight and corruption

Some sub-Saharan African leaders, bureaucrats, and dictators have a history of using (and continue to use) corrupt means to acquire wealth, national funds, and resources, which they bank in countries in the developed world. This flight of capital helps the developed countries but leaves the sub-Saharan African countries poor, especially when most of these funds are never repatriated (returned) to their countries of origin. Multinational corporations, some of them operating out of resource-rich sub-Saharan African countries, also plunder the countries' wealth by using tax havens and other tax loopholes to avoid paying a fair share of local taxes.

Brain drain

Many sub-Saharan Africans have joined the African **diaspora**. Many of the skilled people who leave are pushed out of their countries by several factors, such as: a lack of appropriate infrastructure, lack of technology, working equipment and tools, corruption, lack of recognition and incentives, low salaries, and many more. When these skilled people leave sub-Saharan Africa, they leave with their knowledge and skills, and for many reasons of opportunity and betterment, they often relocate to the developed world. Developed countries then benefit from these skills, and sub-Saharan Africa is left without the necessary expertise; and so the investment made in training these people is also lost. This is a strong factor in increasing the levels of poverty in sub-Saharan Africa.

Structural adjustments

Many **structural adjustment** programmes in sub-Saharan Africa, particularly those prescribed by the International Monetary Fund (IMF) and World Bank, have called for cutbacks in public spending on education, health, and other vital social services. These cuts in the social services, which are related to poverty and its alleviation, as discussed earlier, mean that fewer services will be provided, and poverty is then exacerbated. Some of the policy prescriptions of these so-called 'Bretton Woods institutions', such as privatisation of state-owned entities, removal of farm subsidies, and imposition of user

diaspora: the spread of people around the world, who have left their original homelands

structural adjustment: an economics term that describes a policy to impose conditions for lending and borrowing money by developing countries, by the World Bank and IMF, the Bretton Woods institutions, so-called because they developed out of a 1944 meeting in which 44 countries met to decide how to rebuild the shattered post-World War II economy, and cooperate globally to do so

fees, have proved to be a barrier to poor people's access to basic essential services such as health care, water and sanitation, and have led to widespread hunger.

Unfair world trade

The developed countries, just as in colonial times, continue to receive raw materials and natural resources from sub-Saharan African countries. As these resources are exported in their raw form, they are sold cheaply to the developed countries. The developed countries then process these raw materials into finished products and sell them (sometimes even back to the countries where the raw materials and resources originated) as finished products, at high prices with enormous profits. This increases the dependency of sub-Saharan African countries on developed countries and, in turn, leads to under-development, loss of jobs, inequality, and further poverty in sub-Saharan Africa.

Lack of fundamental freedoms

Exclusion, voicelessness, and lack of participation of poor people in decision-making in matters that impact on their livelihoods, are also known to exacerbate poverty levels. If one is excluded from participation and involvement, the decisions made by the rich and powerful will always reflect self-interest, and burden the poor with more poverty and disadvantage. The veil of secrecy and a lack of access to information is what renders poor people vulnerable to bad policy choices, the result of which could lead to the loss of productive resources, such as land, pasture, or water access rights. Making publicly available all information relating to the acquisition, allocation, and expenditure of public money in a timely, accessible, relevant, and comprehensible manner should be the foundational pillar of all efforts to eradicate poverty.

 Stop and reflect

1 Which are your top five main causes of poverty, and why do you consider those five the most important causes?
2 Some analysts see the brain drain as a brain circulation. They do not see it as a major cause of poverty. What is your view on this? Discuss this with your colleagues in class and see what conclusions you reach. Remember to give reasons for these conclusions.

The relationship between education and poverty

❝ *Education is not a way to escape poverty – it is a way of fighting it.* ❞

Julius Nyerere, former President of the United Republic of Tanzania

The role of education in development and poverty eradication, in close cooperation with other sectors, is crucial, and needs to be exposed and explored. Doing this gives us an idea of how education can be structured and reformed to contribute to poverty alleviation and development. No country can succeed if does not have educated people. Everyone agrees that the single most important key to development, wealth creation, and to poverty alleviation is education. That is why renowned economist, Amartya Sen declared: "To build a nation, build a school" (Engle and Black, 2008). The Department for International Development in the United Kingdom asserts that education is at the heart of development and that countries which have made the greatest progress in reducing poverty are those that have combined effective and equitable investment in education with sound economic policies (DFID, 2001).

How does education contribute to poverty reduction? Although the impact of education on poverty alleviation tends to be indirect, there is no doubt, however, that education is pivotal in breaking the vicious cycle of poverty – which is the reality of most people in sub-Saharan Africa. Education is said to be the single most important key to development, poverty alleviation, and to breaking the poverty cycle, which works like this:

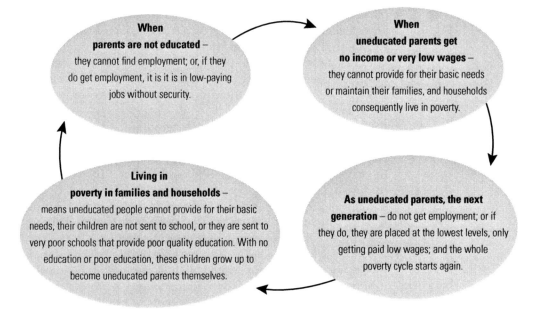

When parents are not educated – they cannot find employment; or, if they do get employment, it is it is in low-paying jobs without security.

When uneducated parents get no income or very low wages – they cannot provide for their basic needs or maintain their families, and households consequently live in poverty.

Living in poverty in families and households – means uneducated people cannot provide for their basic needs, their children are not sent to school, or they are sent to very poor schools that provide poor quality education. With no education or poor education, these children grow up to become uneducated parents themselves.

As uneducated parents, the next generation – do not get employment; or if they do, they are placed at the lowest levels, only getting paid low wages; and the whole poverty cycle starts again.

To break this cycle of poverty, in which many sub-Saharan African families are caught, providing good quality education is an imperative. Such education, particularly for children from poor families, will provide them with the knowledge and skills that employers are seeking. As better educated people, they also have the skills and knowledge needed to improve their quality of life. They are more productive, and, as a result, increase their income and reduce poverty. They use capital, land, and other resources in more efficient ways. They are far more likely to innovate and devise new forms of production, improving their income earning potential (Asian Development Bank, 2006). Consequently, they will find employment and earn good salaries. With the good salaries, they will be able to provide for their needs, and also provide a good education for their children. When their children get a good education, they will go on to get good jobs and decent salaries, finally breaking the cycle of poverty. Education can therefore do a great deal to break the vicious cycle of marginalisation, exclusion and poverty. According to Sukati (2010), education plays, among others, the following roles in poverty reduction:

- *It is a human right enshrined in the Universal Declaration of Human Rights.* The link between education rights and human rights is reinforced, as education operates as a multiplier. Where the right to education is guaranteed, people's enjoyment of all individual rights and freedoms is enhanced. Where the right to education is denied or violated, people are deprived of many other rights and freedoms. So, denial of the right to education triggers exclusion from the enjoyment of several rights, such as exclusion from the labour market, exclusion from social security schemes, exclusion from political participation, etc.
- *It improves the quality of the labour force.* Increased education levels are considered powerful drivers of national economic growth and productivity. Quality education develops knowledge, skills, attitudes, new values, and perspectives. It increases choices and professional competencies, which enable one to become more efficient, more innovative, more productive, and more competitive in the labour market.
- *It reduces inequalities.* When individuals get an education, particularly the poor and marginalised, they are more likely to find higher-paying jobs, getting get higher incomes, and in doing so, reducing the income gap between themseles and the wealthy. This, then, means that access to education increases income equality, and social mobility. As a result, education has been called a great leveller, since it provides a means by which disadvantaged groups can improve their socio-economic conditions.
- *It improves people's health.* There is a relationship between education, health, and poverty. Poor health and the scourge of HIV and AIDS in sub-Saharan Africa have been found to have a profound effect on poverty outcomes, with improvements in health leading to a reduction in poverty. The reasons for this are: a) when people are

healthy, they do not have to spend money on medicines and health services, thus saving money for their other needs; b) when people are healthy, they are more productive and, as they produce more, they get higher incomes; c) when people are healthy, they do not have to take many days off work because of ill health; d) when children are not healthy, their school performance deteriorates; e) educated people can make informed choices, leading to positive health outcomes.

• *It increases and improves research and development skills.* Education, and in particular, higher education, enables people to use and extend their capacities, and provide, promote, and improve the research and development skills, which help improve processes and products. This helps to increase the number and variety of products produced for the market, and results in increased revenues for the benefit of all, and in economic growth and development.

Education can therefore do a great deal to break the vicious cycle of poverty, marginalisation, and exclusion (Tomasevski, 2003; Caillods, 1998). Without education, people are impeded from gaining access to employment, and their low educational attainment prejudices their career advancement, which results in lower salaries that negatively affect their security, especially in old age.

Stop and reflect

1 Does the poverty cycle, as described here, have all the necessary descriptive components, in your opinion? Are there any other components that you feel are necessary but missing, and need to be added? Where do they fit in the cycle described earlier (page 185)?

2 With the current alarming rates of unemployed school leavers, do you think education is still important and necessary? Why?

Education planning models and policies needed to address poverty in sub-Saharan Africa

In 2003, the World Bank published a sourcebook of poverty reduction strategies covering most of the dimensions of poverty; this has become the prime mover behind the Poverty Reduction Strategy Papers (PRSPs). These were introduced in 1999 by the World Bank and the IMF as a new framework to enhance countries' accountability for poverty reduction efforts. They put countries in a good light so that they can access debt relief, and summarise current knowledge and analysis of a country's poverty situation, describe the existing poverty reduction strategy, and then lay out the process for producing a fully developed poverty reduction strategy that involves a broad range of stakeholders. The UNDP (2003) clearly articulates that breaking out of the poverty trap requires a multifaceted approach, and goes on to identify six policy clusters that are crucial. The first of these is investing in human development, where education plays a major role in fostering a productive labour force that can participate effectively in the world economy. Hence (and as also observed in the last section), education is critical in poverty alleviation. For the education system to truly respond to the needs of the poor, and to contribute to the creation of wealth in families, communities, and society at large, it needs to take the issue of poverty into special consideration in the planning of the educational services. What education planning models and policies should sub-Saharan African education systems take into account to address the issues of poverty?

Sukati (2010), following an extensive review of literature, concluded that the planning models that should be taken into account, include:

Providing education for all

School enrolment ratios in sub-Saharan Africa are low, particularly at the higher levels, and do not demonstrate that education is considered a human right. This means that many people are not able to access education and, as a result, cannot break out of the chains of poverty. It should be noted here that providing education for all only at the primary school level, as many sub-Saharan African countries are doing, will have little impact. This is because, as some experts have argued, it is secondary, higher, and adult and lifelong education that provide the skills which have proven to be useful in the labour market. These are the skills that can keep the people above the poverty line, and indeed, enhance their only chance of prosperity.

Providing a good quality and relevant education

It is essential that sub-Saharan African countries provide a good quality education at all the levels: pre-school, primary, secondary, and tertiary. It is the quality and the relevance of the education provided that will make people productive in the labour market. A poor education, and one that is not relevant to the needs of the individual, society, and the labour market, will not produce a productive worker who is equipped to earn an income and get out of the poverty trap. Further, poor education produces individuals who are unable to find employment. So, while teaching the three Rs (reading, writing and arithmetic) is still important and should continue, the curriculum should include other important and relevant subjects in the sciences, practical arts, technical and vocational education, to ensure that it also provides the knowledge and skills that are necessary for employment and self-employment (Sukati, 2010).

Providing inclusive education

When inclusive education is not provided, certain pockets of people, particularly people with special needs, such as the physically challenged, the visually and hearing impaired, etc., are left out of the education system. These could also be children from poor families, children from the rural areas, religious minorities, refugees, or immigrants; it could be girls. When these groups are left out of the education system, or marginalised in any way, they do not get the knowledge and skills necessary for employment. They grow up to be unemployed and unemployable adults who get no income and are destined to live in poverty all their lives. Providing them with education turns this situation around as it equips them with the skills necessary for employment or self-employment, so they can grow and participate in the labour market, get income, and escape from poverty.

Providing an appropriate school curriculum

The world of knowledge, and how it is accessed, has expanded vastly, and hence the need to decide what a necessary and relevant education is, and what it is not. A number of sub-Saharan African countries have experienced the phenomenon of the educated unemployed (the 'diploma disease' according to Dore, 1997), mainly because they offer inappropriate curricula that have not kept up with global developments. The curriculum taught in many schools in sub-Saharan regions has not changed with the times and with the changing environment. When this happens, children are taught and trained for a non-existent world and contemporary environment. They cannot then be absorbed by the labour market and so grow up to be unemployed and, again, live in poverty.

Providing courses on research, innovation, entrepreneurship, and development

School leavers need to be able to improve existing products and processes to make them more efficient and to add value, and/or develop new products that the market needs. This calls for innovative minds, high-level research and analytical skills, and good production and entrepreneurial skills. If sub-Saharan Africa is to escape from the scourge of poverty, such skills are necessary so that Africans can develop new products, produce old ones more efficiently, and be competitive in the global market. These skills seem to have been neglected by sub-Saharan African countries, and unless this is changed, the continent will not be competitive in the globalised world market, and sub-Saharan Africa may continue to lag behind.

Providing qualified teachers and improving teaching methods

The lecture method has long been the dominant teaching mode in sub-Saharan Africa. Other more modern, and innovative and interactive methods, are rarely used. This is mainly because a number of teachers in schools are not trained as teachers and are not qualified in current methodologies. Typically what happens in many countries, is that people who do not do well at secondary school, and are not admitted to a tertiary institution, are engaged to teach because of a shortage of qualified teachers. Without any training in teaching, such individuals simply teach in the same way as they were taught, since they do not know any other methods of teaching. In addition, without having studied further, such teachers will not be qualified in the content of the course they are teaching. Their students therefore do not get proper teaching and end up not acquiring the education they should receive, sometimes even dropping out of the education system.

Developing the role of the teacher

Considering all the issues, models, and trends discussed in this chapter so far, what policies do teachers need to pursue to address the issues of poverty? Teachers live and mix in the communities where they work. They are also in regular contact with the learners in their schools, so they can play an important role in the fight against poverty. Some policies and initiatives that they might apply could be to:

- *Work towards providing access to education for all.* Teachers should work towards actively removing any barriers to access in their schools. This means working with education authorities on the issues that form barriers to education, like: learners who have to walk long distances to reach school; learners who cannot afford to pay high school fees, or who are not admitted to the school because they cannot pay fees; and learners who are not admitted by the school because of space and numbers limitations. On the professional front, teachers can seek to make more efficient use of the available teaching resources, provide additional help to weak students so that they can improve their performance and not fail or drop out; and be aware of and expose the misuse of school funds.

- *Ensure that they foster inclusive education.* Teachers should make sure that all children of school-going age are attending school, and are not hindered in any way. This means that provision is made for the physically challenged, the visually and hearing impaired, for learners with cognitive difficulties and language problems, for girl children, for children from poor families, informal settlements, refugee camps, for immigrant children, etc. All this would help to ensure that inclusive education is provided and no one is excluded or allowed to drop out of school.

- *Offer a comprehensive and relevant curriculum.* In the school, teachers should make sure that the subjects they offer are in line with, and relevant to, the future careers of their learners. It should not just be about teaching a subject because it has always been taught, but because it is a subject that the learner can use in the future. Teachers can influence the education authorities to introduce those subjects that are essential for the twenty-first century, and are relevant to future careers. Where the available school resources lag behind modern trends and developments in the real world, teachers can update these resources, e.g. by making sure prescribed texts are revised and updated, even supplementing them with current information and developments. They can further encourage learners to read and understand information from other resources such as the internet, newspapers, journals, news broadcasts on radio and television.

- *Have good teaching methods that fit the curriculum and subject matter, and inculcate the required values.* Good teaching and learning methods will help learners focus on the lesson, understand what is important, will provide for interaction between learner and teacher, and improve the performance of the learner, reducing failure, repetition and dropping out. Teachers have to strive for excellence in teaching, as though there were a prize for the best teacher. Also, it is necessary that all teachers are qualified for whatever level that they are teaching, and adopt a culture of continuous learning and improvement in their own practice.
- *Provide support for poor children.* Many sub-Saharan African countries have introduced universal, free, primary education in a bid to achieve the MDG goals. Despite this noble gesture, not all primary school-going age children are attending school. Many children are prevented from attending school (or attending regularly) because of numerous other barriers, such as lack of uniforms; costs and means of travel to school; additional school fees; opportunity costs such as being needed to work at home, e.g. looking after cattle or younger siblings; or simply, and most sadly, because of hunger. This then means that to have all children attending school, it is not only free primary education that will solve the problem. There needs to be other support provided to poor children to remove barriers and enable learners to attend and stay at school. This could be in the form of a conditional cash grant, provision of transport, or a school feeding scheme. Without this required additional support, there is no way that sub-Saharan Africa will ever fully achieve the MDGs.
- *Provide health education.* The introduction of health education would help arrest the devastation, in particular, of HIV and AIDS, tuberculosis, malaria, and other diseases, and improve the wellness of the sub-Saharan African people. If they are afflicted by disease, they will have problems teaching and learning. If they do not succeed in school, they will not be employed and will remain poor. The academic performance of children who are not healthy is inevitably poor, but providing health education will help people make informed choices and keep them healthy.
- *Provide for child-friendly schools.* The atmosphere at school should be conducive to learning and should be child-friendly so that children perform at their best, and that repetition and dropping out are eliminated. This could involve the provision of nutritious meals for the children, particularly those who are poor; offering extra tutorial classes for learners who are behind or are under-performing; doing health checks and offering sports and fitness programmes; providing proper sanitation facilities; and, most importantly, making the school a safe and secure place for children to learn.
- *Inculcate appropriate and needed values and attitudes in behaviour, research, innovation, entrepreneurship and development.* When appropriate values are inculcated in a child early on, the child grows up guided by those values and acts in accordance with

them. All the listed values here would help in making sure that children are equipped with the correct values, attitudes, and personal resources to fight poverty.

- *Encourage parental/caregiver involvement in the governance of schools and education of children.* Parents should be concerned about the performance of their children at school, should follow up, and assist with things like homework, projects, behaviour and attitude issues. They should encourage a culture of reading and learning at home, and assist where possible with additional learning materials. Parents should be involved in decision-making at the local school in terms of setting the level of school fees, the use to which school funds should be put, monitoring school performance, and taking measures to identify and assist indigent learners and families.

 CASE STUDY 2

Following the death of both their parents, the Khumalo children were left to fend for themselves. Their thatched roof house started falling apart and no one would help them to repair their home. Since they could not be employed, and had no income or food, the children left their home one by one. Each of the children went his or her own way – the young girls went to the towns to look for ways to make some money, and the boys went to other villages to find work looking after cattle. To get money fast to buy food, the girls became shoplifters and were also drawn into prostitution. The boys became herd boys and lived in families that abused them. They would be severely beaten when the cattle were lost, or when the cattle damaged someone's crops.

With the children gone from their home for over a year, neighbouring people started using their land for farming. Some even sold the land to other people. The children then had no place to call home and had to stay away permanently. As they had not finished school, they could not communicate with one another and they lost touch. They never knew where their siblings were and what they were doing. Without education, none could ever find a decent job, and all remained poor and unable to provide for their needs, or those of their own children when they had them.

1. How can the community and community leaders help orphaned, vulnerable and uneducated members of their community? Base your suggestions in part on what you have read in this chapter, and on your experience as a teacher.
2. Despite finding themselves in the conditions presented in this case study, how could the Khumalo children still turn their situation around? Again, base your answer on what you have read here, and on your own experience as a teacher.

Summary of discussion

Poverty is a major problem faced by the majority of the people in sub-Saharan African countries. In fact, the sub-Saharan Africa region has the highest rates of poverty compared with other world regions. This underlines the crucial importance of addressing this scourge that afflicts so many people. Many families live in poverty and fail to provide for their basic needs of food, shelter, education, health care, and clean water and sanitation. Although there are many causes of poverty in the region, some of them quite complex, almost all of them are within the capacity of the sub-Saharan countries to solve.

Sub-Saharan countries need a critical mass of appropriately educated and trained people to solve the problems that emanate from endemic poverty. Education remains the single most important key to development, and the alleviation of poverty in sub-Saharan Africa. For an education system to be in a position to solve poverty, it has to: i) be relevant, offer quality education for all, and be inclusive; ii) provide an appropriate curriculum with a major focus on science and technology subjects, research, innovation, entrepreneurship, and development; and iii) have a qualified corps of teachers to teach students appropriately, and to mentor new teachers. Educators therefore have an important role to play in all these requirements, and in formulating and implementing relevant policies and practice to ensure that education is effectively delivered, and poverty is eliminated.

Closing activities

1. In your own area and community, do you know of any individuals and families that have changed from being poor to becoming self-sufficient? In your experience, how did they manage to change their standard of living? Write a case study similar to those you have read in this book, illustrating how the individual or household managed to turn their life around.

    Does inclusive education contribute to the reduction of poverty? Write a two-page essay in which you present your argument. Give fully supported reasons (with examples) why it contributes or does not contribute to poverty reduction. Base your essay on what you have read in chapters in this book and on your own further reading. Remember to include a reference list of all sources you consulted.

References

Arimah, B. 2004. Poverty reduction and human development in Africa. *Journal of Human Development.* 5(3):399–415.

Asian Development Bank. 2006. *Policy on education.* Retrieved from: http://www.adb.org/documents/Policies/Education on 13 June 2013.

Caillods, F. 1998. *Education strategies for disadvantaged groups: Some basic issues.* IIEP Contributions (No. 31). New York: UNESCO IIEP.

Christie, P. & Gordon, A. 1992. Politics, poverty and education in rural South Africa. *British Journal of Sociology of Education.* 13(4):399–417.

Department for International Development. 2001. *The challenge of universal primary education: Strategies for achieving the international development targets.* London: DFID.

Dore, R. 1997. *The diploma disease: Education, qualification and development.* 2nd ed. London: Institute of Education, University of London.

Durston, S. & Nashire, N. 2001. Rethinking poverty and education: An attempt by an education programme in Malawi to have an impact on poverty. *Compare.* 31(1):75–91.

Engle, P.L. & Black, M.M. 2008. The effect of poverty on child development and educational outcomes. *Annals of the New York Academy of Sciences.* 1136:243–256. doi:10.1196/annals.1425.023.

Gaventa, J. 2004. From policy to power: Revisiting actors, knowledge and spaces. In K. Brock, R. McGee & J. Gaventa (Eds). *Unpacking policy: Knowledge, actors and spaces in poverty reduction in Uganda and Nigeria.* (pp. 274–300). Kampala, Uganda: Fountain Publishers Ltd.

Harber, C. 2002. Education, democracy and poverty reduction in Africa. *Comparative Education.* 38(3):267–276.

Hemmer, H. & Wilhelm, R. 2000. *Fighting poverty in developing countries: Principles for economic policy.* Brussels: Peter Lang.

Mualuko, N.J. 2007. The issue of poverty in the provision of quality education in Kenyan secondary schools. *Educational Research and Review.* 2(7):157–164.

Republic of South Africa. 2000. *Poverty and inequality in South Africa.* Retrieved from: http://www.INFO.GOV.ZA/OTHERDOCS/1998/POVERTY/ on 13 June 2013.

Sukati, C.W.S. 2010. Reducing poverty: Educational planning and policy implications in Swaziland. *Educational Planning.* 19(2):8–21.

Tilak, J.B.G. 2007. Post-elementary education, poverty and development in India. *International Journal of Educational Development.* 27(4):435–445.

Tomasevski, K. 2003. *Education denied: Costs and remedies.* London: Zed Books.

United Nations Development Programme. 2003. *Human development report 2003. Millennium development goals: A compact among nations to end human poverty.* New York: UNDP.

United Nations Development Programme. 2006. *The millennium development goals report.* New York: UNDP.

World Bank. 2012. *World Bank sees progress against extreme poverty, but flags vulnerabilities.* Retrieved from: http://web.worldbank.org/WBSITE/EXTERNAL/NEWS/0 on 7 April 2014.

World Bank. 2013. *GNI per capita, Atlas method (current US$).* Retrieved from: http://data.worldbank.org/indicator/NY.GNP.PCAP.CD on 13 June 2013.

11

The historical development of inclusive education in South Africa

Melanie Drake

Chapter overview

This chapter addresses the historical development of inclusive education in South Africa. You will be exposed to a brief history of education in South Africa in order to help you appreciate the movement towards this educational approach. Important discussions around why and how inclusive education is important for South African education will also be covered, as well as the educational policies which enhance the adoption of inclusive education. The last section the chapter highlights the challenges facing the implementation of inclusive education in South Africa.

Learning outcomes

By the end of this chapter you should be able to:
- Give a brief historical overview of inclusive education in South Africa
- Summarise the main developments in education that have shaped inclusive education in South Africa
- Understand the human rights culture in South Africa, and its relevance to inclusive education
- Identify the policies that are important for developing inclusive education in South Africa
- Explain the policy–practice gap in South Africa and the challenges of policy implementation
- Outline key barriers to the realisation of inclusive education in South Africa and critically discuss how these can be overcome in the future to realise true transformation in South Africa.

Q CASE STUDY 1

This research took place at a primary school in the Mdantsane Township in the Eastern Cape, South Africa. The school had 990 learners from Grades 4 to 7. The average class size was 68. The school was very poorly resourced with broken desks and windows, a serious shortage of textbooks and no school library, and the computer laboratory was completely dysfunctional.

During a classroom observation, I noticed a girl named Bulelwa. She was a Grade 7 learner who was severely physically disabled. She had spastic diplegia, a form of cerebral palsy, which meant that her lower body muscles were 'stiff and tight', affecting her legs, hips and pelvis. Although she managed to move around with a pair of crutches, her movements were uncoordinated and she battled to stay upright. She also required a lot of space to get up from the broken desk where she sat.

The class teacher asked her to come forward and complete an example on the chalkboard. No one assisted her to get up from her desk. After several clumsy and awkward attempts, she managed to get herself off her chair and to the front of the overcrowded classroom. She balanced on one crutch as she took the chalk and began solving the problem the teacher had presented. Suddenly, the crutch slipped out from under her, and she fell to the ground. Visibly upset, she quickly tried to get up. No one assisted her. The teacher calmly asked her to continue with the problem. The other learners remained at their desks, completing their work. They hardly lifted their heads. I battled to not leap off my chair to help her. In a brave attempt, she pulled herself up, unassisted by anyone in the class. She was upset with the crutch that had slipped from under her, nothing or no one else. She dusted herself off quickly, and finished completing the problem. The teacher praised her correct answer. She moved back to her desk and carried on with her work.

(Adapted from raw fieldwork material, observation notes: Drake, 2012)

How far have we come with inclusive education?

The case study you have just read features an episode in the life of a Grade 7 learner called Bulelwa. Although physically disabled, she attended a mainstream school. In many ways, the case study shows how far South Africa has come in terms of inclusive education. Bulelwa was part of her class. When she fell down, her classmates and teachers were not alarmed. They were so used to her physical disability that it had become part of the classroom 'norm'. She was one of them, and these sorts of things 'just happened'. They all just got on with teaching and learning, and life at school.

South Africa has faced a multitude of challenges and difficulties in education since the change to democracy in 1994. At the heart of this ordeal is a striving towards *access*, *quality* and *equity* in the education sector. The efforts of education movements and inclusive education proponents promised all South African people a single education system for all learners regardless of abilities, needs, or specialised care. The *Education White Paper 6: Special Needs Education – Building an Inclusive Education and Training System* (Department of Education, 2001) addresses support for learners with disabilities and other challenges. However, more than ten years on, this ideal has yet to be realised in many education contexts across the country. Let us go back a bit and look at our history in education to see how far we have come – and how far we still have to go.

A brief history of education in South Africa

We cannot discuss the development of inclusive education in South Africa without reflecting on our unique South African history. Inclusive education has developed out of a country previously founded on the principles of segregation and racial division. Let us take a brief look at the major developments in South African history that have shaped education today.

Institutionalised apartheid is generally said to have started after the 1948 election victory of the Nationalist Party (NP). Apartheid can be characterised by its central policy of 'divide and rule' (by race), which was aimed at ensuring white survival and **hegemony** by dividing non-whites along racial and ethnic lines (Henrard, 2002:19). Two policies are significant in laying the foundations of apartheid education: the Christian National Education (CNE) Policy of 1948 set up whites as the "senior trustees of the native" and saw the task of whites towards blacks as "to Christianize him and help him on culturally" (Article 15 of CNE Policy, 1948, as quoted in Msila, 2007:148–9); and the Bantu Education Act (No. 47) of 1953 which legalised separate (and inferior) education facilities for blacks.

hegemony: domination by one group over others

In the 1980s, as international pressure and sanctions became more intense, and apartheid resistance groups became stronger and more rebellious, there were increasingly high-powered negotiations between the National Party government, the African National Congress (ANC), and other parties from the resistance movements. Eventually, this led to President F.W. de Klerk's speech in 1990 at the annual opening of parliament, which set in motion the protracted constitutional negotiation process leading up to the first multi-racial elections in April 1994, in which the ANC came to power, and the first democratic Constitution for South Africa was adopted (De Klerk, 1994:4–6). The electoral mandate of the ANC was to redress the inherited inequities and inequalities of the apartheid regime. This change transformed all spheres of life for South Africans, the most challenging being the educational context. Education in South Africa was previously profoundly shaped and modelled on the principle of separation and division along racial lines. Policy development and articulation during the ANC's push for democracy in the 1990s were founded on values that would inform all future transformations in South African education, including inclusive education.

The history of inclusive education

Before 1994, the special education system was segregated from the general education system. South Africa was strongly influenced by international trends. In the 1960s, South Africa followed the American model by creating categories for 'exceptionality' based on learner's physical, sensory and cognitive disabilities. Learners were placed in special schools which were mostly provided for white children; special schools were also segregated along racial lines. South Africa followed the 'medical model' of categorising learners. This meant that the deficit was located in the learner and resulted in interventions that tried to 'restore them to the norm'. By the 1980s, there was a move from the strict labelling and categorisation of learners, towards a broader, special needs education (Lomofsky & Lazarus, 2001).

A significant turn was made in the 1990s when there was an international rethinking of 'special needs'. It was considered that a learner's predisposition as well as the immediate environment of the learner needed to be considered. For example, the Human Sciences Research Council in South Africa published a report (1987), cited in Lomofsky & Lazarus (2001), that showed that there was an extremely high incidence of disability in the black population group of South Africa. The HSRC report attributed this to the environmental factors that created disadvantage: factors such as poverty, lack of awareness of and access to medical facilities, exposure to violence, and lack of opportunities for learning. There was a strong relationship drawn between poverty and disability, a vital component in understanding disability in the South African context and history (Lomofsky & Lazarus, 2001). Since then, there has been a major push to integrate special needs schools into general or mainstream education. With the change to a unified general education system, there is growing pressure to ensure inclusion of learners with specialised educational needs into mainstream education.

 Stop and reflect

You are required to interview a family member or a person who was educated during apartheid in South Africa. Make brief, narrative notes during this informal interview and share them with your class. What can we learn from these past experiences?

Here are some questions to guide your interview:

1 What do you remember most vividly about your years at school?
2 What do you think are the most significant changes in education since apartheid education, besides race desegregation?
3 How do the educational challenges now compare to the educational challenges then?
4 Do you remember any children with disabilities or differences that were at school with you? If so, how did they make you feel? What did you learn or realise from these feelings?

Prior to the adoption of democracy and its new educational policies in South Africa, most learners like Bulelwa, who experienced barriers to learning or who had special requirements for learning, were excluded from education, or sent to mainstream schools without any form of specialised support. There was far too little specialised support at a school level, and even worse, no support for colleges or tertiary institutions that were educating teachers. After 1994, it was the South African Constitution and Bill of Rights (Republic of South Africa, 1996) that would ensure this practice did not continue. Let us investigate these two important policies to increase our understanding of how inclusive education was shaped in South Africa.

The South African Constitution

In 1996, the official Constitution of the Republic of South Africa was adopted. The Constitution, which provided the foundations for the new democracy in 1994, details values, ideals, and hopes for South African society. For those South Africans living in poverty, the

Constitution expressed a set of basic human rights that are protected by the state. The Constitution of the Republic of South Africa is a detailed document consisting of a preamble and 14 chapters, containing 244 sections and eight schedules (Republic of South Africa, 1996). The constitutional principles include the values which are to represent South African society, and are to be nurtured, protected, and emphasised in South African schools. The first principle proclaims that the Constitution shall provide for the establishment of one sovereign state, a common South African citizenry, and a democratic government committed to achieving equality between men and women, and especially between people of all races. Another principle includes prohibition of discrimination and the protection of racial and gender equality, and national unity. These principles directly relate to the development of an inclusive education system, as will be described further later in this chapter.

Ten fundamental values are embedded in the Constitution to enable transformation in South Africa. These are democracy, social justice and equity, equality, non-racism and non-sexism, Ubuntu (human dignity), an open society, accountability, the rule of law, respect, and reconciliation. These values bind all South Africans and all schools to the promise of a new society based on social justice and equality, which are fundamental human rights. It is crucial that education law follow the provisions made in the Constitution. The most important of these provisions is the guarantee that all South Africans, including those needing specialised support, are able to receive a basic level of education. In order to facilitate and advance the realisation of the rights detailed in the new Constitution, the Bill of Rights was established and officially enacted in 1996.

 Stop and reflect

What are values? How do you understand values? First make a list of the ten constitutional values described earlier and write your own definition for each. How do each of these values relate to inclusive education? Now discuss your reflections with your class peers.

The Bill of Rights

The ANC saw a Bill of Rights as crucial to the new Constitution. The Bill of Rights is based on the fundamental equality of all women and men, irrespective of race or colour. These were the principles the ANC had fought for over many decades. The Bill of Rights protects a range of civil, political, economic, and social rights, which were denied to the majority of South Africans during the apartheid years. Remind yourself what these rights are by reading the information on the next page:

What are the rights in the Bill of Rights?

- No one may be subjected to slavery, servitude or forced labour.
- Everyone has the right to fair labour practices – workers are guaranteed the right to form and join trade unions, to participate in the activities and programmes of their unions, and to go on strike.
- Everyone has the right to an environment that is not harmful to his/her health or wellbeing.
- Everyone has the right to have access to adequate housing. The state must take reasonable measures to achieve the progressive realisation of this right within available resources. It is contingent upon the state's available resources.
- Everyone has the right to have access to health care services (including reproductive health care) and sufficient food, water and social security. Again, this right (besides emergency medical treatment) is under progressive realisation.
- Everyone has the right to a basic education, including adult basic education. Everyone also has the right to further education, which the state must take reasonable measures to make progressively available and accessible.
- Provided they do not breach any provision of the Bill of Rights, persons who belong to cultural, religious and linguistic communities have the right to enjoy their culture, religion and language. They may form, join or maintain organisations associated with these rights.

The formation of a human rights culture, founded on specific values, reflected in the Constitution and Bill of Rights, is the basis of state transformation in South Africa. Socio-economic rights are vital to an integrated, holistic Bill of Rights, reflecting the needs and aspirations of all South Africans. These rights were intended to enable people marginalised by poverty to have a voice. These rights also ensure that all children are now protected, including children with special educational needs. Socio-economic rights are regarded as crucial to facilitating the fundamental change of South African society (Liebenberg, 2010:27). Together with the Constitution, the Bill of Rights directly impacts on policy formation in the education sphere.

A culture of human rights

Bulelwa, in our case study, would not have had the experience of mainstream schooling if she had gone to school prior to 1994. Her current placement in the school and in her class is founded on the human rights culture that South Africa now upholds. Let us now discuss the culture of human rights in South Africa to get a better understanding of the development of an inclusive education system.

"Human rights has become an elaborate international practice" (Beitz, 2009:1). Since the end of World War II, many international communities have adopted the human rights framework, and it has expanded the way humans generally think about the human rights doctrine. Human rights have developed in three generations, or major stages. *First generation rights* represent civil and political rights; for example, that all people are born equal, regardless of race, gender, language, religion, and social origin. *Second generation rights* include social, economic, and cultural rights; these include things like the right to work, the right to a standard of living adequate for health, and the right to education. *Third generation rights* support solidarity rights, like the right to a clean environment, the rights to have governments cooperate with one another, and the right to self-determination. These are considered collective rights, supporting **autonomy**, as well as social responsibility (Rude, Paolucci-Whitcomb & Comerford, 2005:27).

South Africa's focus on building a culture of human rights for transformation is not unique. Many African and other countries have adopted a human rights culture in an attempt to democratise their states in light of Western society's values and norms. These values and norms are sometimes interpreted by 'other', non-Western countries as the ideal, in light of their own often traumatic and cruel histories. Since apartheid denied this culture in South Africa, the emphasis on realising and making effective the new human rights culture (proposed in new policy) requires a lot of effort in the education of the public (Dlamini, 1997:41). Dlamini stresses that the Constitution and the Bill of Rights has to occupy a central position in the hearts of the people for transformation to occur, and this does not happen automatically. It follows a deliberate process of educating the youth in the values stated in these new policies. "Education has direct relevance to democracy" (Dlamini,1997:43). In order for South Africa to have a participatory democracy, all people, including the weak, poor, and illiterate, need to be involved. Informed participation depends on education (a second generation right in the Bill of Rights). In order for any country to take the issue of human rights seriously, they have to place top priority on education: "There should be massive education of the people in this country [South Africa] in the bill of rights. The bill of rights has to be made accessible to the people. People should be educated on the bill of rights and its provisions. The right place to start is at school [...]" (Dlamini, 1997:45).

Hence, it is important that schools reflect the nature of a human rights culture, starting with representing the diversity of all South Africans, in particular, those previously marginalised, like Bulelwa and other learners with special needs. In 1996, the National Commission on Special Needs Education and Training (NCSNET) and the National Committee for Education Support Services (NCESS) were appointed to conduct research and make recommendations on how learners with special needs could fully access their right to education. We look now at what these committees found out and recommended.

The NCSNET and NCESS (Department of Education, 1997) found vast inequalities in provisions across race groups and rural and urban settings. They estimated that 288 000 school-age children with disabilities were out of school. On top of this, many more children were out of school because of race, language, HIV and AIDS, and for many other socio-economic reasons. In 1997, the Commission proposed that about 50 per cent of learners in South Africa could be considered to have 'special needs'. Hence, the term *'barriers to learning and development'* was suggested, rather than *'special needs'* (Daniels, 2010). These and other important findings will be further discussed in the policy section of this chapter.

Stop and reflect

New policies that informed education change

As future educators, it is important that you understand the education policies that shape our current education system. We have already looked at the South African Constitution and Bill of Rights. In this section, we will unpack the policies that specifically shape education, and particularly describe inclusive education. To enhance understanding, these policies are summarised in Table 11.1 on page 207.

Important education policies in South Africa

After 1994, the new government committed itself to providing and making available the necessary resources and facilities to give everyone a fair chance to succeed at school. This initiative was premised on the official South African discourse about equality, opportunity and redress. These policy documents form the basis of the new structure in education.

In order to redress white–black educational inequality and the growing need for educational access for all South Africans, the new government's first *White Paper on Education and Training* presented in 1995 became the primary education policy document for both the government and society. It is the source of authority on all education programmes, initiatives and action (Bengu, 1997:22). It was the government's attempt to endorse a principled and realistic vision of what education and training would be for all South Africans; first and foremost favouring and expanding access to education:

> The system must increasingly open access to education and training opportunity of good quality, to all children, youths and adults, and provide means for learners to move easily from one learning context to another, so that the possibilities of lifelong learning are enhanced.' (Department of Education, 1995)

The major change in policy, as shown in this statement, is accessibility of education for all South Africans, regardless of colour or ability. The word 'increasingly' suggests awareness that this process may be long and challenging. The first White Paper sets up a framework to redress past inequalities, emphasising the need for participation by civil society (involvement of all members of society) in the education sphere. With regard to redressing support services, the first White Paper recognises that issues of health, social, psychological, academic, and vocational development, and support services for learners with special educational needs in mainstream schools, are all interrelated. Hence the White Paper intended to explore a holistic and integrated approach.

The *South African Schools Act (SASA)* of 1996 commits to a country and an educational system that will not only redress the injustices of the apartheid past, but also commits to eradicating poverty and ensuring the economic wellbeing of society. It acknowledges that the transformation of society, through overcoming racism, sexism, and all other discriminations and intolerances, will be achieved (Vandeya, 2003:194). The Act focuses on decentralising educational control and decision-making. Emphasis is placed on greater community and parental participation in schooling (Sayed, 1999:141). This Act lays the foundations for the development of all South Africans' talents and capabilities, and upholds the rights of all learners, parents and teachers (Bengu, 1997:23). Compulsory exclusion is abolished and, according to this Act, schools must admit learners and serve their educational needs without unfairly discriminating in any way. School governing bodies must give parents of children with special needs the right to a choice of placement. The governing body should also include representation of learners with specialised educational needs (Lomofsky & Lazarus, 2001).

Inclusive education policies

As future teachers, it is important that you are aware of the policies that shape inclusive education, and how these policies impact on what we do in the classroom. Inclusive education in South Africa is not only about addressing disability in the schooling system. It also addresses context issues that face education in South Africa (Walton, 2011). These include poverty, language differences, inflexible curricula, inaccessible environments, inadequate support services, lack of parental or guardian involvement, single-headed and/or child-headed families, and illnesses such as HIV and AIDS.

Policy (Department of Education, 2001) (you will read more about this shortly) describes inclusive education as acknowledging, accepting and respecting that all learners are different in some way and that different learning needs need to be equally valued. It also emphasises the enabling of structures, systems, and learning methodologies to meet the needs of all learners. Importantly, policy also dictates the role of the community and home in inclusive education, not merely formal education stakeholders. It is about changing the attitudes, behaviours, perceptions, and environment to meet the needs of all learners to enable them to participate critically in learning, and to be empowered.

As described in the previous sections, the *NCSNET/NCESS Report* (Department of Education, 1997) is an important document as it was

> **What is the difference between 'mainstreaming' and 'inclusion'?**
>
> **mainstreaming:** describes the process of getting learners to 'fit in' to a particular system that already exists.
>
> **inclusion:** recognises and respects differences among learners and attempts to build on similarities.

founded on empirical research in the South African context. It provides recommendations that have shaped policies regarding inclusive education since then. The vision for this report was an education and training system that promotes education for all South Africans and fosters development of supportive and inclusive schools that will enable all learners to participate actively and become equal members of society (Daniels, 2010).

Firstly, the Report (Department of Education, 1997) identified the key barriers to learning that were described by the Commission. These include:

- **Socio-economic barriers**. Learning breakdown occurred in impoverished communities. This was due to factors such as poverty, underdevelopment, and a lack of basic services which placed learners at risk. The effects of sustained poverty are poor living conditions, under-nourishment, overcrowded housing, and unemployment, all of which impact on learners. Social, political and economic conditions have profound effects on learners' physical and emotional development. These include dysfunctional families, sexual and physical abuse, violence and crime, substance abuse, crime, chronic illness, and HIV and AIDS.
- **Discrimination and negative attitudes**. Prejudice based on race, class, gender, culture, language, religion, and disability become barriers when directed towards learners at school.
- **Inflexible curricula**. Lack of relevant content, lack of appropriate materials, lack of resources, and inflexible teaching styles that did not allow for individual differences, impacted on learners' development.
- **Language and communication blocks**. When the medium of instruction is not the learners' first language, and sign language is not provided for hearing-impaired learners, these factors become key barriers to learning. A lack of alternative communication strategies for non-speaking learners also significantly impacts on learning.
- **Inaccessible/unsafe built environments**. When learners' physical and/or sensory disabilities are not catered for and there are inadequate support services, these factors place learners at risk.
- **Lack of parental recognition and involvement**. Parental involvement is considered vital when addressing barriers to learning.
- **Lack of human resource development**. Education and training of teachers and other role players is crucial for diminishing key barriers to learning.
- **Disabilities**. Physical, neurological, psycho-neurological, and sensory (sign and hearing) impairments, learning difficulties in reading, writing, and mathematics, speech and language difficulties, are considered barriers to learning.
- **Lack of protective legislation and policy**. Policy and legislation are needed to protect all learners, particularly those learners who were previously marginalised and have specialised needs required for learning. (Lomofsky & Lazarus, 2001:311–312)

Stop and reflect

Engage with South African policies (particularly White Paper 6) that address inclusive education, and the many online articles that critically evaluate the state of inclusive education in South Africa (utilise your library's online databases, or simply use Google scholar to access articles). With your class peers, devise a table that compares policy and practice. Use the key barriers described in the NCSNET/NCESS Report (1997) to guide your work. Report back to your lecturer and class on your main findings and discussion points.

The *NCSNET/NCESS Report* (Department of Education, 1997) envisaged certain characteristics of inclusive education in South Africa:
- With a single education system, a range of learning contexts, offering a varied curriculum and support interventions to address learners' diversity, should be provided in the new South African education system. Ordinary contexts need to be transformed to be able to respond to the diverse needs of learners.
- A flexible curriculum is needed that can respond to learners' diverse needs.
- A change in ethos that welcomes and supports a psycho-social environment for learning and teaching through the development of strategies, is necessary.
- Integration of community-based support systems, that build capacity in all aspects of the system to support learners' diverse needs, is important. There needs to be collaboration and integration across all key role players involved in supporting learners with barriers to learning.
- Human resource development is vital, through various training and support programmes for all role players, particularly teachers.
- Adequate financial and other supports as well as other resources are needed to implement the vision of the Report.
- Practical implementation plans that move towards the vision of an inclusive education and training system in South Africa. (Lomofsky & Lazarus, 2001:312)

These recommendations shaped the official policy that was brought out in 2001, *Education White Paper 6: Building an Inclusive Education and Training System*. The inclusive education principle is in accordance with international trends and developments, and acknowledges that learners who experience barriers should not be excluded from the mainstream education system.

Education White Paper 6 makes the shift from the deficit 'special needs' model to a broader focus on 'barriers to learning and development' which involves the system as a whole, not just the learner. Provision is at the forefront of this policy: support for mainstream schools for low-intensity support needs of learners, moderate level support in full-service schools, and intensive support in special schools with high support needs. Special schools were to transform into resource centres for mainstream schools. Again, there is a strong link back to those founding documents, the Constitution and Bill of Rights. The principles of White Paper 6 include human rights and social justice for all learners; optimal participation and integration of all learners, regardless of educational needs; equal access to schools and to the curriculum so that they can meaningfully and fully engage in the teaching and learning process; equity and redress of past inequalities; sensitivity to and involvement of the community; and cost-effectiveness of services provided (Daniels, 2010).The long-term goal of this policy development is to create an inclusive education and training system that will uncover and address barriers to learning, and recognise and accommodate the diverse range of learning needs. So, how exactly is an inclusive education system defined?

According to this policy document, inclusive education and training (Department of Education, 2001:16):
- Is about acknowledging that all children and youth can learn, and that all children and youth need support.
- Is accepting and respectful of the fact that all learners are different in some way, and have different learning needs, which are equally valued and an ordinary part of our human experience.
- Is about enabling education structures, systems and learning methodologies to meet the needs of all learners.
- Acknowledges and respects differences in learners, whether due to age, gender, ethnicity, language, and class, disability, or HIV status.
- Is broader than formal schooling and acknowledges that learning also occurs in the home and community, and within formal and informal modes and structures.
- Is about changing attitudes, behaviour, teaching methodologies, curricula, and the environment, to meet the needs of all learners.
- Is about maximising the participation of all learners in the culture and the curricula of educational institutions, and uncovering and minimising barriers to learning.
- Is about empowering learners by developing their individual strengths and enabling them to participate critically in the process of learning.

 Stop and reflect

The definition of inclusive education is broad and complex. How does this make you feel as a student teacher? Think about how you are going to accommodate learners with barriers to learning in your own classroom. Some of your reflections might be emotional. Discuss these feelings with a classmate, or sit over a lunch break in a small group and brainstorm ideas around being truly inclusive in your approach to teaching and learning. What will the biggest challenges be?

We have summarised and discussed in detail a number of policy documents. Use the table that follows to ensure you understand the progression and development of inclusive education in South Africa. Bulelwa, in the opening case study, enjoyed mainstream education because of these major shifts in educational thinking in South Africa. However, it is not always as simple as designing a policy around a challenging issue. One of the biggest critiques of these policy documents is the capacity of policy to be implemented in South African schools. Let us now look at issues around implementation of these policies in South African schools.

Table 11.1 Overview of inclusive education policies

Policy	Date	Overview	Important features for inclusive education
Constitution of the Republic of South Africa, 1996	1996 (Interim Constitution used 1994–1996)	Founding document, rights containing new principles, values for the new, transformed, apartheid-free South Africa	• Equality between all people • Protection of all people • Redress for previously marginalised groups • People with specialised needs guaranteed primary level of education
Bill of Rights	Officially adopted in 1996	Detailed description of specific rights that all South Africans are entitled to, including first, second, and third generation rights	• Everyone has a right to basic education • Everyone has a right to have access to health care services • Everyone has a right to an environment that is not harmful to his or her health
First White Paper on Education and Training	1995	A primary document on all education programmes allowing open access to education for all South Africans	• Redressing support services • All learners have access to schooling • A holistic, integrated approach for education
South African Schools Act	1996	For government and society. Addresses inequality and educational access for all South Africans. Decentralised control and decision-making for schools.	• More collaboration and participation at school level • Parental involvement encouraged • All learners must be served at school and must be represented at schools without discrimination
NCSNET/NCESS Report	1997	Based on empirical research done in South Africa. Provides strategies for inclusive education system.	• 'Special needs' replaced with 'barriers to teaching and development' • Many environmental, political, emotional and socio-economic factors impact on barriers to learning • Curriculum relevance and teacher training crucial for inclusive education realisation
White Paper 6: Building an Inclusive Education and Training System	2001	Special policy designed to specifically address the specialised needs of learners with barriers to learning. Strong links to Constitution, Bill of Rights, and values of equality and redress.	• Understanding and describing inclusive education • Outlining specific strategies and goals for the adoption of a truly inclusive education system • Encouraging participation of all stakeholders and community members • Espouses medium-term and long-term goals

The challenge of implementation of inclusive policies

As you read the following case study, use the overview of inclusive education policies to remind yourself of the essential features of each.

CASE STUDY 2

Teacher A: You know, I cannot deal with another policy document that I am expected to implement in my class, with no support or training from our EDO [education department official] or from the Department of Education.

Teacher B: What is the point of all this paperwork? It is not like it is going to change anything for us. If they could give us basics, like desks and textbooks first, then maybe we could start thinking about new policies and reports.

Teacher A: I know. These policies take away from my teaching focus and from my time with the learners. I have 70 learners in my home class, and when I teach Social Sciences across a grade, I have over 300 files that I am expected to monitor for one subject!

Teacher B: And don't forget the special reports that we are supposed to keep for the learners in our classes who have barriers to learning. I find that I have no option but to neglect those reports. I don't even know what I would say in it. It is not like I have the time to devise special lessons or activities for these learners.

Teacher A: And some parents want updates, too. Just the other day a parent wanted to know how their child with **dyslexia** was doing in class, and I found it very difficult to even remember what I had done with the learner that week.

Teacher B: It makes me want to give up, to find another career.

Teacher A: I understand. And with each new policy or programme adopted in education, comes a whole new workload for us, as teachers, to accommodate.

Teacher B: Yes, and don't forget the lack of training and development. Remember that workshop we were expected to come to in our school holidays? Or the other one where the course facilitators didn't come because they couldn't find our school? It is like the government doesn't understand what is happening on the ground level, in our schools.

Teacher A: I feel that if they just stopped, and came to witness first-hand the conditions under which we work, then they would have a better understanding of what is happening in our schools and how over-burdened we are as teachers. I just see no light. I feel hopeless, and hopeless for our learners, too.

(Adapted from focus group transcripts: Drake, 2012)

Stop and reflect

Discuss the following questions with a fellow student.
1 Do the teachers in this case study sound happy with their work and the situation in their classrooms? Why or why not?
2 What are three main things that are of concern to these teachers? Explain each one, based on your understanding of the background you have been reading.
3 If you could talk to these teachers, what one question would you ask them? What one thing would you like to tell them?

Schooling is often assumed to be of political and socio-economic benefit in society, but at times can end up reproducing existing inequalities and contribute to violence in society (Harber & Mncube, 2011:234). In South Africa, standards of living are closely associated with race (Woolard, 2002), and poverty is predominantly concentrated among black people (Mubangizi & Mubangizi, 2005). Hence, schools serving well-off communities can charge high school fees in order to maintain excellent facilities and employ more teachers; while schools in poor communities are not able to do so (Harber & Mncube, 2011:236). The Delta Foundation (Delta Foundation South Africa, 2004), which supports educational research conducted by the Nelson Mandela Metropolitan University and disseminated to universities and schools, showed that of the 30 000 plus schools in South Africa, 3 000 are deemed dysfunctional (Delta Foundation South Africa, 2004). These schools are unable to produce an environment for effective teaching and learning. The National Education Infrastructure Management System (Development Bank of South Africa, 2008) described the context that daily teaching and learning occurs in the majority of South African schools: 42 per cent of schools are overcrowded, 3 152 are without water, 1 532 are without toilets, 4 297 are without electricity, 79 per cent have no libraries, 68 per cent have no computers, and 60 per cent are without laboratories. On a so-called normal day, as many as 30 per cent of teachers and 50 per cent of learners will be absent, and blame it on poor physical facilities and intimidation (Mitchell, 2005).

Apart from these daily, real-life challenges, educators are expected to accommodate a broad range of learners' needs in the classroom. As we have seen through the discussion and investigation into the many policies that have founded the development of inclusive education in South Africa, the responsibility ultimately lies with the teacher to support and guide these learners in the teaching and learning process. This is in line with the inclusive education principles of meeting every child's needs within the education system while acknowledging differences in the ways that children learn (Luger, Prudhomme, Bullen, Pitt & Geiger, 2012).

So how do teachers cope with these new demands and considerations? If we consider the conversation between the two educators at the

dyslexia: a difficulty in reading that involves not being able to interpret words or recognise letters and symbols

beginning of this section, we see that teachers do not always cope well with these transformations in the education system, and in their schools. Research suggests that in the majority of cases, teachers are not coping in South Africa, and neither are they in other countries. Teachers play one of the most influential roles in the successful implementation of inclusive education, but research findings suggest that teachers are not well prepared to deal with inclusive education in their classrooms. Inclusive education is thus perceived to place additional demands and stress on teachers, which negatively impacts on the progress of all children in the classroom (Engelbrecht, 2006). Improving the acceptance and recognition of human rights of all South African children, requires an honest reflection on the usefulness of policy to teachers at the ground level. In research findings discussed by Engelbrecht (2006:260), three elements came through as impacting on the development of an inclusive education system at a South African school in a rural community. Although this research represents findings at one school in South Africa, the findings allow us to consider the bigger issues and complexities of inclusive education in typical South African schools.

What three elements impact on the development of an inclusive education system?

1 Diversity is a difficult value to understand. Children with disabilities, as well as those from poverty-stricken backgrounds, are often viewed as being 'different'. Teachers, despite the fact that many of them experienced discrimination themselves during the apartheid era, seem unable to grasp the idea that their own attitudes and opinions towards diversity can contradict basic human rights and equitable access to education.
2 Schools are expected to be democratic institutions, a big move from the conservative, authoritarian school system under apartheid. If staff morale is low, and this is directly related to a non-existent culture of **collegiality** and team work in the school, creating an inclusive school community proves impossible. A culture of collaborative partnerships between teachers, as well as between teachers, learners and parents, is crucial. If this does not exist, then a truly inclusive school community cannot develop.
3 Community involvement is identified by teachers, as well as parents, as being problematic in building an inclusive school community. Aspects of illiteracy, socio-economic deprivation, and extreme poverty cause problems with the development of an inclusive community. Parents are often fatigued from long work hours, and illiteracy prevents them from actively engaging in the education of their children, leaving the school with the sole responsibility for the education of a large number of learners. This impacts on daily, ground-level school life through late-coming, absenteeism, repeating grades, and eventual dropping out.

collegiality: working in a spirit of sharing knowledge and learning from one another

In terms of teaching curricula, and understanding and implementing policy, it is recommended that information, skills training, and advocacy issues about disabilities and their implications need to be included more formally in the curriculum for teacher training, and in schools. Teachers need assistance to include learners with disabilities in the academic and social aspects of school. Also, there is a need for disability-related teaching materials that teachers can use, and do-able ways of incorporating these into the present school curriculum. More collaboration and participation between parents and teachers is also needed for inclusive education to truly be realised in South Africa (Luger et al., 2012).

The difficulties and challenges of developing a truly inclusive education system have been discussed. We have seen that although the policies provide a beacon of hope to the realisation of inclusive education in South Africa, we still face major challenges through the implementation process. This implementation process is vital as a first-level problem-solving step. Teachers have to be considered first and foremost, and they need to get the support and assistance they require to understand primarily what inclusion is all about, and then how to incorporate inclusive strategies in their classrooms daily. Parents also need to be educated and encouraged to participate, which is another important but complex challenge that faces policymakers and government officials. Quite simply, for inclusive education to be realised in South Africa, we, as teachers and future teachers, need to model the collaborative and participatory values that founded the policies.

In the next section, we critically analyse the 'policy–practice gap' in South Africa. This chapter has shown that although we have, in many cases, admirable and revolutionary policies in South Africa, the implementation of these policies is a major barrier to these new transformations being realised by all South Africans.

The policy–practice gap: A critical lens

In the earlier sections of this chapter, we have discussed the many policy documents that have shaped how inclusive education has come about in South Africa. Let us take a step further in our discussion and think carefully about if and how policy impacts on practice, and what the implications are. The policy–practice gap is a phenomenon that significantly influences all spheres of life in South Africa, particularly education.

The changes in educational policy can best be described as a strategy to achieve broad **political symbolism** to mark the shift from apartheid to the new transformed South Africa. The core concepts of equity, access, and redress are repeated many times in the new policies. It is assumed that their meanings are understood by everyone in South Africa, but these have led to ambiguities and confusion.

Jansen (2002) argues that, despite the production of any many new policies in post-apartheid South Africa, there has been little change throughout the country, particularly in schools and classrooms. He proposes that an explanation for this gap can be viewed through the lens of 'political symbolism'. During the period of 1994–1999, when the Constitution and Bill of Rights were formulated and passed, the broader political aim was to settle the apartheid struggle in the political domain, rather than in practice. The period is described as an explicitly ideological–political time, and was dominated by establishing the ideological and political credentials of the new

political symbolism: signs and words that are used to represent a particular political standpoint. This can include many things, like flags, banners, mottos, images, specific colours, acronyms. This term is used by Jansen (2002) and other authors to show how policies were the concrete evidence that could be shown and presented to the South African people, to represent the abstract political shift from apartheid to post-apartheid South Africa

government (Jansen, 2002). This was measured by a rapid departure from apartheid, which resulted in the large number of policy papers, documents, legislation and regulations that were produced. Ultimately, the human rights discourse was the new government's way of achieving a broad political symbolism that moved away from the apartheid legacy. Jansen argues that in most cases, implementation of policy was never on the agenda of the politicians. Unfortunately, it appears that this policy-making tradition has continued, evident in the policies and the discussions we have had in this chapter. There is a desperate need for concrete steps to realise the promises of a truly inclusive education system.

Democratic and human rights education cannot be provided as part of the school curriculum without attention to the pre-service and in-service training of teachers. Schools are the starting points for promoting democracy and human rights values in society. Increased provision of education itself is not enough – literacy and skills are not enough. Sifuna (2000:236) recommends that educators have to realise the need and importance of this type of education. Transforming political talk into practice requires a commitment beyond just knowledge and skills from educators and school stakeholders.

 Stop and reflect

Political symbolism is an abstract term to grasp. Spend some time talking to a classmate about how you understand political symbolism in South Africa. Think of some examples of political symbolism that are perhaps currently in the news (they do not have to be education-related, but it would be useful to your discussion if they are). What challenges do you think political symbolism poses to the South African people? What steps do you think can be taken to turn political symbolism into concrete change, particularly for the inclusive education ideology?

Summary of discussion

Inclusive education in South Africa is specifically framed within a human rights culture, transforming our constitutional values and principles to impact on the immediate rights of excluded learners, and those with specialised needs at school. The South African education system is a single system of education that is dedicated to ensuring that all individuals, regardless of barriers and specialised educational needs, realise their right to education. This is a vast shift from the 'medical model' that predominated in the education system prior to 1994. Inclusive education, as described in the policies, is founded on the values of freedom and equality. This chapter has presented the reader with an overall discussion on the development of inclusive education in South Africa, while remaining critical of the ideological values and beliefs that come with new policies in a new political dispensation. This chapter has also highlighted the difficulties that prevent this realisation, and the challenges of the policy–practice gap and with implementation which dominate inclusive education and many new education policies.

In the next chapter, the author will unpack the realities of inclusive education in the classroom, the real-life discussions that will further enhance your understanding.

Closing activities

Self-reflection
1. Think back to your personal experiences of school. How have these experiences shaped the way you think today? What memories do you need to rethink and analyse to allow yourself to think differently about your role as a teacher in the future? How can you be the best teacher you can be, and add to the South African dream of true transformation?
2. How do you view people who are different? Think carefully about how you understand diversity. Are you really as 'inclusive' as you may think? How tolerant are you of people who are different and require extra, or different, assistance?

Practical applications
3. List steps that you can take to address inclusive education in your classroom. Be realistic, and plot a timeline on how and when you can achieve these steps. Inclusive practices start with the individual, so it is important that you start thinking about this from today. What training is available to you? What books or articles can you read to improve your own understanding and capacity? Who would you speak to, to get a deeper insight?
4. Volunteer some of your personal time to work with children or people who require assistance. This could be at a special school, a home with elderly people or physically disabled people. There will be many institutions in your town or city that would value your time and input. Write an honest journal reflection on how you found the experience. Avoid writing what you think you should write – begin by being honest with yourself. This is the first step in truly understanding an inclusive education approach.

Analysis and consolidation
5. Draw a policy mind map that shows how inclusive education has developed in South Africa, starting with the Constitution. Make notes of your understanding of these policies and what the biggest challenges are to these policies. Avoid looking back in the chapter. Try to use the knowledge you have acquired, and your own understanding, to guide this activity.
6. Prepare an oral presentation for your class based on the literature that you have researched around inclusive education in South Africa. Use this understanding to ask the critical questions and make personal recommendations on how South Africans can

truly move towards an inclusive education system. Allow time for questions and discussion after your presentation. The best preparation for future educators is to start asking the critical questions and having the difficult discussions, in order to truly realise transformation in South Africa.

References

Beitz, C. 2009. *The idea of human rights.* Oxford: Oxford University Press.

Bengu, S. 1997. Foreword. In E.F.J. de Groof & R. Malherbe (Eds). *Human rights in South African education: From the constitutional drawing board to the chalkboard.* Leuven: Acco.

Daniels, B. 2010. Developing inclusive policy and practice in diverse contexts: A South African experience. *School Psychology International,* 31(6):631–643. Retrieved from: http://spi.sagepub. com/content/31/6/631.full.pdf+html on 30 May 2013.

De Klerk, W. 1994. The process of political negotiations: 1990-1993. In B. de Villiers (Ed). *Birth of a constitution.* Kenwyn, South Africa: Juta.

Delta Foundation South Africa. 2004. *Achieving out of the dust: School communities making things happen: A whole school development initiative.* [Video]. Port Elizabeth: Delta Foundation.

Department of Education. 1995. *White Paper on Education and Training (Notice 196 of 1995).* Retrieved from: http://www. education.gov.za/dynamic/ on 20 April 2008.

Department of Education. 1997. *Quality education for all. Overcoming barriers to learning and development. Report of the National Commission on Special Needs in Education and Training and the National Committee for Special Educational Services.* Retrieved from: http://www.education.gov.za/ on 14 January 2013.

Department of Education. 2001. *Education White Paper 6: Special Needs Education – Building an inclusive education and training system.* Retrieved from: http://www.info.gov.za/whitepapers/2001/ educ6.pdf on 10 January 2013.

Development Bank of South Africa. 2008. *Education roadmap: Focus on schooling system.* Retrieved from: http://www.dbsa.org/ Research/ on 14 August 2011.

Dlamini, C. 1997. The relationship between human rights and education. In J. de Groof & R. Malherbe (Eds). *Human rights in South African education: From the constitutional drawing board to the chalkboard.* Leuven: Acco.

Drake, M. 2012. How do the values in new South African policy manifest in a disadvantaged school setting? Unpublished doctoral thesis. Auckland, New Zealand: University of Auckland.

Engelbrecht, P. (2006). The implementation of inclusive education in South Africa after ten years of democracy. *European Journal of Psychology of Education*, 21(3):253–264. Retrieved from: http://0-web.ebscohost.com.wam.seals.ac.za/ on 21 May 2013.

Harber, C., & Mncube, V. (2011). Is schooling good for the development of society? The case of South Africa. *South African Journal of Education*, 31(2):233–245. Retrieved from: http://www.ajol.info/index.php/saje/article/ on 14 November 2011.

Henrard, K. 2002. Post apartheid South Africa's democratic transformation process: Redress of the past, reconciliation and 'unity in diversity'. *The Global Review of Ethnopolitics*, 1(3):18–38. Retrieved from: http://www.tandfonline.com.ezproxy.auckland.ac.nz/doi/pdf/10.1080/ on 20 February 2011.

Jansen, J. 2002. Political symbolism as policy craft: Explaining non-reform in South African education after apartheid. *Journal of Education Policy*, 17(2):199–215. Retrieved from: http://www.tandfonline.com.ezproxy.auckland.ac.nz/doi/pdf/ on 7 October 2011.

Liebenberg, S. 2010. *Socio-economic rights: Adjudication under a transformative constitution*. Cape Town: Juta.

Lomofsky, L. & Lazarus, S. 2001. South Africa: First steps in the development of an inclusive education system. *Cambridge Journal of Education*, 31(3):303–317. Retrieved from: http://0-web.ebscohost.com.wam.seals.ac.za/ehost/ on 21 May 2013.

Luger, R., Prudhomme, D., Bullen, A., Pitt, C. & Geiger, M. (2012). A journey towards inclusive education: A case study from a 'township' in South Africa. *African Journal of Disability*, 1(1):1–5. Retrieved from: http://www.ajod.org/index.php/ajod/article/ on 5 June 2013.

Mitchell, P. 2005. An organisational development intervention in an Eastern Cape school. Unpublished Masters thesis, Rhodes University, Grahamstown, South Africa.

Msila, V. 2007. From apartheid education to the revised national curriculum: Pedagogy for identity formation and nation building in South Africa. *Nordic Journal of African Studies*, 16(2):146–160. Retrieved from: http://www.njas.helsinki.fi/pdf-files/vol16num2/msila.pdf on 21 February 2014.

Mubangizi, J. & Mubangizi, B. 2005. Poverty, human rights law and socio-economic realities in South Africa. *Development Southern Africa*, 22(2):277–290. Retrieved from: http://www.tandfonline.com.ezproxy.auckland.ac.nz/doi/pdf/ on 8 July 2011.

Republic of South Africa. 1996. The Constitution of the Republic of South Africa, 1996. Cape Town. Retrieved from: http://www.info.gov.za/documents/constitution/ on 12 January 2013.

Rude, H., Paolucci-Whitcomb, P. & Comerford, S. 2005. Ethical leadership: Supporting human rights and diversity in rural communities. *Rural Special Education Quarterly*. 24(4):26. Retrieved from: http://ezproxy.auckland.ac.nz/login?url=http://proquest.umi.com/ on 8 December 2010.

Sayed, Y. 1999. Discourses of the policy of educational decentralisation in South Africa since 1994: An examination of the South African Schools Act [1][2]. Compare, 29(2):141–152. Retrieved from: http://ezproxy.auckland.ac.nz/login? on 17 April 2009.

Sifuna, D. 2000. Education for democracy and human rights in African schools: The Kenyan experience. *African Development*, 25(1&2):213–239. Retrieved from: http://www.ajol.info/index.php/ad/article/view/22114/19401 on 7 May 2010.

Vandeya, S. 2003. The jagged paths to multicultural education: International experiences and South Africa's response to the new dispensation. *South African Journal of Education*, 23(3):193–198. Retrieved from: http://www.ajol.info/index.php/saje/article/4933/20620 on 7 July 2013.

Walton, E. 2011. Getting inclusion right in South Africa. *Hammil Institute on Disabilities*. 46(4):240–245. Retrieved from: http://isc.sagepub.com/content/early/2010/11/20/1053451210389033.full.pdf+html on 26 January 2013.

Woolard, I. 2002. An overview of poverty and inequality in South Africa (unpublished briefing paper). Pretoria: Human Sciences Research Council. Retrieved from: http://www.sarpn.org/CountryPovertyPapers/SouthAfrica/july2002/ onn 5 December 2009.

12 Inclusive education in the classroom: Practical applications

Joseph Tchatchoueng

Chapter overview

Diversity in culture, languages, historical experiences, socio-economic status, and both abilities and disabilities among the people who live in South Africa is easily seen in many contemporary classrooms across the country. The presence of this diversity among learners is an important aspect of an inclusive education classroom but does not, on its own, make the classroom environment an inclusive one. Every learner in the classroom has to be able to participate meaningfully in all educational practices before one can refer to a particular classroom as being an inclusive education classroom. Unfortunately, as is often the case in many developing countries, including South Africa, while the physical placement in mainstream schools of learners with disabilities and other forms of learning barriers is often emphasised, the other aspects of developing an inclusive education classroom environment still need serious attention. This is the case because unemployment, poverty, malnutrition, inadequate medical facilities, and high rates of prenatal and early childhood infections make the number of learners with special needs higher in this country than in many other countries with comparable levels of economic development (Landsberg, 2011). The aim of this chapter is to help the reader gain more insight into practices that can lead to the creation and maintenance of inclusive education classrooms. The chapter will also indicate the contribution that the family and the community can make in building inclusive education classrooms.

Learning outcomes

By the end of this chapter you should be able to:
- Describe some of the features of an inclusive education classroom
- Explain how inclusive education is presently practised in South African classrooms
- Establish practical implications of inclusive education for the family and the community
- Outline the support that is in place to assist South African teachers in building inclusive education classrooms
- Critically analyse ground-level issues and challenges related to the practice of inclusive education within the classroom.

What does it take to be inclusive?

In the last chapter you read about the vision and policies that have been put in place to promote and support inclusive education in South Africa. Dishearteningly, you also learned that there is a considerable gap between policy and practice. We have to go into South African classrooms to discover what is really going on as far as making inclusive education happen.

CASE STUDY 1

Three first-year student teachers are tasked with observing, for five days, an inclusive Grade 8 classroom at a neighbourhood school. During the five days that their observation will last, they are expected to take notes on diversity in the learner population, and to observe how teachers and the learners create and nurture an inclusive education classroom environment. Below are extracts from each student teacher's observation notes.

Student teacher A: The learners I am observing are both respectful and daring. They come from different socio-economic and cultural backgrounds to form a genuine learning community in which everyone is encouraged to participate in all class activities. They display a shared feeling of security and belonging through the friendly ambience of the class, and through the posters and the other pieces of art that adorn the walls of their classroom. Observing these learners at work has led me to think that the main feature of an inclusive classroom is the teacher's ability to maintain an atmosphere of participation and care.

Student teacher B: There is this learner in a wheelchair. Apparently, the boy was fine until he had an accident two years ago. The trauma of the accident put him in the wheelchair and still causes him to suffer epileptic crises now and then. The deputy-principal reports that the school governing body has significantly enhanced the human and material resources of the school. Major changes have also been made in the physical environment so that this learner feels welcome and refers to the school as 'my school'.

Student teacher C: I spotted four very bright learners. One of the teachers explained that no one fails maths in her class, and the credit for this success goes to these bright learners: three girls and a boy. She has taught them how to share their knowledge constructively with their peers. They now make themselves available to help others after completing their own activities. "All I did was to acknowledge their potential, and they have become valuable resources in the classroom community," the maths teacher tells me.

1   Drawing from your own life experience and from the above extracts, what changes would you say have taken place within the learner population of an average classroom in recent years?
2   Identify and explain three factors that have triggered the changes that you now observe in the learner population in South Africa.
3   As a future teacher, what skills do you need to acquire in order to handle diversity among learners in the new classroom environment?
4   Work out from the above extracts what some of the features of an inclusive education classroom should be. Describe at least three features.

Graf (2011:11) argues that "removing barriers to learning and giving all children the opportunity to learn as well as they can are fundamental aims of an inclusive education system." The same could be said of an inclusive education classroom; one could re-formulate the sentence as: removing barriers to learning and giving all children the opportunity to learn to the best of their ability are fundamental aims of an inclusive education classroom. What emerges from this quote, which will help the reader better understand the features of an inclusive education classroom, is this: there are two things that an inclusive education classroom is designed to achieve. The *first* is to offer easy physical access to all the learners regardless of individual physical abilities or disabilities. In other words, all learners, including those in wheelchairs, those on crutches, and those with various forms of auditory and visual impairment, should be able to physically access and move around the school and classroom environment without major help from teachers or peers. As the deputy-principal in our case study puts it, it is about making the necessary changes within the school and classroom environment so that all learners can see for themselves that the school and the classroom facilities were designed and built with them in mind. Ultimately, each learner should be able to refer to the school as 'my school'.

The *second* and perhaps the more important goal of an inclusive education classroom is to gear every method, every means of instruction, and every learning strategy towards ensuring that every learner, regardless of disability, socio-economic status, linguistic and cultural background, and regardless of competence in the language of learning and teaching, is able to acquire as much knowledge as possible, and to experience educational success, friendship, and a genuine sense of belonging to the learning community (DoE, 2001 & 2005). Keeping in mind these very important goals of an inclusive education classroom, let us now look at some of the most characteristic features of such a classroom.

Features of an inclusive education classroom

Some of the most important features of an inclusive education classroom are: a supportive learning culture, democratic leadership, reflective teaching, student centeredness, and responsive curricula. As you will see, these features are organised around the qualities that the inclusive teacher should have, the way the classroom environment should be organised, the behaviour expected of learners, and the flexible and adaptable nature of curricula. Let us look at each one of these features in detail.

Supportive learning culture

All learners learn best in an environment in which they feel comfortable, appreciated, and safe. So, inclusive education teachers work toward maintaining a comfortable, pleasant, and safe classroom environment. In order to achieve this goal, one of the strategies that these teachers use is to obtain as much information as they possibly can about each of their learners and about their family background. In fact, details about individual learner's background, and especially about the background of learners with special needs, are essential to provide a supportive learning environment for everyone in the inclusive education classroom. Besides an introductory session during which individual learners have a chance to volunteer substantial information about themselves, teachers often get the additional information they need from parents or carers during contact with them.

Some parents have many concerns about inclusive education, and about its impact on both the education and the holistic development of their children (this includes both parents of children with disabilities and parents of children without disabilities). These concerns have to be dealt with by the inclusive education teacher. So, maintaining a supportive learning environment in an inclusive classroom also goes hand in hand with showing understanding and keeping up a welcoming and friendly attitude toward all learners and their parents. This includes listening respectfully and patiently to their worries and insecurities. It also entails providing them with the necessary explanations with regard to the benefits of inclusive education, and about measures that are being taken to enable all learners to benefit from learning and teaching within the inclusive education classroom environment (Graf, 2011).

Democratic leadership

One of the most important features of an inclusive classroom is the type of leadership that the teacher decides to foster within the classroom environment (DoE, 2011). One would expect, in an inclusive education classroom, the leadership to be very different from the 'sit, fold your arms, listen and obey'-type of approach that is prevalent in more authoritarian settings. In an inclusive education classroom there is, instead, democratic leadership that allows learners to participate in decision-making. This type leadership is evident when, on entering the learning site, one has the same feeling as that experienced by one of the student teachers of our case study: learners are both "respectful and daring". In fact, one should be able to pick up from the décor, e.g. posters and pictures (including learner's own artwork) displayed on the walls, and from the cheerful ambience among learners, that they own the learning space and contribute meaningfully to their learning. For example, they contribute in establishing the rules of the classroom, and in ensuring that everyone gets a fair chance to participate in cooperative activities and in class discussions.

Shared sense of responsibility

For the sake of learners, the inclusive vision and democratic leadership that the inclusive teacher fosters in the classroom is shared with and supported by other teachers, support staff, and members of the community. Each one of these groups of people brings something to the creation of the inclusive education classroom. For example, parents who see the relevance of inclusive education can help with project-based learning, and with preparing the learner to be a resource for the development of the inclusive education classroom. Thanks to the help of such parents, learners of inclusive education classrooms tend to be more willing to assist others, and tend to be more ready to accept assistance from their peers. In collaboration with parents, the other teachers could encourage learners to use the social skills which are gained in the inclusive education classroom within the broader school environment and within the community at large. In short, teachers of inclusive classrooms understand the importance of adopting a team approach to building and maintaining an inclusive education classroom. They are keen to establish a network of support with parents and colleagues that will help them, in turn, cater for their learners. By so doing, they acknowledge that the key to a learner's meaningful participation in educational processes is creative thinking on the part of that learner's support team.

Responsive curricula

Inclusive education classrooms have a population which is very diverse, and which consists of learners with rich prior knowledge and strong readiness for the grade they are in. But these classrooms also have learners with limited prior knowledge and poor grade readiness. Because of these differences in abilities among learners, the establishment of inclusive education classrooms requires that the curriculum be sufficiently adaptable to allow the teacher to respond flexibly to the variation in prior knowledge, levels of readiness, abilities and preferences that learners display in the classroom. Often, barriers to learning arise from the different interlocking parts of the curriculum, such as "the content of learning programmes, the language and medium of learning and teaching, the management and organisation of the classroom, teaching style and pace, timeframe for completion of curricula, the material and equipment that are available as well as assessment methods and techniques" (DoE, 2001:32). All of these are aspects of the curriculum that should be adaptable and responsive to the different learning needs that learners have in the inclusive classroom environment.

 Stop and reflect

1   After reading this section, what would you say some of the essential features of an inclusive education classroom are? Describe them in your own words.
2   Find out and explain two other features of an inclusive education classroom that are not covered in the above section.

What instructional strategies can teachers use in inclusive education classrooms?

There are several teaching and learning strategies that teachers use in an inclusive education classroom. Some of these are: cooperative learning, scaffolding, cubing, problem solving and collaborative co-teaching. As Prinsloo (2001:344) puts it, when selecting teaching and learning strategies, teachers of inclusive education classrooms have two main objectives to fulfil: "meeting the needs of all learners; and actualising the full potential of all learners." Consequently, teachers of inclusive education classrooms prefer teaching and learning strategies that are learner-centered, highly participatory, and that are attached to the principles of experiential learning. They consider the best of these teaching and learning strategies to be those that give learners a great margin of trial and error in the learning process (Harley & Rule, 2013; Jarvis, 1987). The best teaching and learning strategies also allow teachers to take into consideration individual learner's prior knowledge, and to cater for those who experience barriers to learning, like a lack of competence in the language of learning and teaching, under-preparedness deriving from previous grades, and various forms of impairment including visual and auditory disabilities. They give all learners a chance to draw from their talents and areas of strength, to try out and further develop their abilities and skills when completing tasks in small groups or individually. Let us look at only three of the many strategies that have been developed for teaching in inclusive classroom.

Cooperative learning

Cooperative learning describes methods of learning and teaching that allow learners to work together with a strong interest in each other's learning, and in their own. In fact, in cooperative learning groups, individual learners work together to achieve a common goal, and to enhance in the process each other's learning. Johnson and Johnson (1994:13) characterise cooperative learning with this example: "A cooperative spelling class is one where students are working together in small groups to help each other learn the words in order to take a spelling test individually on another day. Each learner's score on the test is increased by bonus points if the group totals meet specified criteria."

Cooperative learning methods are revolutionary and innovative because they try to remove unnecessary and unhealthy competition among learners. Instead, they replace them by developing both the social skills and supportive attitudes that learners need in order to interact successfully across perceived differences and disabilities. According to Johnson and Johnson (2008:9), "cooperative learning tends to result in greater achievement, more positive relationships and greater psychological health." As such, cooperative methods work for teachers who are eager to develop ways of instruction that do not isolate and stigmatise learners with learning barriers, including learners who lack competence in the language of learning and teaching, those who are affected by family problems, those with physical or learning disabilities, and those who just need more time to understand and apply concepts. In cooperative learning groups, interaction is characterised by application of the following principles: positive interdependence, face-to-face inventive interaction, individual accountability or personal responsibility, interpersonal and small group skills, and group processing. We will discuss each one of these principles further after we have explored two other instructional strategies that teachers use in inclusive classrooms. There are a number of different types of cooperative learning techniques; the following strategies, when they involve peer teaching, can also be seen as cooperative learning techniques.

Scaffolding

Gultig and Stielau (2009: 27) write that "scaffolding refers to the help that teachers give learners that enables them to extend their knowledge and to try something they would otherwise not manage on their own." Learning, just like running, is something that no one can do for the learner. But, just as amateur runners need the expertise of a professional coach to understand the rules that regulate professional running, to discover their individual running style, and, more importantly, to be stretched towards their optimal competence, learners need the expertise of professional teachers who can assess their level of understanding of content knowledge, and then set adequate challenges to take them from their present level to the next level of understanding. Professional teachers guide students to the next level of understanding while ensuring that learners find the experience of learning both challenging and enjoyable In a lesson that is adequately scaffolded, the teacher avoids confusing learners with very complex tasks. She ensures that the gap is not too big between what individual learners have already acquired and what they are expected to acquire. The teacher also ensures that this gap is neither too small nor void of the challenge that is so necessary for learners to learn something new. Ultimately, scaffolding is about reflective teaching and qualitative incrementing of learner's prior knowledge. As such, scaffolding learning is about creating a supportive learning environment where learners' fear of taking risks is reduced; where the design of tasks positively influences each learner's learning experience; and where the relationship between the teacher and the learner positively influences the attitude of learners and increases their chance of success.

 Stop and reflect

1 Work out the steps in turning an A4 size sheet of paper into an envelope to take a letter.
2 After you have worked this out for yourself, use a scaffolding (step-by-step) instructional strategy to teach two other students how to turn an A4 sheet into an envelope.
3 What level of support did each of your classmates require from you to achieve this task?

Collaborative co-teaching

Owing to the diversity in cultural, linguistic, and religious backgrounds among learners, and because of the difference in abilities and disabilities in the inclusive education classroom, it is becoming common to have more than one teacher in each classroom. When this happens, the two teachers coordinate their efforts and negotiate the classroom environment by taking on collaborative co-teaching strategies such as: supportive teaching, parallel teaching, **complementary** teaching, and team teaching (Landsberg, 2011).

In supportive teaching, for example, one teacher presents the content and the other provides enrichment such as setting learners activities to consolidate what they have learned from the content teacher. The two teachers may decide to make use of parallel teaching. In doing so, they work in separate groups within the same classroom. This would be the case when, following learners' performance of a task, the two teachers decide to separate them into two groups where they will cater, in one group, for learners who show better understanding of what was assessed; and in the other group for those who are still struggling to understand certain concepts. In certain circumstances, teachers may decide to make use of team teaching. In this case, both teachers share the whole class instruction, or divide parts of the lesson, or provide simultaneous instruction. Teachers of inclusive education classrooms also often make use of complementary teaching (Moletsane, Raymond & Stofile, 2013). Complementary teaching is at play for example, when, following the lesson of the content teacher, the assistant teacher teaches learners academic writing skills or learning strategies like concept mapping. Complementary teaching is also exercised in a situation where, before the content teacher engages learners in the content of a given lesson, the co-teacher works with learners to teach them note taking skills, or to introduce them to the vocabulary that is specific to the new lesson.

complementary: combining two different things to form a complete thing, or whole

 CASE STUDY 2

Clift is blind and, seven days from now, he will start attending a mainstream Grade 6 class where you have been on teaching practice for some time already. Clift is very bright and has done very well in all the courses he has taken in the special school he used to attend. He reads and writes Braille fluently, and the school has already employed an assistant teacher who knows Braille to help with Clift's special education needs.

You and your teaching practice supervisor are meeting the assistant teacher tomorrow to work out collaborative teaching strategies for Clift's instruction. In preparation for this meeting, your teaching practice supervisor, who knows you have just completed your introductory course in inclusive education, has tasked you with the following:

1   Take 20 minutes to draft three collaborative teaching strategies that you will present to the teacher assistant tomorrow.
2   After you have drafted your three strategies, discuss the different steps that should be followed in implementing each of your strategies, with a fellow student.

Principles of inclusive cooperative learning

Positive interdependence

Positive interdependence requires acceptance by members of small learning groups that they "sink or swim together" (Roger, David & Johnson, 1994:13). In other words, each learner needs to be concerned about how well he or she does, but also about how well each other member of the group does. This is because one cannot successfully accomplish the task without the others. In cooperative learning groups, teachers often foster positive interdependence among learners by 1) setting mutual outcomes for the whole group; 2) dividing the tasks among all group members; 3) dividing the resources, information, and materials among group members; 4) assigning various roles to different group members; and 5) rewarding the group for achieving the mutual outcomes (Landsberg, 2011:79). What is emphasised in this description is that in a cooperative learning situation, learners are encouraged to be concerned about the performance of each member of the group, and to nurture a supportive relationship that will help them to achieve the learning outcomes together. Under such circumstances, the possibility is higher that a weak learner will benefit from the attention of more advanced learners and will be encouraged to do better.

Individual accountability or personal responsibility

In a cooperative learning situation, positive interdependence goes hand in hand with individual accountability. Firstly, the group is accountable for achieving its outcomes; secondly, each individual is held personally responsible for completing his or her small part of the group's task and for contributing to the success of the group. Teachers of inclusive classrooms generally ensure individual accountability by providing assessment criteria that also cater for individual contributions to a task.

Interpersonal and small group skills

Working with another person or with a small group of people to complete a task in an inclusive education classroom environment comes with challenges whose nature and complexity cannot be over-emphasised in this chapter. Learners need to be skilled for group activity, and they need to be monitored while using interpersonal skills during such activities. These are skills that they ought to have learned previously and, in the process of working together, they include: taking turns to speak; addressing the other members of the group in a polite way; respecting one another's views; accepting instructions from peers who have agreed to take on facilitating responsibilities for the benefit of the group; expressing either a different view or disagreeing, in a constructive way (Moletsane, Raymond & Stofile, 2013).

Group processing

Small group instruction, just like any other pedagogical methods that are used in an inclusive education environment, is meant to facilitate the process of learning. This is ultimately what it is all about: enabling learning for everyone. Not just learning, but learning to learn with others and learning to respect and support one another in the process of knowledge acquisition. To ensure that this purpose is fulfilled, at the end of a cooperative learning activity, members of the group are encouraged to reflect on how they have done in the task: what have they done well to be successful; and what reasons they would give to explain some of their shortcomings. As Bouwer (2011:80) puts it, "learners need to describe what contributions were helpful and what behaviour should change to improve the functioning of the group." Group processing is therefore about learners reflecting on their work, and finding ways of improving one another's skills in cooperative learning as well as in getting the content knowledge right. Choosing to get learners to work together in cooperative learning groups does not exclude attention to individuals or to the uniqueness of the challenges of each learner. It is to cater for these individualities that the teachers of inclusive education classrooms draw up and adopt an individual support plan (ISP).

Individual support plan

An individual support plan (ISP) maps out the learning challenges that an individual learner faces at a given point in time, and makes suggestions about how that learner could be helped. In the South African context, individual support plans are designed and provided by the class teacher in collaboration with the institution-level support team (DoE, 2005). Individual support plans, as the name indicates, are individualised supports to learners. As such, they vary in length and in complexity, depending on individual learner's challenges. They are often based on learner's performance in an evaluative assessment that determines what knowledge, skills, and attitudes that learner has already achieved. The result of this assessment is then used to put together a number of outcomes that the learner is expected to achieve by the end of the individual support, and to select the appropriate curriculum content for the realisation of these outcomes. The evaluative assessment is also important in helping the support team choose and recommend learning support strategies and methods that are tailored to the learners' challenges, and more importantly, to their learning styles. Bouwer (2011) strongly recommends that assessment of the effectiveness of the ISP be continuous throughout its implementation and that a final assessment of the learner's performance be done at the very end of the implementation of the support plan to find out whether the intended outcomes have been achieved.

CASE STUDY 3

Jana is 12 years old and, since her birth, lived with her parents on a farm in a quiet Afrikaans community in the great Karoo, South Africa. She attended an Afrikaans-medium primary school where she did reasonably well in basic English but still does not speak or write it fluently. While on holiday, her parents died in a tragic accident. Jana has now relocated to a small town in the vicinity of Durban where she lives with her aunt. For high school, Jana's aunt is willing to send her to a boarding school that offers instruction in Afrikaans but the teenager wants to attend an English-medium high school. Her aunt has explained to her the challenges of taking instruction in a language one has not yet mastered. She tells Jana is that she will struggle with using writing to demonstrate what she knows. But the teenager is convinced that if her friend Mpulo, who is an isiZulu home language speaker, has been able to succeed in an English-medium school, so can she.

A week from now, there will be a meeting of the institutional-level support team at the school where you are going for your teaching practice. There are different cases that need practical individual support plans and the coordinator of the ILST has tasked you with reflecting on and proposing a practical individual support plan for Jana's situation.

Your task, she says, consists of designing a PowerPoint presentation limited to 12 slides. Your presentation should first inform your audience about the nature of Jana's case as well as the academic challenges that she is likely to encounter in her new school. Second, your presentation should suggest a practical way of supporting Jana's English language development, as well as her entire academic journey.

 Reviewing what we know

This section elaborates on some of the teaching and learning strategies that teachers often use in inclusive education classrooms. Some of these preferred learning and teaching strategies include: cooperative learning, scaffolding, cubing (which you will read more about in Chapter 13), problem solving and collaborative co-teaching. Teachers' preference for these learner-centered pedagogies comes from a desire to cater for every learner and to make learning a differentiated yet enjoyable and meaningful activity for those who take part in it. As we have seen, what these teaching strategies have in common is that they are learner-centered, highly participatory and attached to principles of experiential learning which gives learners a large margin of trial and error in the learning process (Harley & Rule, 2013; Moletsane, Raymond & Stofile, 2013). The strategies also take into account individual learner's prior knowledge and cater for those learners who experience barriers to learning, like the lack of competence in the language of learning and teaching, under-preparedness in previous grade and various forms of impairments.

 Stop and reflect

Working with a partner, draft a cooperative learning activity in which you ensure that all 36 learners in a Grade 6 inclusive education classroom get to learn about the different types of pollution, in a Natural Sciences lesson.
1   Take into consideration the difference in learning abilities among your learners.
2   Decide on the appropriate type of groupings, and on a suitable group size.
3   How is this type of grouping appropriate to ensure that learners with different levels of readiness or with different learning abilities get to learn significantly from this activity?
4   Break down the task into its different parts, and decide what each group should focus on.

5 Assign a role to each group member.
6 Provide a rubric to guide learners in completing the task. Make sure that your rubric encourages both group effort and individual contributions.
7 How will you maintain discipline and ensure that everyone is gainfully occupied? Provide some guidelines or 'rules' that everyone agrees to.

How can families and communities support inclusive education classrooms?

Many parents share their children's daily lives and have close experience of their intellectual capabilities and learning difficulties. As such, they are in a good position to understand many of their children's educational needs. Such parents have a lot to offer in building inclusive education classrooms. So much so that the Department of Education (2005) encourages them to get involved in supporting teachers in building inclusive education classrooms. They could do so, for example, by documenting for the school their experience of their children's needs, and by sharing their expectations about what the school should do for their child. Telling a teacher that your child is a third language speaker of English, and your expectation is that the child be given a chance to participate daily in class activities to improve her proficiency in the language of learning and teaching, could help the teacher plan a lesson with that particular learner in mind. Parents are also encouraged by the Department of Education to join institutional support teams, and to help in designing and implementing an individual support plan for their children. They are further encouraged to foster inclusive education practice by attending conferences and meetings on inclusive education, and by joining a parents' organisation that offers them both emotional support and a space for sharing ideas. This section is written with the current South African environment, where many parents are not well informed about the principles of inclusive education, in mind. It suggests that schools need to provide these parents with opportunities for a better understanding of the principles of inclusive education, a good grasp of physiological impairment and learning disabilities, and a better understanding of the importance of working in collaboration with both the teacher and the school.

Fostering more informed attitudes and beliefs

Within the South African context, many parents are far less well educated than teachers and might find schools very intimidating environments where they would rather not venture. This is certainly one of the reasons why many parents are not involved in the life of schools in rural, township, and peri-urban areas. Swart and Pettipher (2011), as well as Prinsloo (2001), recommend that for their own growth, inclusive schools and inclusive classrooms need to empower such parents through workshops and professional training that will help them to better understand inclusive education, the legislation and policies around it, and the opportunities it brings to children's education. The thinking behind this suggestion is that it is only through a better understanding of inclusive education and its benefits for their children's education that parents can become informed partners to teachers of inclusive education classrooms.

Advocates and activists of inclusive education

According to the South African Department of Education (2001), the empowerment of parents through educational encounters should allow them to challenge outdated approaches and prejudices around disabilities and inclusive education in the community. Such training should also empower them to take up their role as activists and advocates of inclusive education. What this means is that parents need to be able to lobby on behalf of their children, both for better facilities and services, and for the rights of children with disabilities to be protected in mainstream schools. In the same vein, in their paper entitled 'Until somebody hears me: Parental voice and advocacy in special education decision-making', Hess, Molina & Kozleski (2006) hold the view that implementing inclusive education in classrooms demands the interactive participation of all role players, including teachers, managers, parents, learners, and community members. According to these authors, there are some very specific roles that parents can play in support of their children's education. One such role is to serve on the school governing body where they will be able to ensure that legislation and policies of inclusion are put into practice in a way that benefits their children.

Support and collaboration

As Swart and Pettipher (2011:21) put it, "support is the cornerstone of successful inclusive education." The Department of Education (2001), through its *Education White Paper 6: A guide to parents and communities*, recommends that parents establish a network to help foster inclusive education in schools. Through this network, parents could assume responsibility for secondary matters, like getting a local taxi organisation to provide transport to school for their children. Parents could also help the school by joining the institutional level support team to investigate how specific support can be obtained for children with some forms of disability to be fully included. They could also collaborate with the school and the district to find ways in which educators might cope better with different learning needs. Furthermore, parents can volunteer to assist the educator where they need help. Finally, the document encourages parents to be positive about their own children and their potential from the outset. It says they should take part in organised initiatives to raise awareness about inclusive education and become "agents for positive change" (Department of Education, 2001).

Stop and reflect

1   What are three things that the family can do to help foster inclusive education classrooms?
2   What are three things that the community can do to help foster inclusive education classrooms?
3   As a teacher of an inclusive education classroom in a peri-urban area, how would you go about ensuring that parents understand the principle of inclusive education, and join you in building an inclusive education classroom? Support your strategy by citing relevant literature.

District-based and institution-level support

Through the official document *Education White Paper 6* (2001) and through its three complementary booklets: *Guidelines for district-based support teams* (2005); *Guidelines for the implementation of special schools as resource centres* (2005); and *Guidelines for the implementation of full service/inclusive schools* (2009), the Department of Education has introduced a number of support services to help teachers in implementing inclusive education in South African classrooms. At district level, this support is managed by a district-based support team. In essence, district-based support teams have the obligation to provide the schools that fall within their area of influence with a coordinated professional support service that, according to the Department of Education (2001:8), "draws on expertise in further and higher education and local communities, targeting special schools and specialised settings, designated full-service and other primary schools and educational institutions."

The Department of Education (2001) requests that district-based support teams cater for learners according to their needs rather than their impairments. To ensure that this is done, a flexible scale is provided to the assessment team of each district-based support team to rate learners' needs, ranging from 1 meaning 'low-intensity support' to 5 meaning 'high-intensity support', and to allocate schools to these learners and provide for them accordingly. It is important to note that despite indicating five levels at which learner needs can be rated, the Department of Education (2005:11,13) specifically mentions only three levels of support namely: "high, moderate and low levels of support." So 2, 3 and 4 may be understood to stand for different degrees of moderate-intensity support.

Learners who are identified as being in need of high-intensity support should be catered for in special schools as resources centres (discussed in the next section). Learners who need a moderate level of support are expected to be catered for in full-service schools; and those who need only low-intensity supports are assigned to ordinary schools. As Landsberg (2011:70) writes, "the Department of Education accepts that a high level of support could be flexible and that learners could move into a lower level of support and therefore to another school, depending on the success of the support received." According to the Department of Education (2005:17–18), the local needs of learners within district schools should dictate the composition of the support services provided within that district. Such services could include: support personnel such as psychologists, medical doctors and support teachers; curriculum specialists, management specialists, administrative experts, specialised staff of special schools, other government experts, non-governmental organisations, parents, caregivers, and other community role players.

System of support of education districts

Each district-based support team coordinates a system of support that consists of special schools, full-service schools, ordinary schools and the district based support team itself. The different types of schools (special schools, full-service schools, and ordinary schools) that belong to this system of support all have slightly different facilities, and human resources with varying expertise. These differences are intended to lower the costs of running the system of support within the district, and to allow the designated schools to work together and to complement one another.

Special schools as resource centres (SSRC)

Special schools as resource centres (SSRC) are the most highly equipped of all the schools within the district. As such, they cater for learners identified as needing high-intensity support. In districts where they are currently available, their resources are integrated into the district-based support team to provide full-service schools and ordinary schools with specialised professional support related to the curriculum, assessment and method of instruction (DoE, 2008). The following is what the Department of Education (2008: 21–23) perceives the function of SSRC within the district to be. "SSRCs are meant to function as an integrated and coordinated part of the district-based support team and to provide professional support to full-service and ordinary schools. They are expected to assist schools in the implementation of strategy on screening, identification, assessment and support. They should provide specialised professional support in curriculum, assessment and instruction to neighbouring schools." This, as Landsberg (2011:72) sees it, includes "training teachers regarding barriers to learning, management of inclusive classrooms, development of learning support material and assistive devices, guidance to parents, early childhood intervention and therapeutic support to learners with impairment in mainstream schools." SSRCs are also expected to assist in the mobilisation of children and youth who are not yet in schools. It is also their function to make their human and material resources available to the community, and to use them, for example, to increase people's awareness of the rights of children with disabilities; on inclusive education; and on similar programmes. SSRCs also partner with non-governmental organisations, parent organisations, and teachers' unions to advocate for the better treatment of learners with impairments, and to channel the expertise and resources of such organisations toward serving full-service schools, ordinary schools, and the local community (DoE, 2008). One of the major challenges faced by SSRCs is the gap between this vision and the implementation of that vision. Because of the shortage of human and physical resources, SSRCs have not yet been built in many districts. In the districts where they are built, there is often shortage of human and material resources to maintain quality services at these centres (DoE, 2011).

Full-service/inclusive schools

The Department of Education (2009:7) presents full-service/inclusive schools as being "first and foremost mainstream schools that provide quality education to all learners by supplying the full range of learning needs in an equitable manner." The Department makes provision for at least one full-service school per education district and expects it to cater for learners in need of moderate to high levels of support. Here are, according to the Department of Education (2009:7–16), the functions of full-service/inclusive schools: providing teachers and learners within the district access to moderate levels of support, resources and programmes; making available, on a regular basis, experienced learning support educators to specific schools. The roles of these experts include consulting and working with teachers, parents and various outside agencies to ensure success (Landsberg, 2011). Full-service schools also have the responsibility to assist other schools within the district, with knowledge, information and assistive devices regarding barriers to learning. This includes providing opportunities for blind learners to learn Braille, and to access computer software that reads the electronic version of the course material to them. Full-service schools assess and refer learners to special schools for services and equipment which they cannot adequately provide themselves. They also assign to ordinary schools learners whose needs have become less demanding as a result of successful provision in full-service schools. Finally, like special schools, full-service schools are also expected to work in close collaboration with the district-based support team to coordinate support within the district (DoE, 2009). One major challenge of this structure is that they often lack human resources, and both technical and assistive devices that are necessary to implement the vision of inclusive schooling system in South Africa (Walton, Nel, Hugo & Muller, 2009).

Ordinary schools

Also referred to as mainstream schools, ordinary schools are those that cater for learners who are rated as being in need of low-intensity support. Teachers at ordinary schools are supported in building and maintaining inclusive education classrooms by experts of all the other constituents of the district support system (i.e., the district-based support team, and both special schools as resource centres and full-service/inclusive schools). A learner who, in an ordinary school, is suddenly in need of a moderate or high level of support can either be retained and catered for in the ordinary school with the help of professionals from the district support system, or can be moved to a better-equipped school until the learner is able to cope again in an ordinary school.

What learning support is available within the schools themselves?

Learning support for the building and maintaining of inclusive education classrooms within schools consists principally of institutional-level support teams and professionally trained general education teachers. In some schools, this support also includes teacher assistants.

Institutional-level support team (ILST)

The Department of Education (2001 & 2005) asks of every school, regardless of whether it is a special school as resource centre, a full-service/inclusive school, or an ordinary school, to establish a support team to assist individual teachers in providing support to learners who need it. The Department (2005:34) refers to this team as an institutional-level support team (ILST); and with the word 'institution', it designates both schools and tertiary institutions of learning. Landsberg (2011) observes that in some provinces, and only for the sake of convenience, institutional-based support teams are commonly referred to as school-based support teams. The composition of institutional-based support teams varies according to the available human resources of particular schools. Often, the team is made up of experts from the community, special schools as resource centres, full-service/inclusive schools, and both psychological (or counselling) and medical services.

The purpose of the institutional-based support team is to allow schools to have a team approach in the provision of support to learners who need it. According to the Department of Education (2002:47–48; 2005:35) the functions of the institutional-based support team consist of: a) seeking and making available all support pertaining to the development of learners, teachers and the curriculum; b) identifying and designing strategies to address barriers to learning and other needs identified among students or within the school; c) ensuring that teachers are exposed to the possibilities of in-service training geared toward the identification, assessment and support of all learners; d) building systems for the promotion of quality communication between learners and teachers and between teachers and parents, school and NGOs, school and medical facilities, and school and the justice department, to name but a few; e) adapting existing and developing new learning programmes and teaching strategies for class teachers to try out in their attempt to support their learners (Landsberg (2011:73). It is also the role of institutional-level support f) to promote parental involvement; and g) to monitor and support learners' progress. One major challenge related to institutional-based support teams is that the majority of South African schools still do not have such a team (DoE, 2011). This is attributable to teachers' lack of training in inclusive methodologies, teacher overload, and the lack of parental involvement (Donald, Lazarus & Lolwana, 2010).

Teacher assistants or classroom assistants

Teacher assistants or classroom assistants are presently a huge source of support in many South African schools. The Department of Education (2009:23) recommends their appointment in full-service schools and in ordinary schools where they are needed. Often, they are appointed to help the main teacher cater for some of the specific needs of learners with disabilities. The tasks of teacher assistants are specified in the *Guidelines for full-service/inclusive schools* (DoE, 2009) and include: assisting with the identification of barriers to learning within the classroom and in individual learners; implementing programmes designed by the institution-level support in collaboration with the therapist and the teacher to respond to specific barriers to learning; assessing learners' performances in consultation with the learning support teacher and all therapists involved; and participating in the evaluation of the effectiveness of programmes and related interventions. Ultimately, professionally trained teachers constitute the most important resource in the building and nurturing of inclusive education classrooms.

Professionally qualified teachers

A professionally qualified teacher, whether for general or special education, is undoubtedly the most important asset in an inclusive education classroom. His or her role as set out by the Department of Education (2000) in the official document, *Norms and standards for educators*, includes being a: mediator of learning; interpreter and designer of learning programmes; leader, administrator and manager of the classroom community; assessor; community member and pastoral caregiver; and learning area/subject/discipline/phase specialist. It is useful to gain more insight into these roles, by revisiting the document on *Norms and standards for educators*. As you will discover (or re-discover), the roles that are both formally and informally recognised as relating to those of the teaching profession, establish the new generation of South African teachers as assets for building the inclusive education classrooms that are intended to actualise the full potential of every learner, and to foster social justice.

Reviewing what we know

This part of the chapter looked at both district-based and institutional supports, as conceived by the Department of Education, to assist and equip teachers of inclusive education classrooms within the South African context. At district level, the support is managed by a district-based support team that has the duty of providing every school within its area of influence with a coordinated professional support service. Each district-based support team is asked to enhance and diversify the service it offers to foster inclusion at local schools by drawing on expertise in further and higher education, and by making use of key human resources that are often available within local communities. The differentiation in services available at district level is too often dependent on the availability of institutional resources such as special schools and specialised settings, designated full-service, and other primary schools, and educational institutions (Department of Education, 2001). District-based support teams use a flexible scale system, ranging from 1 for 'low-intensity support' to 5 for 'high-intensity support', to determine the needs of individual learners and suggest ways of catering for these learners. What determines the type of support to learners is their needs, and not their impairment. So learners who are identified as being in need of high-intensity support should be catered for in special schools as resource centres. Learners who need a moderate level of support are expected to be catered for in full-service schools. Learners who need only low-intensity support are assigned to ordinary schools. The second aspect that we looked at in this part of the chapter is the support for inclusion at the level of institutions of learning. Such support consists of institutional-based support teams whose purpose is to allow schools to take a team approach in the provision of support to learners who need it. At school level, this support also comprises teacher assistants and professional teachers themselves.

Stop and reflect

1 Work with a partner and discuss your understanding of following:
   • Learners who need high-intensity support
   • Learners who need a moderate level of support
   • Learners who need low-intensity support.
2 Student teacher B in Case study 1 at the beginning of this chapter speaks of noticing a learner in a wheelchair who has an additional health issue, frequent epileptic crises. Using the flexible scale that the Department of Education provides to measure the level of educational need of learners, would you say that this learner needs high-intensity support, a moderate level of support, or low-intensity support? Justify your answer.

Ground-level issues and challenges to the practice of inclusive education in classrooms

Inclusive education is a new movement in school reform and, as such, is bound to come with challenges. This section examines some of these challenges with a specific focus on those that affect the implementation of inclusive education in the great majority of South African classrooms.

Lack of funding

A lack of sufficient funding from the Department of Basic Education, coupled with the low socio-economic status of the great majority of parents and caregivers, constitute two of the major challenges to establishing inclusive education classrooms in South African schools. This shortage of financial support has led to many delays, including the delay in the implementation of district-based and institutional level support structures, as announced by the Department of Education in 2001. In fact, according to Landsberg (2011), and Wildmane and Nombo (2007), by 2007, district-based support teams did not exist in all nine provinces. Today, many districts in the country still do not have a functional district-based support team. In addition, the plan to implement at least one full-service school and one special school as resource centre in each education district has also been delayed in many districts. Furthermore, because of the lack of financial means, these support structures are built far apart from one another in many rural areas. The distances between support structures in some rural areas has weakened the network of support that is expected between special schools, full-service schools, ordinary schools, and the district-based support team in these areas. Finally, as Prinsloo (2011:30) argues, "education in the poverty-stricken communities of South Africa is hampered by a lack of order in the communal structures, a culture of vandalism, a short-term orientation towards time, a powerful and negative peer group influence, (e.g. on the Cape Flats and in inner-city slums), a non-stimulating milieu, insecurity, language deficiencies, poor orientation towards school, and clashes between the value orientations of the family and the school." In such conditions, inclusive education can only be promoted by resilient professionals and equally resilient learners (Christie, 1998).

Discrepancy between teacher training and the demands of inclusive classrooms

Another ground-level issue related to the implementation of inclusive education in some South African classrooms is that often, the professional development of teachers is inadequate in equipping them with the skills to handle large classes, to manage learners with special needs, and to cater for learners with special needs in large classes (Swart & Pettipher, 2011; Prinsloo, 2011). In fact, many teachers complete their studies without having been exposed to a model of an inclusive education classroom, and without being taught how to handle, collaboratively, learners with special needs in the ordinary classroom. With this range of learners to cater for (often in overcrowded classes), they struggle to find a balance in attending to the needs of all learners. As result, they often display the following limitations: failure to include all learners in all activities; failure to involve parents, and to adequately respond to the grievances of those parents who find it problematic that their children are being taught in the same classroom with learners who have some form of disability; failure to recognise when additional support is needed and to seek this support timeously; and failure to establish learner support teams and to cooperate with other teachers, school support staff, and with the district (Lamport, Graves & Ward, 2012).

According to Swart and Pettipher (2011:22), the challenge of underprepared and limited teachers could be resolved through adequate exposure of trainee teachers to inclusive education classrooms and through substantial workshops for in-service teachers. As they put it, "for educators to teach in an inclusive school and to collaborate with one another, they need to acquire, through pre-service and in-service experiences, a common vision, conceptual framework and language, and a set of instructional and technical skills to work with the needs of diverse learners". However, the development of such skills in the new generation of teachers can only be accomplished through a model of staff development that is school based and context focused. This point is shared by Ainscow (1999) who suggests that teachers' professional development is more responsive to the challenges encountered in inclusive classrooms when it takes place within both the inclusive school and the inclusive classroom context, and addresses day-to-day concerns of inclusive teachers.

The wide range of barriers to learning in the South African context

Because of unemployment, poverty, malnutrition, inadequate medical facilities, the high rate of pre-natal and early childhood infections, the number of learners with special needs is even higher in poor and in developing countries like South Africa. The presence of this wide range of barriers to learning in the classroom may negatively affect the provision of quality education for all learners if support structures are not in place to help with including every learner. The situation is made critical by the wide meaning given to the concept 'learners with disabilities' or 'learners with special educational needs' in the South African context. As Prinsloo (2001:345) observes, in the South African context, the concept 'barriers to learning' includes "not only the barriers linked to physical and intellectual disabilities, but also the barriers caused by economic and emotional deprivation, as well as social exclusion." In fact, learners whose education requires additional planning and modification in order to assist them to learn, are also referred to as learners who are experiencing barriers to learning. This increases the diversity that the teacher has to cater for.

The number of learners with severe barriers to learning in the same classroom

There is very little certainty about how many learners with severe disabilities can be catered for at one time in the same inclusive education classroom. A typical inclusive education classroom may have up to four learners with disabilities, some of whom are often not as cognitively developed as their classmates. Because of this difference, the teaching and learning process that targets them puts more demand on the teacher, and sometimes proves to be less effective than it could be. Also, depending on their disabilities, some of these learners may disrupt the classroom with behaviour issues. Given that in many South African classrooms it is already a challenge to cater for the needs of all the learners because of a general lack of resources, overcrowding, and learner under-preparedness from previous grades, with learners who have special needs, the work becomes even more difficult (Morrow, 2007; DoE, 2005).

Other ground-level issues relating to the implementation of inclusive education in South African classrooms include: the HIV and AIDS pandemic, the increasing number of orphans, teenage motherhood, illiteracy, the high rate of violence perpetrated against women and children, the shortage of educational and managerial expertise, "the lack of training of personnel at provincial level and the lack of commitment of those already employed" (Landsberg, 2011:74). Last but not least, there is a very limited presence of teacher aides or special needs educators in schools. The shortage of these educators makes it difficult to transfer skills and expose both student teachers and in-service teachers to models of inclusive education classrooms.

Finally, it is important to note that the discussed issues and challenges to the practice of inclusive education in the classrooms are not unique to South Africa; they are also found in all other countries that have had the courage to foster the implementation of inclusive education in their classrooms. Of interest to us is the fact that these challenges reveal that it takes a lot of dedication, training, compassion, and patience on the part of the teacher to create and maintain an effective inclusive education system. In fact, accommodating and catering for learners across the educational and developmental spectrum ranging from typically developing learners through to mild and severely disabled learners in fully functional inclusive education classrooms demands committed and resilient education stakeholders.

Stop and reflect

Many educators and researchers are convinced that inclusive education is the way of the future, and are working at and trying out different strategies to help make its implementation a smooth process.

1 Choose a school that you attended as a learner for at least two years. Briefly describe its composition and demographics. (Remember, you do not have to name it or reveal its identity if you prefer not to.)

2 What are some of the challenges that, as an inclusive teacher, you are most likely to encounter if you were appointed to teach in the school you have chosen?

3 Formulate a possible solution to each one of the challenges that you have identified within your chosen school.

Summary of discussion

Some of the most important features of an inclusive education classroom that were covered in this chapter include: the establishment of a supportive learning culture within the classroom, the fostering of a democratic leadership style, the implementation of reflective teaching pedagogies, the fostering of learner centeredness, and the implementation of responsive curricula. In order to ensure that every one of their learners acquires as much knowledge as possible, and experiences educational success, friendship, and a genuine sense of belonging to the learning community, teachers of inclusive education classrooms will typically use teaching and learning strategies that are: learner-centered, highly participatory, and attached to the principles of experiential learning. These teachers consider the best teaching and learning strategies to be those that give learners a large margin of trial and error in the learning process. We covered the following teaching and learning strategies in this chapter: cooperative learning, scaffolding, and collaborative co-teaching.

As we observed in this chapter, the task of creating and maintaining inclusive education classrooms is very demanding and teachers require the support of the family and the community to realise their effort. But it is only through a better understanding of inclusive education and its benefits for their children that parents can become informed partners to teachers; schools therefore need to find channels to inform parents and the community about inclusive education so that they become active and informed collaborators with teachers. The Department of Basic Education makes provision to help teachers of inclusive education classrooms both at district and at institutional level. At district level, this support is managed by a district-based support team. Each district-based support team coordinates a system of support that involves special schools, full-service schools, ordinary schools and the district based support team itself. These schools each have slightly different facilities, and human resources with varying expertise. These differences are intended to lower the costs of running the system of support within the district, by allowing the designated schools to work together and to complement one another. At institutional level, this support consists mainly of institutional-level support teams and of professionally trained general education teachers. In some schools, this support may also include teacher assistants.

The final part of this chapter explained some of the ongoing challenges to the establishment of inclusive education classrooms. These remain a lack of adequate funding; the mismatch between teacher preparedness – both at training and in-service levels – to meet the demands of teaching in inclusive classrooms; the very wide range of barriers to learning experienced by South African learners; and the sheer number of learners with different needs within an average classroom. Added to these challenges is the wider context of adverse socio-economic conditions that many South Africans face. We concluded, however, by pointing out that although there are many demands and challenges, teachers with commitment, resilience and resourcefulness can face and overcome them.

Closing activity

Work with a partner.
1. Draw a chart showing the support system that is in place at district level for teachers of inclusive education classrooms.
2. Draw another chart indicating the support system that is in place at institutional/school level for teachers of inclusive education classrooms.

References

Allen, D. & Tanner, K. 2005. Infusing active learning into the large-enrolment biology class: Seven strategies, from the simple to the complex. *Cell Biology Education*. 4:262–268.

Biklen, D. 1992. *Schooling without labels: Parents, educators, and inclusive education*. Philadelphia: Temple University Press.

Bornman, J. & Rose, J. 2010. *Believe that all can achieve: Increasing classroom participation in learners with special support needs*. Pretoria: Van Schaik.

Bouwer, C. 2011. Identification and assessment of barriers to learning. In E. Landsberg, D. Kruger & N. Nel (Eds). *Addressing barriers to learning: A South African perspective*. Pretoria: Van Schaik.

Burgstahler, S. 2007. *Equal access: universal design of instruction*. Seattle: University of Washington. Retrieved from: http//www.washington.edu/doit/ on 26 June 2013.

Chataika, T., Mckenzie, J., Swart, E. & Lyner-Cleophas, M. 2012. Access to education in Africa: Responding to the United Nations Convention on the Rights of Persons with Disabilities. *Disability and Society*, 27(2):385–398. Retrieved from: http://dx.doi.org/10.10 80/09687599.2012.654989 on 2 December 2013.

Christie, P. 1998. Schools as (dis)organisations: The 'breakdown of the culture of learning and teaching' in South African schools. *Cambridge Journal of Education*. 28(3): 283–300.

Cohen, J. 2000. Inclusion and belonging. *Independent Education*. 3:10–12.

Department of Education. 2000. *Norms and standards for educators*. Government Gazette, 415 (20844). Pretoria: Government Printers.

Department of Education 2001. *Education White Paper 6: Special needs education: Building an inclusive education and training system*. Pretoria: Department of Education.

Department of Education. 2002. *Draft guidelines for the implementation of inclusive education* (Second draft). Pretoria: Department of Education.

Department of Education. 2005. *Developing district-based support teams: Guidelines for practice*. Pretoria: Department of Education.

Department of Education. 2008. *Guidelines to ensure quality education and support in special schools and special schools as resource centres*. Pretoria: Department of Education.

Department of Education. 2009. *Guidelines for full-service/inclusive schools*. Pretoria: Government Printers.

Department of Education. 2011. *Guidelines for responding to learner diversity in the classroom through curriculum and assessment policy statement*. Pretoria: Government Printers.

Donald, D., Lazarus, S. & Lolwana, P. 2010. *Educational psychology in social context: Ecosystemic applications in southern Africa*. Cape Town: Oxford University Press Southern Africa.

Gardner, H. 1983. *Frames of mind: The theory of multiple intelligences*. New York: Basic Books.

Graf, M. 2011. *Including and supporting learners of English as an additional language*. New York: Continuum International Publishing Group.

Gultig, J. & Stielau, J. (Eds). 2009. *Getting practical about classroom-based teaching for the national curriculum statement*. Cape Town: Oxford University Press Southern Africa.

Harley, A. & Rule, P. 2013. Exploring access as dialogue in an education and development certificate programme. In R. Dhumpath & R. Vithal (Eds). *Alternative access to higher education: Underprepared students or underprepared institutions?* Cape Town: Pearson.

Henson, K.T. 2004. *Constructivist teaching strategies for diverse middle-level classrooms.* Boston, MA: Pearson.

Hess, R.S., Molina, A.M. & Kozleski, E.B. 2006. Until somebody hears me: Parental voice and advocacy in special education decision-making. *British Journal of Special Education.* 33:148–157.

Jarvis, P. 1987. *Adult learning in the social context.* London: Croom Helm.

Johnson, D.W. & Johnson, R.T. 1994. *Leading the cooperative school.* Edina, MN: Interaction Book Company.

Johnson, D. W., Johnson, R.T. & Holubec, E. 2008. *Cooperation in the classroom.* 8th ed. Edina, MN: Interaction Book Company.

Johnson, D.W. & Johnson, R.T. 2008. Social interdependence theory and cooperative learning: The teacher's role. In R.M. Gilles, A. Ashman & J. Terwel (Eds). *The teacher's role in implementing cooperative learning in the classroom.* New York: Springer Science+Business Media. 9–36.

Krüger, D. & Yorke, C. 2010. Collaborative co-teaching of numeracy and literacy as a key to inclusion in an independent school. *South African Journal of Education.* 30(2):293–306.

Lamport, M.A., Graves, L. & Ward, A. 2012. Special needs students in inclusive classrooms: the impact of social interaction on educational outcomes for learners with emotional and behavioural disabilities. *European Journal of Business and Social Sciences.* 1(5):54–69.

Landsberg, E. 2011. Learning support. In E. Landsberg, D. Krüger & E. Swart (Eds). *Addressing barriers to learning: A South African perspective.* (69–86). Pretoria: Van Schaik.

Landsberg, E., Krüger, D. & Swart, E. (Eds). 2011. *Addressing barriers to learning: A South African perspective.* (xvi, 533). Pretoria: Van Schaik.

Mitchell, D. 2008. *What really works in special and inclusive education: Using evidence-based teaching strategies.* London: Routledge.

Moletsane, M., Raymond, E. & Stofile, S. 2013. Instructional approaches for inclusive classrooms. In C.F. Pienaar and E.B. Raymond (Eds). *Making inclusive education work in classrooms.* (132–153). Cape Town: Pearson Education South Africa.

Morrow, W. 2007. *Learning to teach in South Africa.* Cape Town: Human Sciences Research Council.

Ntombela, S. & Raymond, E. 2013. Inclusive education in South Africa and globally. In C.F. Pienaar and E.B. Raymond (Eds). *Making inclusive education work in classrooms.* (2–17). Cape Town: Pearson Education South Africa.

Prinsloo, E. 2001. Working towards inclusive education in South African classrooms. *South African Journal of Education.* 21(4):344–348.

Prinsloo, E. 2011. Socio-economic barriers to learning in contemporary society. In E. Landsberg, D. Kruger & N. Nel (Eds). *Addressing barriers to learning: A South African perspective.* Pretoria: Van Schaik.

Swart, E. & Pettipher, R. 2007. Understanding and working with change. In P. Engelbrecht & L. Green (Eds). *Responding to the challenges of inclusive education in Southern Africa.* Pretoria: Van Schaik.

Swart, E. & Pettipher, R. 2011. A framework for understanding inclusion. In E. Landsberg, D. Kruger & N. Nel (Eds). *Addressing barriers to learning: A South African perspective.* Pretoria: Van Schaik.

United Nations Educational Scientific and Cultural Organisation (UNESCO). 1994. *The Salamanca Statement: A framework for action on special needs education.* Paris: UNESCO.

Van Niekerk, T. & Wolwaardt, J. (Eds). 2010. *Oxford South African Concise Dictionary.* 2nd ed. Cape Town: Oxford University Press Southern Africa.

Walton, E., Nel, N., Hugo, A. & Muller, H. 2009. The extent and practice of inclusion in independent schools in South Africa. *South African Journal of Education.* 20:105–126.

Wildeman, R.W. & Nombo, C. 2007. Implementation of inclusive education: Where are we? *Idasa Occasional Papers*, 1–35, March. Accessed at: http://www.idasa.org.za on 17 June 2013.

Barriers to formal learning in South Africa

Moshweu Mampe

Chapter overview

In this chapter, we discuss the barriers to formal learning in South Africa. Specifically, we analyse what these barriers mean to formal learning in Africa, as factors that hinder teaching and learning. We contextualise barriers to formal learning in South Africa, describe typologies of barriers to formal learning, investigate the causes of barriers to formal learning, and suggest strategies to facilitate formal learning, as well as policy issues around formal learning.

Learning outcomes

By the end of this chapter you should be able to:

* Compare and contrast the differences between mild intellectual disability, and moderate to severe intellectual disability in terms of cause, characteristics, and appropriate processes of teaching and learning.
* Describe how to accommodate a learner who experiences intellectual disability requiring cognitive stimulation.

CASE STUDY

Pius is seven years old. He lives in a small rural village in the north of North West Province where he attends a local primary school. The surrounding community is generally quite poor, although a number of parents have smallholdings, some run tuck-shop businesses, and a few are farmers. Pius's own parents are very poor. The primary school Pius attends includes learners from a range of different backgrounds. The languages commonly heard in the school include English, Setswana, Afrikaans, and some isiXhosa. His class, a combined Grade 1 and 2, has 45 learners. The teacher, Ms Masilabele, who is newly qualified, has found it difficult to handle the mixed levels but she is making a determined effort to meet the different needs in her class.

Pius has not coped well at school. Although this is his second year of study, he is still not meeting some of the expected Grade 1 outcomes. His main difficulties appear to be in the area of language, as well as his general behaviour. Although he is seldom absent from school, he is generally not a healthy child. He often has a cold and runny nose. Ms Masilabele is very concerned about him. Although she has taken the problem to the school support team (SST), where various suggestions have been offered, none seemed to work so far. Because personnel from the district-based support teams (DBST) do not manage to visit schools situated in rural areas like this very often, no help has come from them to date.

Ms Masilabele says Pius's language development is very poor in both Setswana and English. Both languages are spoken at his home, although English is the main language he uses with his peers. He often does not appear to understand what she or his peers are saying and she sometimes thinks he is deliberately ignoring her. His own speech sounds are poorly formed, he has a limited vocabulary and poor language development, and he struggles with even the basics of reading and spelling. Surprisingly, his mathematics is quite good, particularly when he is working with concrete objects and doing sums in his book. He is able to do quite detailed drawings and artwork.

His behaviour is very disruptive in the class as a whole. He tends to shout a lot and is very short tempered with other learners. As a result, learners tend to reject him and he now has few friends in class. Since he really wants to be accepted by the others, this has made his situation worse and he will do almost anything to draw attention to himself. He laughs too loudly at anyone's jokes, pulls faces and generally 'plays the fool' much of the time, although he is clearly quite intelligent.

(Adapted from Donald, Lazarus & Lolwana, 2010)

1   How would you explain Pius's poor school achievement?

2   How would you explain his classroom behaviour?

3   How do you think the language situation in this case study affects Pius?

4   What do you think would be of most immediate help in this situation?

What is the problem? Identifying barriers to learning

In classrooms throughout South Africa learners like Pius present themselves every day in the expectation of learning, and, effectively, of achieving their basic human right of a formal education. Although the systemic essentials are in place – classrooms with desks and chairs, textbooks and other learning materials, qualified teachers and other support staff – many learners, like Pius, will encounter hindrances and obstacles that prevent them from achieving their potential. In this chapter we try to identify and fully describe these barriers to formal learning. Then we search out answers and responses to the problem they present to our learners, and indeed, to the entire formal education system.

The meaning of barriers to formal learning

Barriers to formal learning are those factors which lead to the inability of the education system to accommodate diversity. These factors result in a learning breakdown, which prevents learners from accessing educational provision (Landsberg, Kruger & Swart, 2011:19). Such factors may be located within the learner, within the school, within the education system, or sometimes within the broader social, economic, and political context (Department of Education, 2008:8).

Physical barriers to formal learning

Physical barriers to formal learning are caused by congenital factors, i.e. those conditions present at birth, which may be genetic in origin (inherited from parental genes), or health-related (caused by specific problems, illnesses, or infections that occur during pregnancy), or injuries from accident and violence (Donald, Lazarus & Lolwana, 2010:304). Most of these causes are much more common in disadvantaged social contexts, especially because of a lack of adequate health and safety measures in the communities concerned.

Intellectual barriers to formal learning

Intellectual barriers to formal learning have a broad and complex set of possible causes, namely, problems with understanding, remembering, reasoning, and other higher cognitive functions. It is one of the most urgent areas of specific learning need in South Africa (Donald et al., 2010:311). There are three main groups of causes, namely, physical, familial, and contextual. These causes often overlap and frequently reinforce one another.

Physical causes are due to actual damage to, or inadequate formation of the brain. Donald et al. (2010:312) identify them as follows:

- **Genetic abnormalities.** These include **Down's syndrome** and other more rare genetic abnormalities.
- **Specific congenital problems.** There is a range of these problems, most of which are quite rare. However, malnutrition, alcohol abuse (leading to foetal alcohol syndrome, or FAS), or syphilis, affecting the pregnant mother and hence the unborn child, are most common, and of particular concern in the South African context.
- **Birth problems.** Oxygen deprivation for various reasons at birth is an especially prominent cause of brain damage.
- **Infection affecting the brain after birth.** Some examples are encephalitis and meningitis, as well as untreated human immunodeficiency virus (HIV) infection through mother-to-child transmission.
- **Severe head injury.** This is the result of accident or violence before or at birth, or in early childhood.

Familial causes are multiple, but one example is when a child is born into a family of generally low intellectual ability. It is likely that he will inherit a similar limited ability. This then interacts with a generally limited degree of intellectual stimulation in his family, thereby increasing the problem.

Contextual causes are generally more complex. These relate to an interaction of physical and familial factors that, in turn, are related to contextual disadvantages. Such a combination of contextual disadvantages includes malnutrition, health risks, parental stress, and the consequent limited stimulation of the child in a very deprived environment, which is a major risk to her general, and especially cognitive development (Donald et al., 2010:312).

Sensory barriers to formal learning

Sensory barriers to formal learning are complex in nature. The causes of sensory barriers to formal learning are either congenital, or the after-effects of specific diseases and infections. Eye infections in the case of vision, and middle ear infections in the case of hearing, are more common in the disadvantaged social context. Children frequently do not get the necessary early medical treatment. Exposure to diseases such as **rubella** during pregnancy is a particular concern because of their effects on the sensory development of an unborn child (Donald et al., 2010:306).

Down's syndrome: a congenital disorder causing intellectual impairment and physical abnormalities

rubella: an infectious viral disease, also known as German measles

Neurological barriers to formal learning

Neurological barriers to formal learning occur in the area related to the physical functioning of the brain and nervous system. The two common barriers to formal learning in this category are cerebral palsy and epilepsy.

- **Cerebral palsy** results from permanent damage to the cerebral cortex of the brain. Although the damage itself does not change, different neurological effects evolve as the brain develops. The damage may be caused by head injuries, problems during birth, or a particular disease or infection in early development. Tuberculosis and meningitis are examples of such infections (Donald et al., 2010:308).
- **Epilepsy** is due to damage to different areas of the brain. The damage may be substantial, as in a brain tumour. It is more commonly caused by factors that have deprived the brain of sufficient oxygen at some stage. The resulting damage causes susceptibility to an abnormal discharge of electrical energy, which characterises epilepsy in its various forms (Donald et al., 2010:309).

Extrinsic barriers to formal learning

extrinsic: describes something that is not essential or inherent; the opposite of intrinsic, which describes something that is essential, an inherent part of the functioning or nature of something

Extrinsic barriers to formal learning that are still located within the system are lack of access to basic services, lack of human and material resources, inappropriate and inadequate provision of support services, inflexible curriculum, and language of learning and teaching. They are described as those factors which lead to the inability of the system to accommodate diversity. This leads to a learning breakdown which prevents learners from accessing educational provision (Landsberg et al., 2005:17). From a systemic approach, factors that can create barriers to formal learning may be located within the educational system and within the broader social, economic, and political context. Examples of systemic barriers to formal learning are as follows:

- **Inaccessible and unsafe schooling environment.** Learners with barriers to formal learning must have access to the physical environment of any school, and this includes the surrounding terrain, school buildings, classrooms, and equipment. Besides access, the concern is also about safety and health. Most of the schools in South Africa, particularly in rural areas, are physically inaccessible to a large number of learners. Learners with barriers to formal learning are not always accommodated in many such schools. Engelbrecht, Green, Naicker and Engelbrecht (1999:47) suggest three important aspects relating to access, particularly when dealing with learners with barriers to formal learning. *Firstly,* access refers to all aspects of the curriculum that facilitate successful learning, including the learning programmes, the medium of teaching and learning, classroom management and teaching practices, materials and equipment, assessment procedures, quality assurance, and curriculum development approaches. *Secondly,* access refers to the ability of the psycho-social environment, including the culture and ethos of the school, attitudes, human relations and the way in which the school and the classroom are managed, to facilitate positive learning and development for all learners. *Thirdly,* access refers to the physical environment of the school, which makes it possible for entry and engagement in the education process.

- **Child abuse.** According to Donald et al. (2010:230), child abuse is a particular concern to teachers and is a disturbingly common and serious social problem in South African society. Donald et al. (2010:230) report that in 2006, 700 cases of child abuse or neglect were reported to the Children's Courts over six municipalities in the Western Cape. Child abuse, especially if sustained, poses direct risks to the physical, social, and emotional development in a child. Donald et al. (2010:231) note that child abuse may take four different forms, including: sexual abuse, physical abuse, emotional abuse, and neglect.

  · **Sexual abuse** involves any sexual activity, from touching to full intercourse, by an adult or adolescent, on a child who developmentally is not able to understand fully or give consent to the activity. Sexual abuse occurs within the family, commonly by the father, stepfather or temporary partner, grandfather, older siblings, or other relatives (Donald et al., 2010:231). It may also occur outside the family through people in charge of the child, including teachers, caregivers in children's homes, and child supervisors, or through strangers. Donald et al. (2010:231) maintain that with the current HIV and AIDS pandemic, it is particularly disturbing that child sexual abuse in South Africa has not only increased, but has also contributed to the spread of HIV infection. There are a number of complex and increasing reasons behind this, such as cultural beliefs and practices, together with increasing poverty, that are clearly implicated in the prevalence of sexual abuse (Donald et al., 2010:231).

  · **Physical abuse** is regarded as common and is serious in its consequences for child development. It involves intentional acts of physical hurt on a child. Physical abuse can also mean sadistic practices like tying or locking up a child, or burning her with a cigarette or other hot objects. Tragically, it could also include actual murder, which is often linked to sexual abuse (Donald et al., 2010:231).

  · **Emotional abuse** is the most common form of abuse, which may have the worst effects on the development of a child. This involves those in proximal relationships with a child, most often parents, caregivers, teachers and sometimes peers, in the form of bullying, or engaging in patterns of behaviour that are consistently destructive of a child's emotional and psychological wellbeing. The most common patterns of emotional abuse include emotionally negating, rejecting, isolating, terrorising, corrupting, and humiliating a child (Donald et al., 2010:231).

- **Neglect** means the failure on the part of a child's parents or caregivers to provide for a child's physical needs, such as food, shelter, clothes, and medical help (Donald et al., 2010:232). Neglect actually often relates to extreme poverty or psychological inability in the primary caregiver, usually the mother, to provide consistently for her own needs as well as those of the child.

The listed types of abuse can prevent learning or even cause learners to drop out of school. Violence in homes and communities is also seen as a barrier to learning. The child is distracted by what may happen when he goes home and cannot concentrate on learning.

- **HIV and AIDS pandemic.** According to Donald et al. (2010:249), the HIV and AIDS pandemic has devastating effects on individual adults, children and youth, on families, on schools, on community and society as a whole. It is regarded as a catastrophic social problem. Effectively, the HIV and AIDS pandemic means that children are dealing with parents and siblings who are chronically ill and dying, as well as often heading up households themselves.

Causes of barriers to formal learning

Tselapedi (2009:6) succinctly states that most barriers to formal learning for learners arise from different aspects, and are as follows:

Socio-economic barriers

Socio-economic barriers exist in South Africa where there is an inadequate number of schools. The educational needs of the population are not easily met, and there are often insufficient human and material resources for a number of learners. Effective learning depends on resources. Many learners arrive at school hungry because parents are not employed and cannot afford to buy food. It is impossible for such learners to concentrate on learning to read, write, spell, and do mathematical calculations if they have not eaten for a day or more. Swart and Pettipher (2005:16) and Green (2008:10) mention that inadequacies in the provision of education are linked to other inequalities in society such as urban or rural disparities, as well as inequalities arising from discrimination on the grounds of, for example, gender, race, and disability.

Lack of access to basic services

Lack of access to basic services appears as the most dominant barrier to learning. Pettipher (2009:15) maintains that, in rural areas in South Africa many learners cannot reach their nearest school because there are no transport facilities. Lack of access to adequate medical treatment means that some learners are absent from school for a long period of time because of ill-health. Lack of access to health centres also seems to be a problem that threatens the education system in South Africa. A lack of even basic amenities in schools and homes, such as electricity and toilets, creates an unhealthy environment, which places learners and educators at risk.

Inter-sectoral collaboration

The inclusive system of education emphasises the collaboration of various government agencies such as the Departments of Health, Social Services, Correctional Services, Justice, Public Works, Safety and Security, Child Protection Units, local government unions, as well as non-governmental organisations, in order to meet the needs of all learners, with common divergent contexts and activities. Therefore, it becomes clear that inadequate inter-departmental collaboration also prohibits effective learning. In *Conceptual and operational guidelines for the implementation of inclusive education* (Department of Education, 2005), it is argued that a lack of access to other services, such as welfare and communication services, also affects the learning process and leads to learning breakdown.

Poverty and underdevelopment

Poverty has a great impact on the education system, learning processes, and on learners themselves. There are a number of factors which lead to poverty, but the most dominant one is unemployment. Unemployment deprives families of resources to satisfy basic needs, such as a place to live and nutritious food. Learners living in poverty are highly vulnerable to the health and safety risks associated with malnutrition, which leads to an inability to concentrate at school, and other symptoms, which affect the ability of learners to engage effectively and meaningfully in the learning process (Donald, Lazarus & Lolwana, 2010:319). Furthermore, learners living under such conditions are subject to increased emotional stress which adversely affects learning and development. In many cases, such conditions encourage learners to leave school early and to risk their lives by engaging in criminal activities such as theft, hijacking, or even becoming homeless street children.

Inappropriate and inadequate provision of support services

Inappropriate and inadequate provisioning of education services may also be a barrier to formal learning. Some of the barriers to formal learning emanate from the system itself. This inhibits the work of people who are trying to address barriers to formal learning, since they should be focused on the problems of learners rather than taking up time with those of the system. The Department of Education (1997) emphasises that the type of intervention recommended may lead to a learner being removed from a learning environment rather than addressing the existing problems within that environment. Another problem is that most schools which are situated in rural areas are rarely supported by education support services as you read in Chapter 12. Naicker (2008:39) believes that the inadequate distribution of these services may further disadvantage a learner rather than contributing to effective learning.

An inflexible curriculum

An inflexible curriculum is also seen as one of the most significant barriers to formal learning for the majority of learners at schools, even if it is well implemented. The Department of Education (2001:19) briefly states that barriers to formal learning arise from different aspects of the curriculum, such as:

- content (i.e. what is taught)
- language or medium of instruction
- how the classroom is organised and managed
- methods and processes used in teaching
- learning materials and equipment that are used
- assessment strategies.

An inflexible or inappropriate curriculum cannot meet the diverse needs of all learners when it fails to deliver a match between the learner and their needs, in any of these aspects. The key components that need to be examined (or re-examined) are the style and tempo of teaching and learning, what is taught, classroom management, and the materials and resources that are used for teaching and learning (Tselapedi, 2009:7).

Language and communication

The language of learning and teaching (LOLT) used in different schools can be a barrier to many learners. Given the diverse language environment of South Africa, it is inevitable that some learners will be attending schools where teaching and learning takes place in a language that is not the learners' first (or home) language. Communication is essential for learning, and learners who cannot communicate or understand educators or their peers will experience great difficulty with the learning process (Tselapedi, 2009:7). Learners who are taught in their first (or even second) additional language will always be at some disadvantage, which could lead to a learning breakdown. The DoE (1997) argues that such learners are subject to low expectations (their own and their educators'), discrimination, and lack of cultural peer groups. Further, their teachers often encounter difficulties in providing the kind of support they need, possibly because it is beyond their competence or understanding, or perhaps simply because of time and capacity constraints. Besides language, a failure to communicate may present as a great barrier to formal learning, and this can occur in both formal and informal settings.

Strategies to facilitate formal learning

Cooperative learning

Wessels (2010:9) defines cooperative learning as an opportunity to learn through the expression and exploration of diverse ideas and experiences in cooperative company. It is another way to use available resources in a group to deepen understanding, sharpen judgements, share ideas, and support one another, while participation in a group constructs new knowledge and skills. Cooperative learning activities include listening, telling, sharing, discussing, arguing, convincing, persuading, enquiring, teaching, explaining, informing, and encouraging one another in a group.

Face-to-face learning is the ideal condition for cooperative learning which is holistic, interactive and interdependent.

Wessels (2010:9) explains the advantages of group work in cooperative learning as follows:
- Group work helps learners to learn to work cooperatively.
- Learners actively participate in purposeful activities, such as a role-play dealing with returning damaged goods to a shop.
- There is a face-to-face interaction that makes the learning process more personal. Learners interact socially and they develop communication skills, such as listening, sharing, advising, and persuading.
- Group work reinforces skills previously taught, which may give learners the opportunity, for example, to practise introducing people to one another.
- Group work allows learners to discuss and clarify issues in their home language. They also have the opportunity to practise what they want to say in an additional language, within a supportive group. If group members have been coached to be supportive,

working in groups will help to build self-confidence and a positive attitude towards the additional language.

• Discussions and planning develop higher-order thinking skills, such as logical reasoning, open-ended problem solving, synthesis and analysis.

• Group work helps learners to pool their resources and to respect one another's strengths and weaknesses. They learn from one another and thus become more understanding and tolerant of others.

• During group work teachers circulate and monitor the progress of an activity, assessing learners continually. General errors are identified and dealt with at a later stage.

• Cooperative learning allows learners to become 'knowers', rather than just 'assimilators'.

With these advantages, cooperative learning can lead to dramatically improved academic achievement and the development of higher-order thinking skills, especially for low-achieving learners. It is an effective way of including learners with barriers to formal learning among groups of high-achieving learners. It also improves the attitude of teachers and learners towards learners with barriers to learning, hence motivating those learners to achieve in mainstream schools. And finally, goes a long way to improving social relations, social skills, and self-esteem among all learners.

Scaffolding

Bornman and Rose (2010:82) explain scaffolding as a technique that can help teachers organise how to teach and provide meaningful contexts linked to the child's stage of development. Therefore, scaffolding can be implemented in classrooms where learners with diverse intellectual differences are involved. There are a number of activities that the teacher can use to scaffold learning, for example:

This teacher is scaffolding her lesson by using visual references as much as possible, and explaining what to look for, to her learners.

• Projects can start off small and then gradually be built up to become larger and more complex, as learners' skills increase. As an alternative to mind maps, which may be used to get a project started, teachers can later help learners to make research grids for more complex tasks.

- During teaching, the teacher always models activities or assignments to be done.
- During activities that involve writing in the classroom, the teacher may provide more specific support in a group for those learners who find it difficult. She might, for example, suggest headings and sub-headings to help learners organise their ideas in writing.
- Teachers should allow more time to complete in-class work. Some learners who work very slowly might be paired with learners who work more quickly, and who can encourage them to finish.
- Learners who cannot finish on time because they are too precise, or uncertain about the task, can be seated next to learners who work at faster pace.
- Teachers should provide a visual scheme to help learners understand the specific content that is being taught in the lesson. As with modelling, she can draw on the chalkboard, or use pictures and diagrams to support and illustrate what she is teaching.

Cubing

Bornman and Rose (2010:78) describe cubing as a versatile differentiation strategy that can be used to explore different aspects of a topic, and to add novelty to the instructions given by the teacher. Learners often enjoy this strategy as it challenges their problem-solving and thinking skills, while providing opportunities for sharing ideas about the subject. The cubing strategy works in the following ways:

- Primarily, learners have the opportunity to share ideas about the topic or subject of the lesson.

Cubing is a strategy that asks learners to think about a concept from a number of different perspectives.

- A cube consisting of six sides is used; the strategy involves using the instructions on the six sides to talk about a topic or concept from a number of different angles. Each 'side' instructs the learner on what to do: e.g. describe, compare, associate, analyse, apply, or argue.
- Each instruction follows the same levels as Bloom's taxonomy of learning, but may be reworked to apply to the topic or concept being taught.
- Learners' involvement in the lesson starts with 1) recognising and recalling facts (rote memory); and moves on to 2) understanding the facts by comparing them; 3) applying facts to a given situation; 4) analysing information by breaking facts up in smaller parts; 5) evaluating the information by making judgements, and arguing for or against a statement; and 6) creating new facts by applying them to new situations.

- Rolling the cube adds excitement and interest to an activity; because they get to try out answering in a number of different ways, from different perspectives, learners get the most learning and enjoyment out of the activity.
- The strategy can be used in diverse classrooms where not all the learners are able to read at the same level.

Collaborative co-teaching

Collaboration in teaching is seen as the cornerstone for forming partnerships among teachers in teaching (Landsberg et al., 2011:241). This process requires a collaborative ethic, involving time and effort of each partner. It requires two teachers teaching together in the same classroom, usually taking turns with different parts of the lesson. The expertise of the subject teacher and inclusive skills of the learning support teacher are combined to teach a diverse group of learners in the same classroom. Co-teachers perform tasks jointly, including planning and teaching, developing instructional accommodation, monitoring and assessing learners, and communicating learner progress. Landsberg et al. (2011:83) indicate that it can be done in the following alternative ways:

- The whole class is taught by the subject teacher, while the learning support teacher provides support to certain learners.
- Parallel teaching is employed, where the class is divided into groups of mixed ability, and taught simultaneously by both teachers.
- Alternative teaching is carried out, where learners who struggle with certain concepts are included in one small group. While the subject teacher teaches the bigger group, the learning support teacher re-teaches the smaller group by means of different teaching strategies for better understanding.

 Stop and reflect

Imagine yourself in a co-teaching situation in a class that has a disruptive learner who does not pay attention during the lesson. In what ways do you think co-teaching would benefit disruptive learners. Also highlight the benefits to you as a teacher, and to the entire class.

Policy issues relating to barriers to formal learning

The *White Paper on Education and Training in a Democratic South Africa* (1995) is the key policy document in our discussion. In this policy, the Department of Education and Training introduced key initiatives to respond to diverse learners' needs. These initiatives included 1) the culture of learning, teaching and service (COLTS) initiative, which is now called the Tirisano programme; 2) the National Qualifications

Framework (NQF); 3) Curriculum 2005, based on outcomes-based education (OBE); and 4) a new policy on language in education.

The White Paper on Education and Training and the South African Schools Act of 1996 created the necessary basis for policy and legislation to facilitate a paradigm shift to inclusive education.

In the White Paper on an Integrated National Disability Strategy, strategies for access to the curriculum for learners with impairments were described, further emphasising and supporting the paradigm shift from a medical model of disability to a socio-critical model, based on the premise that society must change to accommodate the diverse needs of its entire people.

The Constitution of the Republic of South Africa, 1996 provides a base for development of inclusive education in South African education. With regard to education, the Bill of Rights (Chapter 2 of the Constitution) provides that everyone has the right to basic education. The South African Schools Act 108 of 1996 also provides that everyone has a right to basic education. The National Education Policy, Act 27 of 1996 promotes access and inclusivity. *Education White Paper 6* of 2001 proclaims a policy of inclusive education, the goal being the advancement of human rights as well as social and environmental justice. In the national strategy on Screening, Identification, Assessment and Support (SIAS) of 2008, the Department of Education sets out to implement, in an incremental way, the main elements of an inclusive education system. The emphasis is on identifying learners who experience barriers to formal learning and development within the education system so as to provide additional support to enhance participation and inclusion. Barriers to formal learning as captured by Education White Paper 6 were taken as a point of departure in writing this chapter. The focus is mainly on support within the classroom.

It should be noted that while the National Curriculum and Assessment Policy Statement (CAPS), a comprehensive policy document, replaced the Subject and Learning Area Statements, Learning Programme Guidelines, and Subject Assessment Guidelines for all subjects listed in the National Curriculum Statement Grades R–12 in 2010, the original principles for inclusive education in the policy document, Curriculum 2005, still hold.

 Stop and reflect

Consider the range of causes of intellectual disability. What do you think are the priorities for prevention in your social context? More importantly, what can you see yourself doing about this, as a future teacher situated in a community? Write your response as a proposal to your provincial education authority.

Summary of discussion

This chapter has tried to set out the main causes of barriers to formal learning. An understanding of different barriers to formal learning helps teachers to reflect continually on why certain learners have difficulty in learning; to look not just at the learner, but also at his context; and then to work out what type and level of support he needs in order to learn. Different strategies were described and the advantages of using them in inclusive classrooms was explained.

PART 3 Understanding inclusive education

Closing activities

1. Identify a learner who experiences barriers to formal learning in your classroom (or a classroom where you have recently taught). Develop a case study of the learner by analysing the barriers to learning in terms of the bio-ecological model (Landsberg et al., 2011; Tabane, in Chapter 5 of this book). You could use the case study at the beginning of this chapter as a model. Develop a set of questions about your case study that can be answered by a fellow student.

2. Design an individual support plan for a learner who experiences difficulties with her first additional language. This learner has a limited vocabulary and speaks in very short sentences, or single phrases. Because her reading ability is poor, she does not understand what she has read, and this is impacting on her other subjects (Landsberg et al., 2011; Ramohai & Moreeng, in Chapter 4 of this book). Your plan should include at least one of the strategies you have read about in this chapter.

Further reading

Bornman, J. & Rose, J. 2010. *Believe that all can achieve: Increasing classroom participation in learners with special support needs.* Pretoria: Van Schaik.
> This local book gives further details on all teaching strategies discussed in this chapter, including collaborative co-teaching.

Donald, D., Lazarus, S. & Lolwana, P. 2010. *Educational psychology in social context: Ecosystemic application in southern Africa.* 4th ed. Cape Town: Oxford University Press.
> This book is of high priority in ecosystemic applications in South Africa.

Landsberg, E., Kruger, D. & Swart, E. 2011. *Addressing barriers to learning: A South African perspective.* Pretoria: Van Schaik.
> This book is of immediate relevance on the typologies of barriers to formal leaning in South African context.

Kirk, S.A., Gallaghar, J.J., Anastasiow, N.J. & Coleman, M.R. 2006. *Educating exceptional children.* Boston (MA): Houghton Mifflin.
> This book provides the basics on how to educate learners with barriers to formal learning.

Winkler, G. Modise, M. & Dawber, A. 2004. *All children can learn: A handbook on teaching children with learning difficulties.* Cape Town: Francolin.
> This book is of immediate relevance to teaching children with learning difficulties.

258

References

Bornman, J., & Rose, J. 2010. *Believe that all can achieve: Increasing classroom participation in learners with special support needs.* Pretoria: Van Schaik.

Department of Education. 1996. *National Education Act 27 of 1996.* Pretoria: Government Printers.

Department of Education. 1997. *Quality education for all: overcoming barriers to learning and development.* A report by the National Commission on Special Needs in Education and Training and the National Committee for Education Support Services. Pretoria: Government Printers.

Department of Education. 2001. *Education White Paper 6 – Special needs education: Building an inclusive education and training system.* Pretoria: Government Printers.

Department of Education. 2002. *Revised National Curriculum Statement Grades R-9.* Pretoria: Government Printers.

Department of Education. 2005. *Conceptual and operational guidelines for the implementation of inclusive education: Special schools as resource centres.* Pretoria: Government Printers.

Department of Education. 2008. The national strategy on screening, identification, assessment and support (SIAS). Pretoria: Government Printers.

Donald, D., Lazarus, S. & Lolwana, P. 2010. *Educational psychology in social context: Ecosystemic application in southern Africa.* 4th ed. Cape Town: Oxford University Press.

Engelbrecht, P., Green, L., Naicker, S. & Engelbrecht, L. 1999. *Inclusive education in action in South Africa.* Pretoria: Van Schaik.

Green, L. 2008. Theoretical and contextual background. In P. Engelbrecht & L. Green (Eds). *Promoting learner development: Preventing and working with barriers to learning.* Pretoria: Van Schaik.

Jacobs, M., Vakalisa, N.C.G. & Gawe, N. 2011. *Teaching-learning dynamics.* 4th ed. Cape Town: Pearson.

Kirk, S.A., Gallaghar, J.J., Anastasiow, N. J. & Coleman, M. R. 2006. *Educating exceptional children.* Boston MA: Houghton Mifflin.

Landsberg, E., Kruger, D. & Nel, N. 2005. *Addressing barriers to learning: A South African perspective.* 1st ed. Pretoria: Van Schaik.

Landsberg, E., Kruger, D. & Swart, E. 2011. *Addressing barriers to learning: A South African perspective.* 3rd ed. Pretoria: Van Schaik.

Naicker, S. 1999. Inclusive education in South Africa. In: P. Engelbrecht, L. Green, S. Naicker & L. Engelbrecht (Eds). *Inclusive education in action in South Africa*. Pretoria: Van Schaik.

Republic of South Africa. 1996. *Constitution of the Republic of South Africa, 1996*. Pretoria: Government Printers.

Swart, E. & Pettipher, R. 2005. A framework for understanding inclusion. In E. Landsberg, D. Kruger & N. Nel. *Addressing barriers to learning: A South African perspective*. Pretoria: Van Schaik.

Tselapedi, O.J. 2009. *Inclusive education: Providing ongoing support*. Mafikeng: Government Printers.

Wessels, M. 2011. *Practical guide to facilitating language learning*. 3rd ed. Cape Town: Oxford University Press.

14

Language as a barrier to learning in South African classrooms

Juliet Ramohai and Boitumelo Moreeng

Chapter overview

Simply put, language is the way that people use to communicate. It is a uniquely human function. It is also a very important tool to help people acquire and share ideas and views about different issues. Communication between different people allows them to get to understand one another, to gain knowledge about different issues, and to build on their existing knowledge. The opposite is the case when people use a language that they are not competent or comfortable in, to communicate. No, or very little, meaningful engagement can happen, few ideas can be shared. The focus in this chapter will be on how language in the context of the South African classroom can act as a barrier to learning. Specifically, the chapter will look at:

- The history of language in education in South Africa
- The different ways in which language can be a barrier in the classroom
- The impact of language as a barrier on the teaching and learning process
- Providing suggestions on how to deal with language as a barrier in the classroom.

It is in line with *Education White Paper 6: Building an Inclusive Education and Training System in South Africa* (DoE, 2001), that this chapter discusses the barriers that language can create in the learning and teaching process in our classrooms in South Africa. Education White Paper 6 reiterates the need for equal access through the clear goal of inclusiveness in South African schools. It states: "Our long-term goal is the development of an inclusive education and training system that will uncover and address barriers to learning, and recognise and accommodate the diverse range of learning needs" (2001:45).

Learning outcomes

By the end of this chapter you should be able to:

- Define the role that language plays in the teaching and learning process
- Demonstrate an understanding of the history of language within the South African education context
- Critically discuss the different barriers that language creates in classrooms
- Analyse the impact that language barriers have on learners within the classroom context
- Demonstrate an understanding of the different ways in which we can minimise the impact that language barriers have on learners in classrooms.

Read the following case study and answer the questions that follow:

CASE STUDY 1

Bronder Primary School is located in the suburbs of the big city of Withof. Bronder is a former Model C Afrikaans-medium school which catered for the all-white Afrikaans-speaking community in the area. With the current South African education landscape, in which racial segregation in schools no longer exists, the school has opened access to a diverse group of learners from different geographical and language backgrounds. The school is also no longer an in an exclusively white Afrikaans suburb because of the movement of other race groups into the area recently. So the school has been constrained by the demands of the education system through the South African Education Language Policy to cater for the language needs of all the learners within the school. As a result of these demands, the school management team, in consultation with their other stakeholders, decided to do away with Afrikaans and adopted English as the only language of instruction. English has been phased in from Grade 1 in the past five years. Grades 6 and 7 are still taught in Afrikaans.

 Stop and reflect

After reading the case study, ask yourself:
1   Why was it necessary for the school to change its language policy from Afrikaans to English?
2   Describe Bronder Primary School before the language changes were implemented.
3   What brought about the changes at the school?
4   How have these changes affected the school's education landscape?
5   Do you think that within the changing education landscape it will now be easier or more difficult for you as an educator to teach in a township or rural school, for example? Motivate your answer.

Bantu-speaking people refers to a large and diverse group of African people in and around central and southern Africa who speak linguistically related languages. Some South Africans are uncomfortable using the term 'bantu' which became racially loaded when it was adopted by the apartheid regime to refer to black people. However, throughout Africa it is accepted and used as the linguistically correct descriptive term.

A brief history of language in South African education

The current status of languages in South Africa can be traced through the historical development of South Africa itself, stretching as far back as pre-colonial times. From about 2 000 years ago, different groups of Bantu-speaking people moved from the central parts of Africa to settle in various regions around the southern part of the continent (Prah, 2007). African languages survived and developed side by side into two large groups that were eventually classified into the Nguni languages (isiZulu, isiXhosa, isiNdebele, SiSwati, Tshivenda); and the Sotho languages (Setswana, Sesotho, Sepedi). The arrival of Europeans in southern Africa from the mid-seventeenth century had a great influence on the settlement patterns of the different African groups. First came the Dutch and later followed the English, both of whom entered into an intense competition for dominance over the next century. From this point, the medium of instruction in South African schools revolved around English and a form of Dutch that later became Afrikaans, with an almost complete neglect of African languages. Education, then, was synonymous with learning in English, or what later became Afrikaans. After 1948, Afrikaans began to dominate as a result of the drive to forge an Afrikaans national identity based on the policy of apartheid, as instituted by the Nationalist Party in government. The apartheid system used the Group Areas Act (No. 41 of 1950) and later the Bantu Homeland Citizenship Act (No. 26 of 1970) to keep people divided according to racial and ethnic lines, as well as linguistic groups.

It is now well established that the Soweto uprising of 1976 began as a result of people's (mainly school students') resistance to being taught in Afrikaans. In 1974 the government had instituted the Afrikaans Medium Decree making it compulsory for certain subjects to be taught only in Afrikaans in black schools. These subjects included mathematics, arithmetic and social studies. English could only be used for the teaching of general science and practical subjects. Many black youth associated Afrikaans with the oppressive apartheid regime and preferred to be taught in English.

After the 1994 democratic elections, the post-apartheid government embarked on a process of unifying the nation on the principles of multiculturalism, multiracialism, multilingualism, and respect for diversity. The South African Constitution (1996), recognises 11 official languages, to which the state guarantees equal status. These include: Afrikaans, Setswana, English, isiNdebele, SiSwati, isiXhosa, Tshivenda, isiZulu, Sesotho, Sepedi, and South African Sign Language. The implication is that no language should be given priority at the expense of another language, as was previously practised under apartheid.

> **code-switch:** the practice of moving from one language to another in the course of a conversation, lecture or lesson, sometimes using less formal language in the alternate language, in order to express oneself better, or make a meaning clearer

Language challenges within the classroom

Before we analyse the barriers that language might create, let us look at what actually goes on in some classrooms. Read the following case study and then do the activity that follows:

 CASE STUDY 2

Cedric is a 52-year-old teacher who received his teacher training in a previously Afrikaans-medium teacher's college. He has been teaching at Bronder Primary School for 20 years. For 15 years of his teaching experience at Bronder he taught solely in Afrikaans. When the school changed over to English in the last five years, he had to adapt to the new language of instruction. Cedric is now encountering many problems with learners' understanding during his class presentation.

 *Cedric:* My learners frustrate me so much. They always look blank in class like they don't understand when I present a lesson. They complain about my accent and pronunciation. I don't think those issues have anything to do with their lack of understanding. I have been teaching for 20 years and my learners in previous years always passed well. Surely there isn't anything wrong with my teaching? I think it's the quality of learners who get enrolled in our school currently. When this school was still Afrikaans, I did not encounter this kind of problem, and in any case, that is the language I am most comfortable with. Right now, I can't even **code-switch** when I explain because most of the learners don't even understand Afrikaans.

Palse is a 26-year-old teacher who is also teaching at Bronder Primary. She joined the school a year ago after completing her education degree at a predominantly black university. She comes from a rural area and moved to the area around Bronder when she got this teaching post.

Palse: My learners find it difficult to understand when I use English only, in class. The majority speak Sesotho as their home language, and some are Afrikaans-speaking. I am from a Zulu background myself, so I cannot use any other language to try and clarify concepts. At varsity most of us were Zulu so some concepts are easy to explain in isiZulu because our lecturers would also explain them in isiZulu for us to understand. This current environment is frustrating. Maybe if I had been teaching for a long time, I would know how to approach these learners. Sometimes they feel that I speak too fast and inaudibly, and at times they say I use words that are too difficult. And half of the time I have to explain terms to them, even the simplest! This takes up so much of my teaching time. I don't know what to do!

Thato is 34 years old. She was redeployed to Bronder two years ago when the farm school where she was teaching closed. For most of her career, she taught at the same farm school after obtaining her advanced certificate in education 13 years ago. At the farm school, the medium of instruction was Afrikaans, but learners mostly spoke Sesotho as their home language. This made it easy for Thato since she was also Sesotho speaking. Before Bronder, Thato would use mainly Sesotho in her class presentations.

Thato: My learners say that most of the time they don't understand because my presentation is not clear. We argue so much on the appropriate use of English terms. At times during class presentations, they keep correcting my use of words and expressions. This really turns me off! I mean, I have been a teacher for 13 years, and yes, I might have been educated in an Afrikaans school, but I did my courses in English at tertiary level. How difficult can it be to teach a Grade 5 learner in English? Besides, I teach maths not English, and this English is only for communicating ideas which I feel I am doing well. I tried to revert to explaining in Sesotho or Afrikaans, but now they do so badly in tests!

 Stop and reflect

After reading Case study 2:
1   Identify the challenges in the language of instruction that each one of the three teachers faces, which contribute to barriers in understanding/learning for their Grade 5 learners.
2   Write a short report (one page) in which you discuss the contributing factors to the challenges that the teachers face.

These guidelines will help you to analyse the case study. In your analysis think about:
- The number of years of teaching experience for each teacher
- The attitude that the teachers have towards learners who are struggling
- Teacher competence in the language of instruction
- The influence of the school's language history
- The teachers' own language background.

Language as a barrier to learning

Since it is the primary means of communication, language plays an important role in the teaching and learning process because it enables the teacher to send out the message about the learning content to the learners. It enables her to give instructions, to explain, to ask questions, to respond to learners' questions and observations, and to give feedback. However, the way in which the teacher uses language can become a barrier to effective and meaningful teaching. In the following section we will look at how language can be a barrier to effective teaching and learning, by focusing on the following agents – the teachers and the learners.

Teachers

Competence and knowledge of LOLT

Most schools in South Africa use either English or Afrikaans as the medium of instruction. So it is logical to expect that all teachers have received training in these languages in which they are expected to teach. The reality is that not every teacher is competent in these languages, particularly additional language speakers, and this in itself impacts negatively on communication within the classroom.

In some instances, the teacher's vocabulary in the second language is limited. This forces the teacher to code-switch between the language of instruction and her home language, making it even more difficult for learners to understand the lesson. This happens especially in cases where learners within the classroom come from diverse language backgrounds and cannot all understand the teacher's home language. Reverting to mother tongue in a multilingual class could create barriers for learners whose home language is different from the teacher's mother tongue. Teachers might revert to their mother tongue when presenting a class because they lack competence or confidence in the language of instruction, or they lack the language proficiency to support learners in acquiring academic literacy, or simply that they are not trained to teach through the medium of the second language (Landsberg, 2011).

home language and **mother tongue** are used to mean the same thing in this context, i.e. the language that one is 'born into' and which is primarily used in one's home environment

 Stop and reflect

Think about your own situation in the school in which you teach, or the school that you attended as a learner. Describe the ways in which a teacher's lack of competence in the language of instruction could lead to barriers in learning.

Teachers' cultural background and socialisation

The teacher's personality contributes to the way language is used in the classroom. If the teacher is warm and welcoming, learners will feel able to participate and to talk in class. The opposite happens when the teacher is strict and inflexible. In this case, learners will not be free to contribute or to ask questions in class. Learners are very quick to sense what the teacher likes or dislikes, and they respond accordingly.

Another important factor that might inhibit the meaningful use of language in the classroom is whether the teacher is monolingual or multilingual. The South African situation, as depicted in the earlier section of this chapter, is a multilingual and multicultural context. Therefore most South African classrooms are likely to be multilingual by nature. A teacher who knows only one language will tend to limit the extent to which learners, especially those who are not confident in the LOLT (language of learning and teaching), participate in the classroom. The learning environment will be enhanced by the teacher's basic knowledge of, and appreciative attitude towards, all the languages that are spoken by the learners in the region where the school is located. This could result in meaningful code-switching that would deepen the quality of learning taking place in the classroom; more learners will participate in classroom discussions and ask questions where necessary. Here we are not encouraging the teacher to move away totally from the LOLT, but we allow that learners will make more meaning of concepts being studied in a language that they already understand. If teachers 'borrow' some words from the other languages present in the classroom, learners could more easily make associations between these concepts in their mother tongue and the language of instruction.

Linked to the personality of the teacher, is the way in which the teacher uses language in the class in terms of the receptivity of the learners. In some instances, the teacher's use of language in class might not be congruent with the learners' level of understanding (Nel & Muller, 2010). Learners in different grades are at different levels of language development, so a teacher has always to consider the choice of words and level of language used when communicating in the classroom. The teacher should also be aware of his accent, pronunciation, articulation, and intonation as these might also impact on how learners make meaning of what is being presented. Although these language features are often not taken seriously by teachers, and may be regarded as having little impact on learning, they are central to the learning process. For example, if the teacher's accent in English has an American, or French, or Indian influence, and the learners are from a rural area where they are not even much exposed to South African English, they will find it difficult to follow the teacher's presentation.

Stop and reflect

1 Take time to listen to one another's accents in your class. How do different accents impact on your level of understanding?
2 Reflect on the different accents of your lecturers. In what ways does this have an influence on the way you understand their presentations?

The way in which a teacher has been socialised and whether she comes across as a warm, welcoming person who likes to work with diverse learners, a person who enjoys conversations with people, knows how to talk to children, is approachable, has a sense of humour, is always encouraging, and has a positive outlook on life, will all, in most cases, make for a vibrant classroom. In this kind of classroom learners will be encouraged to participate, to present their ideas, to ask questions, and to have group discussions. The teacher will create a safe space for learners to make mistakes and to learn from them. Inability to express oneself in the LOLT, or making mistakes, is not ridiculed, but is understood to be part of the learning process.

In addition to the issue of personality, the use of language that discriminates, stigmatises, and shows prejudice on the basis of race, gender, culture, language, or religious orientation, should never be used. The use of this kind of language will result in reduced and restricted participation from learners.

Type of training received

The type of teacher training received, and the environment in which training took place, has an impact on whether the teacher will understand and appreciate issues of diversity, multiculturalism and multilingualism. The more inclusive the environment where the teacher trained, and the environments she was exposed in pre-service, all have the potential to make teachers more conscious about issues of diversity. Teachers from such environments are more likely to be familiar with strategies that are responsive to the diverse needs of learners.

Assessment

Assessment is included as a point on its own to emphasise its importance. Through assessment, learners are admitted into different programmes, they are promoted to the next grade, and they are certified competent. Furthermore, continuous assessment is used as a teaching and learning opportunity to improve both teaching and learning, not only to evaluate learners and determine their advancement. It is also used to diagnose learners' abilities, problems, and prior knowledge; to monitor learners' progress in mastering concepts, from recall of factual information to formal thinking. All these assessment processes are language dependent and therefore centre on the choice and use of language. Teachers have to design questions and activities using the language of instruction. When these are not properly phrased, or are pitched at a level higher than that of the learners, learners' problems and areas for improvement are wrongly diagnosed or missed, and the wrong conclusions about learners' potential might be reached.

Stop and reflect

After reading this section on teachers' challenges in using language within the classroom, refer again to Case study 2 (on pages 263–264). How would you further describe the challenges that Cedric, Palse and Thato from Bronder Primary are encountering?

Learners

In the classroom learners use and are exposed to language when they have to read and interpret information, respond to questions orally or in written form, ask questions in class, participate in group discussions or in whole class activities. Study the following excerpts and then do the activity.

Teacher only give me small work to do becos I am leming English. But I can do more work. I dont speech good but I am cleever. So I can lern more English so Teacher must give me more work.

Excerpt 1: Sample from a learner's essay

Excerpt 2: Most learners are afraid of writing.

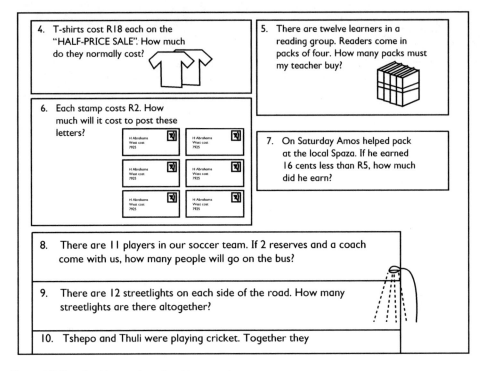

Excerpt 3: Sample of learners' word problem exercises

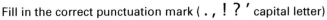

Fill in the correct punctuation mark (. , ! ? ' capital letter)

Excerpt 4: Helping English second language learners to deal with punctuation

Activity 1

With a partner, spend about 20 minutes going through all the excerpts, and identify the challenges that each excerpt depicts. Also think of the ways in which you with your learners could minimise the impact of some of these challenges in your classroom. Share these strategies with the class after your discussion with your partner.

Consider the following questions in your analysis:

- In Excerpt 1, what can you say about the teacher's attitude towards the learner, which may be inhibiting the learner? How do you assess the overall expression of the learner in the excerpt?
- In Excerpt 2, why do you think the learners' enthusiasm is dampened by the fact that they will have to write about their learning experience after the field trip?
- In Excerpt 3, look carefully at the words used in the word sums. How could these words create a barrier to understanding the questions for second language learners?
- In Excerpt 4, what could have contributed to the learners' lack of understanding of punctuation? In what way do you think the learners' understanding of punctuation in his or her home language would have helped in understanding and completing the task in English? Provide an example if you can.

Possible problems for learners learning in a second language

- *Learners' lack of competence and proficiency in the language of learning and instruction*

From looking at the excerpts at the beginning of this section, you will have noticed that the learners' knowledge, competence, and proficiency in the language of instruction all have an adverse effect on the learning process within the classroom. Some of the problems that you identified might have been the result of a lack of competence in the LOLT, including limited vocabulary, learners' failure to adequately express themselves in the language of instruction, and a failure to interpret written text. This lack of competence in the LOLT clearly has an impact on how learners perform in the classroom, and on the views that the teacher holds about the learners. This could be in terms of whether they are performing at an acceptable level or not, and, more importantly, whether they are capable of performing at an acceptable level.

Learners' problems with the language might also be worsened by the fact that learners are taught in a second (or additional) language: they consequently have difficulties making meaning of the language used for instruction. This can further impact negatively on the learners' self-esteem and self-confidence in speaking and writing in the language of instruction. Learners in these kinds of spaces sometimes experience a sense of frustration as they feel that their own language and cultural experiences do not have a place in formal learning. The learners who use a second language as a language of learning sometimes face the challenge of being undermined by a teacher and their peers who can express themselves fluently in the language. They are often stereotyped as non-performing and slow, which leads to a withdrawal from expressing themselves using the language of learning.

• *Learners have to learn in a monolingual environment*

In cases where the learners are strictly exposed to a monolingual classroom environment through the LOLT, where even for discussion and concept clarification no multilingual approaches are used, they might not fully engage with what is being taught. As has been indicated earlier, if teachers are not trained in multilingualism, they often fail to offer support to multilingual learners in their classroom. As a result, learners are forced to remain in a monolingual environment in which transfer of knowledge from their own language is not taken into consideration.

One other aspect that monolingual classrooms fail to consider is that learners' level of language development differs according to their age and background environment. Younger learners who are not yet fluent in their home language may find it difficult to fully grasp concepts in the second language. So, instruction that disregards this fails to consider that the acquisition of vocabulary is dependent on learners' level of development in both languages. If learners are exposed to language and terms that they cannot make sense of, they tend to get frustrated, to miss the intended message in the lesson, which compounds as a problem when they fail to develop good conceptual frameworks.

• *Learners have other barriers to learning*

The problem with language use and its impact on the quality of teaching and learning also includes learners who are deaf (or hearing impaired), or learners that have difficulties with speaking. These learners are always neglected and their needs are not usually fully catered for. Most instruction focuses mainly on oral language and not much is done to accommodate learners who are hard of hearing and those that have problems with speaking, even in an inclusive classroom. As a result, these learners struggle and find it difficult to fit into this kind of environment where their special needs are not considered. Consider the experience of the learner called Larry in the following case study.

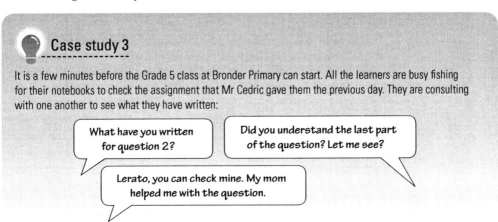

Case study 3

It is a few minutes before the Grade 5 class at Bronder Primary can start. All the learners are busy fishing for their notebooks to check the assignment that Mr Cedric gave them the previous day. They are consulting with one another to see what they have written:

> What have you written for question 2?

> Did you understand the last part of the question? Let me see?

> Lerato, you can check mine. My mom helped me with the question.

Everyone is busy, except for Larry, who is sitting alone quietly at the front, looking at his own notebook. He has a hearing problem and other learners tend to ignore him.

Mr Cedric comes in and shouts: 'I hope you have completed your assignment. We will work out the answers on the board. Lerato, come and show us what you have for the first question.'

All the learners listen as Lerato explains. Then some start talking amongst themselves and they check their books to see if they have same answers. After they complete the assignment, Mr Cedric announces that they are going to write a test on the content of the assignment, the next day.

Larry does not speak to any other learner throughout the lesson, nor do they speak to him.

Work in pairs to answer the following questions:
1 Look closely at what learners are doing as they wait for Mr Cedric to come to class. What are they busy with?
2 Larry is not joining in the discussions going on among his classmates. Why is this?
3 Read the case study again with your partner and identify some of the things that the learners and Mr Cedric do which act as a barrier to Larry's inclusion in class.
4 With your partner, write down at least five ways in which you as a teacher would ensure that you create an inclusive environment in which Larry would feel a sense of belonging, and be able to engage in the teaching and learning process.

Appropriate learning and teaching support material

The teaching and learning process can be enhanced by the use of teaching and learning support material (LTSM) in the form of textbooks, reference books, pamphlets, posters, charts, chalkboard, radio presentations or podcasts, CD, DVD and video presentations, cellphones, smartphones, tablets and computers, and the internet. These are mainly used by both the teachers and learners to look for information, to do research, to study, and to make notes on what they learn. These learning aids use language in a written or oral form.

When any of these media are used, care should be taken to ensure that the material used is in line with the learners' level of development, and that the choice of language used is appropriate. The language of these resources could be at a slightly higher level than the level at which the learners are currently functioning so that they are challenged and 'stretched' to learn. However, if it is at too high a level, understanding could be impeded, leading to misinterpretation of the content which, in turn, leads to performance problems during tests and examinations.

The value and usefulness of the material could also be impeded by the teacher's failure to include explanations, definitions, and summaries that help in making the language used more learner-friendly and compatible with the level of learners. If audio-visual material is going to be used, it should also be audible enough for everyone to hear, and the pronunciation familiar with what learners are used to. It should also be visible to all learners, even if this means they have to take turns viewing the material (e.g. on a computer screen or tablet). These may seem obvious points, but in large class situations the benefits of good resources are limited unless the teacher can organise access for everyone.

The LTSM used in the classroom should also respond to the language diversity in the classroom. Teachers could use more simplified versions of the teaching and learning material that could be better understood by all learners, including those who have difficulties in the additional language.

Time allocated to complete tasks

The time that is allocated for the completion of an activity or topic could also present a problem for second language learners. Piaget's theory of cognitive development (Sigelman & Rider, 2012) indicates that learners have different information processing skills at different ages. This means that the speed at which different learners process information varies significantly. In the case of the second language learner, there is already a problem with understanding and interpreting the text because of a language barrier, which compounds the difficulty for the learner to process the given information within the normal time. The learner is not only expected to process the information within a given time, but also to provide the correct response to the questions asked. This is especially the case in timed tasks like tests and exams. Unfortunately, sometimes this problem is overlooked and learners are labelled as slow when they do not finish tasks.

Some strategies for helping teachers and learners

The following suggestions are aimed at minimising the barriers that might be caused by language use in the classroom and also at improving learners' competence in the LOLT.

Teacher training

The ways in which teachers are trained, and the kind of in-service training that they are exposed to, has an impact on the kind of teacher that they become. Teachers who are trained in a multiracial, multicultural and multilingual environment tend to be more appreciative of diversity. They become aware of the different languages used in specific areas and regions. Some training institutions encourage **dynamic bilingualism** for their students to enable them to understand another language apart from their own home language, with the aim of using it actively and effectively when communicating, especially in the classroom (Garcia, 2009). It is only those teachers that have been trained to do this who can effectively engage their learners in a learning experience where different languages are accommodated and used effectively.

dynamic bilingualism: a language practice that uses two or more languages at a time to increase the effectiveness of communication; users switch between and adjust the languages used to their communicative needs

The teacher's ability to be reflective about the language used in the classroom is also important. This process of self-reflection on the part of the teacher is important during the initial training phase, and also during the formative years of teaching. It allows teachers to be aware of their limitations in the use of LOLT and other languages in the classroom. As a result, teachers might want to engage in self-development initiatives in order to improve on their knowledge, competence, confidence, and skills to meet the language demands of the multilingual learners in their classrooms. They need to be equipped with skills in how to use language optimally and flexibly to present classes and assess the learners effectively within the teaching and learning process.

Planning

Another way of dealing with language as a barrier in the classroom is through planning. Planning for the teaching and learning process can be done at different levels. In this section we focus on lesson planning. In preparing for a lesson, teachers have to consider different issues that might impact on or enhance the quality of teaching and learning. These include taking into consideration the different language needs in the classroom. This could be done through variations in the class presentation. For example, the use of different teaching approaches that include using images, diagrams, and other media could enhance understanding. This is especially useful in a class where there are hearing-impaired learners. The approaches should be extended to the writing of examinations and tests, where learners could also be allowed to use alternative presentations of their ideas, for example, orally or by drawing rather than writing.

Content-based teaching approach

The teacher could adopt a content-based approach by spending more time on the whole learning experience rather than on the language issues. This means that the teacher needs to adopt a content-oriented teaching approach when dealing with a class of children from linguistically diverse environments who are exposed to the use of an additional language as the language of instruction. The topic being taught is the focus, and the language 'finds a way, or ways' of making this meaningful and comprehensible. In this case, the language or expression becomes a non-issue, and the teacher focuses on the understanding of the content. Teachers can promote inter-group communication and understanding. The best way of doing so is through mother tongue-based bilingual education and the promotion of **individual multilingualism**. This is the rationale for the official language education policy of 'additive bilingualism' (i.e., the addition of another language and maintenance of the first language, or mother tongue). The teacher therefore could confidently opt for a multilingual approach knowing it is in line with this policy requirement.

individual multilingualism: the ability of an individual to use more than two languages fluently

The use of learners' own language could be strongly fostered when learners develop posters for the walls around the classroom. Learners could be encouraged to post their research, information gathered from field trips, and interesting material from the internet on these walls. If learners are allowed to present the information in their own language, they would be further encouraged to participate in research and field trips. In addition, all learners will get to appreciate and try to understand the diverse languages within their classroom. In this way, no language will be viewed as inferior and this will boost all learners' confidence in engaging in these language-rich exercises.

Learners who can express themselves in many languages will develop the kind
of inclusive classroom they have pride and ownership in.

Teachers' use of assessment

The use of assessment is also very dependent on the use of language. Typically, learners have to listen and respond verbally to questions as well as reading, and responding in writing to questions. The type of instruction words used, the type of questions (such as those requiring recall of exact words), expressing an argument or an opinion, evaluating a situation, all require learners to demonstrate a particular level of language proficiency and development.

As has been indicated earlier, the time that is allocated for the completion of the section or topic could also present problems for second language learners. Since there is already a problem with the interpretation of the text due to a language barrier, there is a need to allocate enough time for the tasks and activities when learners do the activities.

The use of alternative assessment procedures can also help in minimising the impact of language as a barrier in the classroom. This could include an assessment where a teacher uses alternative systems as sources of information. The sources of information could include parents, peers, and other school personnel. Through scaffolding (which you explored thoroughly in earlier chapters), everyone can contribute to meaningful learning by learners. In using this approach, the teacher needs to employ multiple procedures and to assess the learners, based on relevant information collected from these different sources.

Learners can be given tasks such as observation, interviewing people outside the classroom, checklists, and other procedures that work in a multicultural classroom. The content included here could be close to that of the prescribed textbook but, by using additional multiple sources and different procedures, understanding and effective learning are achieved. The procedures should be based on content that is not completely new, and be accompanied by the skills learners require in a particular subject. For more effective approaches in this case, learners from diverse linguistic backgrounds could work in groups, and in different contexts. These groups, where possible, should consist of at least one learner whose first language is the language of instruction, or a learner who has proficiency in this language. When learners interact in such groups, they all have the opportunity to enhance their vocabulary and conceptual understanding of the LOLT. This is because they are focused on the subject or task, but the right amount of language support is also available.

Learners should also be allowed to demonstrate their knowledge in different formats, not only orally or in writing; for example, they might use role play or drama, they could develop collages and posters with available visual material, or draw diagrams and flow charts. This approach is not only beneficial to learners who have problems in the language of instruction, but more importantly, learners who have hearing and speaking problems can benefit greatly from alternative assessment procedures. Using alternative approaches will give these learners a chance to express themselves in a way that makes it easier for them to become effective participants in the teaching and learning process.

Learners' improvement in the language

One's ability to improve in a language is determined by a person's level of interest in the language. Learners should therefore be encouraged to take the initiative in improving their competence in the LOLT. Learners can improve their language competence by taking more responsibility for their learning. They should be less dependent on the teacher and engage in more intensive self-study. Learners' willingness to do extra reading and research will increase their vocabulary. In turn they will become more confident in explaining terms, using new expressions and reading different kinds of texts. Increased self-study will further enhance learners' self-esteem and general confidence. Learners can also be encouraged to keep journals of their learning experiences. They can use this to explain their learning experiences in order to make sense of them, to write about their difficulties, to describe how they sought help or solved a problem, or to keep a record of the strategies they use in dealing with their challenges. Not only will this enable learners to express themselves in a safe and private psychological space, but it will increase their knowledge of themselves, their studies, and their general proficiency in language.

Teachers also have an important role to play in minimising the impact that language can have as a barrier in the teaching and learning process. The use of personal and shared stories which centre on learners' cultural and familiar experiences can help a great deal in learners making meaning of the content being taught. This process of **concept transfer** plays an important part in making learners' experience of learning more meaningful and engaging.

concept transfer: in this context, means using a familiar situation or common language to make a concept more understandable

The kind of environment that is created and experienced by the learners is also important as it impacts on the manner in which language is used in the classroom. An environment in which learners feel safe and are able to learn from the mistakes they make in speaking and writing in a particular language, will encourage learner participation during activities. It will further minimise problems emanating from language use in the classroom. An environment where learners are also allowed to use their own language to make meaning of what is taught is encouraged where possible.

Keeping journals

As suggested earlier, learners should be encouraged to keep journals that describe and explain their learning experiences. Ideally, these journals should be in the LOLT so that they can learn to express themselves in the language. The advantage of keeping a journal is that it is a private exercise in which learners feel safe in expressing their frustrations about the learning process, their difficulties, their achievements, and the strategies they use, or intend to use, to deal with their language problems. In the journal, the learner could also keep a record of the new concepts learned, and a thorough description of the concept using the LOLT. Learners can make changes to what they write in their journals whenever they feel that they have a better explanation of the concept. The journals should not only be used in the English class but can be used for other subjects as well. For example, learners can write maths formulae in their journals and explain these in their own words, so that they can understand them. They could start their own science concepts dictionary. They should, however, always be encouraged to do so using the LOLT.

Other strategies

Other strategies and approaches that could be used in fostering a language-friendly classroom include:

- The teacher's willingness to expose the learners to the language as used in new technologies such as Google, Twitter, and other social media. The teacher should orientate learners on how to access material from internet websites. This will help learners to become familiar with the 'languages' that are used in real life and current technology, which are also rapidly infiltrating the education sector.
- Availability of language resources such as dictionaries and thesauruses, which could assist learners with vocabulary. Learners can be taught the skills of using dictionaries and thesauruses, how to compile their own vocabulary lists, how to develop their vocabularies contextually.
- Interpretation services in classrooms, where financially viable. These interpreters (who may include sign language interpreters or even skilled parents) could assist in multilingual classrooms where learners are allowed to express themselves in different languages.

Summary of discussion

In this chapter, you have learned about the role that language as a communicative tool plays within the classroom. The chapter has shown the ways in which the process of teaching and learning suffers when problems arise in this communicative act within the classroom. The issues that have been highlighted demonstrate that the teacher and the learner depend on each other to ensure that they counter the impact that language problems within the classroom can create in the teaching and learning process. Among the barriers that have been discussed in the chapter are lack of competence in the LOLT, both for the learner and the teacher, the negative impact that the teacher's and learners' cultural background and socialisation could have on the learning process unless managed creatively, and the limiting effect of inappropriate learning and teaching support material on the way in which the teacher and the learner interpret and understand both written and spoken texts. The chapter does not, however, only focus on the barriers to learning. Rather, it tries to provide practical suggestions to assist teachers to deal with the language barriers that interfere with meaningful and successful learning within the inclusive classroom.

Closing activities

To test your understanding of the chapter, work on these activities on your own, and then share your understanding in a group or class:

1. After studying the content of this chapter, reflect on your own teaching practice and the ways in which you as an educator can unintentionally create language barriers in your classroom. List two or three behaviours or attitudes to look out for and avoid if possible.

2. In the chapter, what problems relating to the language of instruction have been discussed? Identify three that interest you and explain why.

3. The stated problems are not exhaustive. Think of other problems that language creates in a classroom and add these to the ones discussed. Remember to identify and explain each of your added problems. Draw from personal experience as far as possible.

4. After reading the chapter, how can you show the interdependence between the teacher, the learner, and the learning materials, in the creation and solution of the language problems within the classroom?

5. Analyse the history of language in the South African education system by briefly describing the situation before 1994, and since then. How do you think the changing education landscape further perpetuates language barriers in schools?

6. Study the following excerpts from learners' essays. By applying any strategies that you have learned in this chapter, show how you would help the learner to overcome the language difficulties as depicted here. The essays are on the topic, 'How I spent my weekend.'

My weekend was very nice. I said to my father could you fetch my cousins? And I ate and ate but I waited too long. But my food was very nice. I played with my cousin exactly when they arrive.

I said lets play pellow fight and my older cousin said if we beat you hard don't cry. And I didn't cry. We where enjoying ourselves. I went to the kichen and my mother said call your cousins because their food is ready. And I said ok.

And I called them. They said that pellow fight was very fun. I ate but I didn't finishe my food. So I said "Mom give Sindi my eggs. Then my mother said fine.

My mother is Lindi. we are going for a weekend. My granny was very exited. she was even singing. The bus we took was very slow. My brother criyed because the bus was moving to slowely.

My sister was very, very exited, and she even took all her clothes. My mother said to my sister that she must not take all of her — clothes, she must leave a few at home.

My brother stopped criying when we arrived where we were going. My sister made a loud noise, and I said you are making noise!!!!. And we spent the weekend very nice.

I posted a card on top of the television. The poster was about mother's day, I mean the headline of the poster. In my weekend I was with my mom. Sunday we celebrated mother's day. On saturday we watched Mtn Sama Awards (MSA).

On sunday I cleaned again. I also cooked a nice meal for my mother. I felled asleep on saturday when I was watching Mtn Sama Awards (MSA). The learners where my mom is working camed. They seated down in the lounge and the other one said "happy mother's day mom then my mom said "thank you." The end.

Thank you very much!!

Excerpt 5: Grade 7 learners' essays

References

Coelho, E. 2003. *Adding English: A guide to teaching in a multilingual classroom*. Toronto: Pippin Publishers Ltd.

Department of Education. 1997. *Education White Paper 3: A programme for higher education transformation*. Pretoria: DoE.

Department of Education. 2001. *Education White Paper 6: Special needs education – Building an inclusive education and training system in South Africa*. Pretoria: DoE.

Garcia, O. 2009. *Bilingual education in the 21st century: A global perspective*. Oxford: Blackwell.

Landsberg, E. 2011. *Addressing barriers to learning: A South African perspective*. Pretoria: Van Schaik.

Nel, N. & Muller, H. 2010. The impact of teachers' limited English proficiency on English second language learners in South African schools. *South African Journal of Education*. 30:635–650.

Prah, S. 2007. *Challenges to the promotion of indigenous languages in South Africa*. Cape Town: Foundation for Human Rights in South Africa.

Sigelman, C.K. & Rider, E.A. 2012. *Life-span human development*. 8th ed. Belmont (CA): Cengage Learning.

Statistics South Africa. 2012. *Census 2011: Census in brief*. Pretoria: Statistics South Africa.

Glossary

Afrocentric philosophy a way of thinking from an African perspective, based on the principles of inclusivity, cultural specificity, critical awareness, committedness, and political awareness

antithetical when two things are not compatible with one another

assimilation the process of absorbing and integrating people, ideas or culture

attribution when something is seen as belonging to, or caused by someone

canon a general rule or principle that sets a standard, by which something can be judged

collegiality working in a spirit of sharing knowledge and learning from one another

complementary combining two different things to form a complete thing, or whole

concept transfer in the context of education, means using a familiar situation or common language to make a concept more understandable

cultural capital non-financial assets like intellect and education that enable one to advance in life

cultural hegemony in sociology, a situation where one group's identity, values and views dominate over all other groups'

defendant a person who is accused of a crime and has to appear in a law court

dialectic the action of opposing social forces, or concepts

diaspora the spread of people around the world, who have left their original homelands

discourse a formal written or spoken discussion of a subject

disinterested impartial, not taking sides or influenced in a particular direction

dissonance not being in harmony with something, clashing, not fitting in

Down's syndrome a congenital disorder causing intellectual impairment and physical abnormalities

dynamic bilingualism a language practice that uses two or more languages at a time to increase the effectiveness of communication

dynamics the influences or forces that make something shift or change

dysfunctional not working or behaving properly; being unable to deal with normal social relations

dyslexia a difficulty in reading that involves not being able to interpret words, or recognise letters and symbols

emancipatory able to set free someone or something, especially from legal, social, or political restrictions

epistemology the theory of knowledge; what is meant by knowledge itself and what is means to know something; knowing what it is to know

explicit when something is made clear and precise

extrinsic describes something that is not essential or inherent; the opposite of intrinsic, which describes something that is essential, an inherent part of the functioning or nature of something

fault-line a geological term that means a place in rock formations where breaks or displacement occur; in a sociological sense, it refers to issues which divide and disconnect people

firing a technique in making clay objects in which pots are dried and baked

fragile environment a place or community that is in constant danger from, e.g. the elements (rain and flooding, extreme temperatures, etc.), or fires, or even removal by local authorities; typically, it is an informal settlement, or 'squatter' camp

function notions, such as role, contribution, or importance of a theory, to the generation of knowledge

functionalism an approach in social psychology that interprets phenomena in terms of the functions they perform within a whole system

gratuitous unasked for; describes something that is done for no good reason

growth in economics, growth is a measure of a country's economic expansion and development over a period of time, usually a year

hegemony dominance by one group over others

hermeneutic to do with interpretation, especially of religious or literary texts

heterogeneous not of the same kind; different in nature and type

humanism a concept in social psychology which relates to an approach that studies the whole person, and the uniqueness of each individual

impulsivity prone to acting without thinking

in loco parentis Latin for 'in the place of the parent', or standing in for the parent

inclusion in education is an approach that recognises and respects differences among learners and attempts to build on similarities

individual multilingualism the ability of an individual to use more than two languages fluently

iterative describes something that is done or stated repeatedly

kinaesthetic describes being aware of the position and movement of all parts of the body

laterally when you think laterally, you solve problems 'sideways' – indirectly and creatively; this is often contrasted with vertical thinking, which involves logical deduction only

leveraging using elements in a situation to achieve other desired outcomes

mainstream the normal course of human ideas, values, activities, and developments in society

mainstreaming describes a process in education of getting learners to 'fit in' to a particular system that already exists

marginalisation a condition of always being on the outside, or left out of the mainstream of social, cultural and economic life

median income refers to the income level earned by a given household, where half of the households in a particular area or region earn more, and half earn less; it is a measure used instead of the average or mean household income because it can give a more accurate picture of an area or region's actual economic status

mediate to play a role or have an influence in a situation or on behaviour

normative relating to a standard or norm

paradigm a pattern or model of something that represents the beliefs and theories that constitute it

phenomenon a representation of concepts, events or facts; in an educational context, phenomena (plural) are those things one is interested in understanding

political symbolism signs and words that are used to represent a particular political standpoint; can include many things, like flags, banners, mottos, images, specific colours, acronyms, and slogans

positivism a philosophy which emphasises things that can be seen and observed, rather than those based on abstract reasoning or speculation

putative generally considered, or reputed to be

reciprocate to return (e.g. love, affection, attention) to someone who gives it

redistribution a plan to address economic inequities through, e.g. taxes, land ownership, social grants, etc.

replicability able to be copied exactly, or repeated over and over in the same way

respite relief from something unpleasant

restorative justice when perpetrators offer victims acceptable apology and compensation (in the form of action, service or money) either within a legal context, or with the help of an arbitrator

rubella an infectious viral disease, also known as German measles

sanctioned allowed, approved or supported

sovereignty in this context, the complete authority or absolute rule

stagnation a term in economics that describes a situation when there is no growth or development happening

structural adjustment an economics term that describes a policy to impose conditions for lending and borrowing money on developing countries; instituted by the World Bank and International Monetary Fund (IMF)

theoretical orientation the direction or angle from which a study or research investigation is projected; also, the angle from which you want others to view the study

topology the way in which the parts of something are arranged

worldview a representation of one's way of seeing and reasoning about things in the world and about life, influenced by one's thoughts and beliefs

Index

Page numbers in bold refer to figures (diagrams) and tables.